T0283619

CONTOURS OF ISRAELI POLITICS

HANNAH M. RIDGE

CONTOURS OF
ISRAELI POLITICS

*Jewish Ethnicity, Religious Nationalism,
and Democracy*

TEMPLE UNIVERSITY PRESS
Philadelphia • Rome • Tokyo

TEMPLE UNIVERSITY PRESS
Philadelphia, Pennsylvania 19122
tupress.temple.edu

Copyright © 2025 by Temple University—Of The Commonwealth System
   of Higher Education
All rights reserved
Published 2025

Library of Congress Cataloging-in-Publication Data

Names: Ridge, Hannah M., 1991– author.
Title: Contours of Israeli politics : Jewish ethnicity, religious
   nationalism, and democracy / Hannah M. Ridge.
Description: Philadelphia : Temple University Press, 2025. | Includes
   bibliographical references and index. | Summary: "Examines race, ethnic
   politics, and relative group status in the Israeli context by studying
   ethnic differences in the Israeli Jewish population"— Provided by
   publisher.
Identifiers: LCCN 2024016404 (print) | LCCN 2024016405 (ebook) | ISBN
   9781439925836 (cloth) | ISBN 9781439925843 (paperback) | ISBN
   9781439925850 (pdf)
Subjects: LCSH: National characteristics, Israeli—Political aspects. |
   Ethnicity—Political aspects—Israel. | Jews—Israel—Identity. | Group
   identity—Israel. | Israel—Ethnic relations—Political aspects.
Classification: LCC DS113.3 .R54 2025 (print) | LCC DS113.3 (ebook) | DDC
   305.892/405694—dc23/eng/20240823
LC record available at https://lccn.loc.gov/2024016404
LC ebook record available at https://lccn.loc.gov/2024016405

♾ The paper used in this publication meets the requirements of the
American National Standard for Information Sciences—Permanence
of Paper for Printed Library Materials, ANSI Z39.48-1992

Printed in the United States of America

9 8 7 6 5 4 3 2 1

To Kelsey

Contents

ILLUSTRATIONS AND TABLES

FIGURES

TABLES

Acknowledgments

This book developed through a fortuitous confluence of events. In July 2020, I heard about Mara Ostfeld and Nicole Yadon's work on skin color and marginal group membership in American politics in the Minority Politics Online Speaker Series (MPOSS). In a subsequent discussion of Judaism and Israeli politics with colleagues, I remarked on Ashkenormativity, which led to my speculation that a parallel dynamic was at work. That idea became a digital sticky note. Peter Feaver's support for a pilot study and an APSA Summer Centennial Research Grant made my surveys possible (IRB approvals at Duke University and the University of Chicago). I am also grateful to the European Social Survey and the Pew Research Center for access to their data.

This manuscript was written during my time at the University of Chicago Center for Human Rights and Chapman University. Earlier stages of this research were presented at the American Political Science Association, Middle East Studies Association, Midwest Political Science Association, and American Association for Public Opinion Research annual meetings; at UChicago's MEHAT workshop; and (bringing things full circle) at MPOSS. I am indebted to Kelsey Ridge, Avital Livney, Amanda Sahar d'Urso, Stephanie Shady, So Jin Lee, Orit Bashkin, Chagai Weiss, Maha Raziq, Rebecca Alpert, Aaron Javsicas, and the anonymous reviewers for their insightful comments on earlier versions of this work and the survey questionnaire. The book is much richer for their advice.

CONTOURS OF ISRAELI POLITICS

1

INTRODUCTION

THE STATE OF ISRAEL will be open for Jewish immigration and for the Ingathering of the Exiles; it will foster the
development of the country for the benefit of all its
inhabitants; it will be based on freedom, justice and peace
as envisaged by the prophets of Israel; it will ensure
complete equality of social and political rights to all its
inhabitants irrespective of religion, race or sex; it will
guarantee freedom of religion, conscience, language,
education and culture; it will safeguard the Holy Places of
all religions; and it will be faithful to the principles of the
Charter of the United Nations.

—ISRAEL'S DECLARATION OF INDEPENDENCE (MAY 15, 1948)

When the termination of the British Mandate in Palestine introduced a United Nations–approved two-state structure for Israel/
Palestine, the provisional Israeli government issued a Declaration
of Independence. Eretz Israel, the signatories announced, was the "birthplace
of the Jewish people" that was (re)claimed by a "natural and historic right"
and UN resolution, which the declaration calls an "international sanction."*
The declaration called for Arab inhabitants of the new state "to preserve peace
and participate in the upbuilding of the State on the basis of full and equal
citizenship" while appealing to the diaspora to support Israel "in the tasks

---

* Language around the State of Israel is incredibly freighted. While the Israeli government
refers to the establishment of the "Jewish State" or the "State of Israel," Palestinian communities may use the term *Nakba* (Arabic for catastrophe) to describe what they see as the destruc-
tion of Palestine. In parallel fashion, describing the contestation over the territory in former
Mandatory Palestine as a "conflict" is potentially controversial, both for denying that the question has been normatively resolved or for seeming to minimize the violence. The term *conflict*
is used here because it is the common English reference and because of the ongoing disputa-
tion. The phrasing Eretz Israel has been used for Mandatory Palestine and for more expansive
territories, historically and now. It is used here because it is the language used in these documents. The text refers to the State of Israel, and Gaza and the West Bank are referred to, in keeping with international recognition and the sources here, as the (Occupied) Palestinian Territories. Where speakers, including survey respondents, appealed to other terminology (e.g.,
Judea and Samaria, Greater Israel), the phrasing is preserved.

of immigration and upbuilding." The declaration calls then for the lifting up of one group—Jewish (potential) nationals—while asserting the equality of the other groups, the non-Jewish inhabitants (and occasional citizens) of the territory. These several agenda points were functionally at odds with one another from the start. That ethno-religious distinction, however, is not the only tension created by this conception of the State of Israel.

Eretz Israel was to be a Jewish state. This presents both a religious and an ethnic assertion, as people can be ethnically and religiously Jewish, without necessarily being both at the same time. Some nonreligious people come from Jewish family lines—lines that may or may not make them Jewish under *halakha* (Jewish law[1]), since Judaism is passed matrilineally. Religious Jews may be members of other ethno-racial communities who have converted into Judaism. Thus, by identifying Israel as a Jewish state, these documents invoke both religious and ethnic communities. Each of these blocs shows internal diversity: the religious and the secular and the ethno-racial subgroupings of Jews. How should the state handle the (non)religiousness of the Jewish community? How should the ethnic diversity within the Jewish population be incorporated into the Israeli identity?

A bright line is drawn around one part of this identity—religion. Jewish and Israeli law have means of demarcating Jews from non-Jews. Nonpracticing and even atheistic individuals can be counted in the fold. The non-Jewish residents of Israel—largely Muslim but also Christian and Druze—are decidedly separate. A clear hierarchy is then established for those for whom this country is supposed to be a homeland and those for whom it is not—even if they are holders of supposedly coequal citizenship. The declaration offers these non-Jewish Israelis freedom of religion and equal political rights, but it is not their place of Ingathering. This point was affirmed in the 2018 Basic Law, which states that the "State of Israel is the nation state of the Jewish people" and that "the right to national self-determination in the State of Israel is exclusive to the Jewish people."

Certainly, there are scholars, activists, and citizens who would assert that Israel has not lived up to the declaration's promise. The non-Jewish inhabitants are not equal in this system. Palestinians are at a lower stratum, and non-Jewish citizens of Israel are not treated equally (Azoulay and Ophir 2012). However, this book is not focused on the distinctions between the Jewish Israelis and the Palestinians. Substantial and ongoing work has highlighted those in-group/out-group disparities. Instead, this text focuses on the hierarchies within the upper stratum—Jewish Israelis—and the sociopolitical impact of blurring that bright line between the in-group and the out-groups. Glossing over intragroup hierarchies risks missing nuances of experience with political significance.[2]

Although Judaism is an ethno-religion and one can think of "Jewish ethnicity," there is not one single Jewish ethnicity. There are Jews of European extraction (i.e., Ashkenazi Jews), Jews of North African and Asian extraction (i.e., Mizrahi/Sephardi Jews), and Jews from other areas (e.g., Ethiopian Jews). Middle Eastern Jews have also been called Arab Jews.[3] They hail from Muslim-majority countries, like Yemen and Morocco. By being both Arab (or at least affiliated with Arab states) and Jewish, these individuals blur the supposedly impermeable line between the in-group and the out-group. This book focuses on the sociopolitical ramifications of this liminality. Namely, these groups face greater pressure to assert their in-group membership (Jewishness) and are more likely to protect the status privileges of that group than prototypical group members (Ashkenazim) are. They may even protect Jewish nationalism at the expense of democracy.

No one Jewish ethnic group constitutes a clear majority of Jewish Israelis by itself. However, in the formation of Israel, sociological and anthropological researchers report, European Jews were seen by political figures, veterans, and teachers as culturally superior by virtue of their Westernness. Israel's "new Jew" would be "western," "masculine," "secular," and "clean" (Khazzoom 2008, 33). The others were to "melt" or assimilate into the secular, Western brand of Jewishness. This phenomenon has been dubbed *Ashkenormativity*. In total, the hierarchy privileges certain kinds of Jews over others while holding the Jewish population over the non-Jewish population. Despite the political assertions of equality within and between groups, these citizens are still subject to discrimination. Thus, they are marginal members of their religious national community.

Marginal group membership theory addresses this positionality. The concept of an "in-group" "extends to any social identity with which a gatekeeper in question self-affiliates," including religion or ethnicity (Branigan et al. 2017, 14). Within that in-group, some members are less "in" than others. These people are faced with performing their group identity on the basis of how they are perceived by others, how they want to be perceived, and what social consequences result from their performances. Will they be seen as part of the in-group or part of an out-group? Which do they prefer? If they want to be included in the group, marginal group members are then called upon to demonstrate their loyalties (Ellemers and Jetten 2013). They have to make strategic choices to control their classification—to the extent that they can.

This study integrates marginal group membership theory and Ashkenormativity to demonstrate the political implications of Mizrahi/Sephardi Jews' liminal position for their political preferences. The focus is on their preferences toward a religious state, Israeli democracy, and state security. In the course of identifying these attitudes, it demonstrates their relative experiences of social inclusion and exclusion and the ways that has colored their engagement with the government or sense of the government's connection to them and to those like them. Their social experience within the hierarchy frames their attitudes.

Marginal Jewish Israelis are more likely to identify exclusion and discrimination in their society. Although they may not personally identify as discriminated against, they are more likely to recognize the discrimination against Mizrahi and Ethiopian Jews in Israel. They see the marginalization. In keeping with asserting their group identity and promoting in-group privilege, which protects their personal privilege, such as it is, they report greater interest in Judaism, place greater value on Jewish tradition, and are more invested in keeping Israel as a Jewish state. The relative preference for Jewish nationalism means occasionally valuing it more than liberal democracy. These ethnicized issue preferences thus extend into overarching preferences for the ethno-religious state. Thus, while the Jewish–non-Jewish cleavage is central to Israeli politics, intra-Jewish diversity is still pertinent to our understanding of Israeli politics.

Marginal Group Membership Theory

Group identity can be formed out of just about anything, which means an in-group/out-group distinction can be formed around any identity. Group belonging is regularly infused with emotional and social significance. Even arbitrary classifications can trigger in-group favoritism; this is the "minimal group paradigm" (Tajfel and Turner 1979; Turner, Brown, and Tajfel 1979; Marques et al. 1998). Most memberships—and the associated favoritism and animus—are far from random. They pertain to persistent and salient identity elements (e.g., race, religion, gender). Furthermore, individuals hold a "collective self," which is to say a "self defined in group terms and connected to fellow group members" (Hogg and Reid 2006, 9). The individual does not experience in-group or out-group status in isolation. Many personal features and socialized experiences shape and perpetuate individuals' (inter)group awareness.

Theoretically, more numerous social divisions make assigning favoritism and privilege more challenging (Hartstone and Augoustinos 1995), and more complex social identities encourage intergroup tolerance (Roccas and Brewer 2002; Brewer and Pierce 2005). In that case, one might expect a diverse society to equalize intergroup treatment. Racialized politics, however, show that multiparty structures can efficiently form and exploit us-versus-them dichotomies in the face of substantial diversity.

The group that forms—although it is recognized by group members and/or observers as constituting an identity—is not necessarily cohesive. If a group of people is divided on the basis of wearing solid-colored or patterned shirts, then each member may be fully on one side of the divide or the other and be seen by all observers as belonging to that side. If a group is established by nuanced criteria, however, gradations of group belonging can develop.

Not all members of that group, even if they fit the criteria, would be equally part of it either objectively or subjectively. Some group members may feel or be seen by others as less connected to it if they only meet some criteria. Even if they meet objective standards, they may not fit the expectations of that group as much as other members do. This is especially possible if some accepted criteria are considered more important than others for group identification. The individuals who most fulfill the expectations or requirements of group membership—or who fit them best among several potential fit options—would be considered the *prototypical* group members.

In social identity theory, in identifying the group, individuals hold a concept of a prototype in their mind. It is built on "fuzzy sets" of attributes (Hogg and Reid 2006, 10) rather than "an objective reality" (Hornsey 2008, 209). Often these attributes are those that "accentuate intragroup similarities (assimilation) and intergroup differences (contrast)" (Hogg and Reid 2006, 10). For instance, race groups have distinct skin-color prototypes. However, other attributes, including some that are shared across group boundaries, may still be associated with the group prototype. For instance, several groups may include traits such as "intelligent," "brunette," or "strong" in their description of their prototypical member.

Those individuals who are not prototypical, for one reason or another, can be considered marginal group members. Somehow, they are on the outskirts of the group classification. Notably, this distinction is not about transitioning into membership. Marginal members of the group are members, but they are nonprototypical members. This distinction between the prototypical and the marginal group members is at the core of marginal group membership theory.

To maintain the shirt analogy, consider the following case. All patterns qualify individuals for the patterned-shirt group. However, a star pattern could be perceived as best, and polka dots considered a close second. Star-shirt wearers would be prototypical group members. Striped shirts would constitute a patterned shirt, but the stripes are less like star shapes than polka dots are. The stripe wearers would then be the marginal group members.

The features that determine centrality are context dependent, even for otherwise overlapping group labels or identities. Circumstances like geography, diversity, and prevalence determine the prototypifying traits. For instance, the prototypical Christian is Coptic in Egypt but Anglican in England and Catholic in Italy. The salience of a dimension would also change with context. While abstaining from alcohol may distinguish a Latter-day

Saint in a Christian-majority context, it would not be distinguishing in a Muslim-majority context.

Once prototypes are formed, they can become reinforcing (Hogg and Reid 2006). The prototypes set the norms for the group. Group members then typically conform to those standards, perpetuating a group norm. Norms do not even have to reflect majority preferences to be perpetuated as long as members think a majority of the group—or of the prototypes—ascribes to it. People who strongly identify with the group, regardless of prototypicality, may strengthen group norms by performing them to assert group membership. Prototypical group members have greater latitude to transgress norms. In a context in which norm observance is not necessary to assert identity, the ingroup norm can decline (Hogg and Reid 2006). For instance, religious service attendance may not be necessary to mark religious identity in a religiously homogenous community; attendance may be necessary to assert group membership in a religiously diverse community or for those whose affiliation could be doubted.

Marginal group membership is demonstrable in studies of race and ethnicity. Substantial scholarship on race and ethnic politics has been conducted on the American public; however, many of these principles can be extended to other countries. This study contributes to that expansion.

Research has regularly incorporated discrete racial or ethnic categories. The simplicity of these variables obscures the complexity of the formation and implementation of these identities: "Adding race as a statistical control in quantitative models is now a common practice that signals disciplinary concern with the importance of race and ethnicity; but paradoxically, the ease of statistical controls offers the dangerous potential for reifying race as a category for social analysis without a concordant focus on what 'race' and 'ethnicity' mean" (Hitlin, Brown, and Elder 2007, 588). This is particularly pertinent when different evaluations of race—self-identified race and observer-identified race—lead to different empirical findings (Saperstein 2006).

Increasingly researchers are addressing the inequalities and differences *within* groups to account for marginality. Colorism, unequal treatment based on skin color within a racial group, has been well traversed. Skin color influences employment, marriage patterns, and perceived beauty. It also shapes perceptions of group status both within and across groups. White people may demonstrate interracial colorism by privileging lighter-skinned people of color. Within groups, colorism can also be used to articulate true membership. In consequence, darker-skinned individuals in the United States have worse socioeconomic, health, and criminal justice outcomes based on these biases, even within racial groups, "while light(er)-skinned BIPOC [Black, Indigenous, and people of color] often feel their racial authenticity and allegiance challenged" (Strmic-Pawl, Gonlin, and Garner 2019, 291; see also Lemi and Brown 2020).

Colorism can also apply to marginal white people. Darker-skinned white Americans recognize that they are not the prototypical white person (Yadon and Ostfeld 2020). This also makes them less likely to be coded as white by observers, which entails a loss of privilege. For instance, a study on police behavior found that the probability of arrest was constant for Black men across skin tones but that darker-skinned white men were more likely to be arrested than lighter white men (Branigan et al. 2017). The nonprototypicality is pushing them toward the positionality of an out-group. This possibility and the fear of it drives political preferences.

Positionality also manifests in the strength with which group identity is held, and holding these identities has multiple valences. These identities operate at the personal level; they are part of how people experience society. Ethnic origin does not itself determine individual identities or the strength with which those identities are held. For instance, white Americans hold uneven levels of attachment to their white identity, separate from their racial prejudice (Jardina 2019). Some people hold their ethnic or racial identity more strongly. Society can inform how citizens identify and express their ethnicity, although those individuals may self-categorize in ways society does not describe them (Hitlin, Brown, and Elder 2007). In addition to a personal racial identity, people also have a "street race," a race group they are tacitly assigned by other people who encounter them (López et al. 2018). That act of ethnic or racial classification informs how they are treated. Furthermore, the individual's cultural ethnicity, which is formed as part of this conversation between the individual and society, can be separated from the individual's "political ethnicity": "the significance of this aspect of identity is subject to change and continuous reinterpretation" (Herzog 1985, 46). Not all group members will engage—consciously—politically on that dimension or do so to an equal degree. In total, the lived experience of group membership and social participation shapes the identification process and the politicization process.

Identification also influences how people are treated. Thus, there are feedback effects between the social conception of race and personal identity (Saperstein and Penner 2014). For instance, immigrant generation, education, region of residence, gender, and age affect how interviewers racially code survey respondents (Saperstein 2006). Some ethnic groups, such as the Italians and Irish in the United States, have been socially "whitened" over time. Aaron J. Hahn Tapper, Ari Y. Kelman, and Aliya Saperstein (2023) document the intentional construction of white identity among American Jews. Such evolutions can shape personal and observer classifications and attachments. The lived experience of race in society, including whether or not individuals are treated as members of the groups with which they identify, leads to nuanced political preferences. Thus, the level of groupishness—marginality versus prototypicality—is politically relevant. It can drive political behavior as well as political preferences and beliefs.

Marginal group members must act to affirm their group membership for several reasons. Marginal members are more likely to have deviated from core group norms in some way, and some marginal group members do seek to exit the group. Those who wish to remain can signal this choice by conforming or overconforming on other features. Marginality and inclusivity are then dynamically adjudicated by continual performance (Ellemers and Jetten 2013). Mutual recognition as group members takes maintenance for marginal members.

Access to social and economic privileges attendant on group membership require people to conform to group patterns that reveal membership (Hitlin, Brown, and Elder 2007; Telles and Paschel 2014). For some marginal group members, such as mixed-race individuals or people with nonprototypical skin tones, the choice of which group to identify with or to present publicly may be a strategic action. Historically, the opportunity to pass as white offered substantial benefits to Americans of color, and nonprototypical minorities sometimes took advantage of their liminal position to shift their classification.[4] Non-white Americans often favor identification with their group, rather than attempting to be perceived as part of another racial or ethnic group (Ostfeld and Yadon 2022b). Affirming their connection to their group—including having their connection affirmed by other people—promotes their own cognitive identity concordance (Saperstein and Penner 2014). Marginal group members may demonstrate "as much loyalty to the group as core members, if not more," especially if they are striving for "greater group inclusion" (Ellemers and Jetten 2013, 4). To the extent that some marginal group members will be content on the margins and will not engage in group-affirming thinking or behaviors, those choices would work against finding any effects.

This demonstration of group identity and group loyalty manifests in citizens' policy preferences. This has been shown with respect to skin color. Skin color influences the sense of linked fate, the belief that what happens to the individual is highly related to the condition of other group members (Lemi and Brown 2020; Dawson 1994). Those with a more prototypical group appearance have more reason to believe their experiences will be informed by being identified with their group by both in-group and out-group members. Objective skin color matters more for members of some groups than others. For instance, it matters more for members of the majority group if the boundaries are blurring (Ostfeld and Yadon 2022b). The higher-status groups' marginal members' politics will reflect their lived experience of marginality. Conversely, in lower-status groups with permeable boundaries, individuals will shift their self-conception toward the group with which they would prefer to be identified by others. Their objective skin color would then be less connected to their politics than their self-assertion. Among Latino Americans, researchers have identified a pattern of claiming lighter skin among conservatives (reporting themselves closer to the—in their minds—prototypical Republican) and claiming darker skin among liberals (reporting themselves closer to the—in their minds—prototypical Democrat) (Ostfeld and Yadon 2022a). Darker skin is perceived as being "more authentic" by some group members (Ostfeld and Yadon 2022b, 77). Thus, they seek to align their ethnic self-evaluation and their political identity.

Prototypicality influences voters' perceptions of political figures. For instance, lighter-skinned Black women candidates are seen as less likely to support progressive policies or "Black Nationalist views" compared to candidates with darker skin; the same is true for potential candidates with textured hair as opposed to straight(ened) hair (Orey and Zhang 2019). When presented with potential minority candidates, liberal voters favor darker-skinned candidates, who could be prototypically construed as more liberal, while conservative voters favor lighter-skinned candidates (Weaver 2012). Prototypical leaders are also afforded more latitude to assert, influence, or evolve group norms than nonprototypical group members who become leaders (Hornsey 2008; Hogg and Reid 2006).

Individuals who identify with their group are more likely to act in its interests than those who do not have a strong group identity. For instance, strong white identity can make white Americans more likely to support policies that favor (in their minds) white people (Jardina 2019). If members are too strongly connected to the group by emotion or by observable characteristics to move out of it, then they may develop beliefs in which their group compares favorably to out-groups, particularly those lower in the social order, and they are more likely to "devalu[e] dimensions that reflect poorly on the ingroup" (Hornsey 2008, 207). Marginal group members can take group defensiveness even further. If they see that their group is under threat, then marginal members can be drawn closer to the group to enhance its numbers and sense of security or they can be "call[ed] on to display their loyalty" (Ellemers and Jetten 2013, 13). This can push marginal group members to pursue politics that favor the in-group.

White people are the current racial majority in the United States. Darker-skinned white people have less white privilege than paler whites. Darker-skinned white people "feel particularly unstable given their relatively lower position within the White racial group," so they do not feel like the "prototypical" white person and thus "work harder on behalf of the group and adopt more extreme attitudes and behaviors than prototypical group members" (Yadon and Ostfeld 2020, 1375–1376). This behavior signals their membership in the dominant group and their nonmembership in the other groups. They place greater value on their white identity, and they adopt more conservative positions on racialized issues (1382). Nicole Yadon and Mara C. Ostfeld (2020, 1388) describe this as "boundary protection" for their identity category.

In parallel fashion, the prototypicality of Western Europeans has been argued as a cause of out-group denigration by Eastern Europeans. Ivan Kalmar (2022) argues that "racism" within Europe against Central Europeans for being "white but not quite" encourages Central Europeans to support illiberal policies against migrants from the Middle East and North Africa (MENA). While Arabs are coded as white in some countries, they were not white enough or Christian enough for those states. Members, including marginal members, who enforce group norms or protocols may earn group approbation (Marques et al. 1998). However, that is not always the case. For instance, many Western Europeans criticized the Central European governments' immigration policies as conservative, while confirming that these were European states and non-European immigrants. Furthermore, the policies could earn the governments' local support by affirming their Europeanness.

Where individuals feel that their groups' status is under threat, they may act to protect it. Compare this to a ramp and to a staircase. If a sliding scale model faces people with a potential slide into lower status, then they have an interest in protecting categorical privilege. For instance, nonprototypical white people benefit more from the perpetuation of white privilege than from a system relying on actual skin lightness. On a ramp, they might be in danger of sliding down in social standing; in fact, they may be lower on the ramp than some people of color. However, if there are levels, then being on the white stair could keep them a step above those other people. Marginal members of dominant groups, then, benefit from a firmer boundary. Strong identifiers are more reactive to group threats (Pérez 2015). Such identifiers are also more attentive to intergroup hierarchies and more willing to engage in intergroup discrimination (Hornsey 2008). If the marginal members are emphasizing their membership to themselves, then they stand to be even more reactive to group threats and to be more protective of the group.

Marginality, though, is different from group identification. Marginal group members are still being identified with the group, either because of some objective characteristic or because of their own or others' estimation. However, marginal group members may not be identified with a group by other individuals as readily as prototypical members are. Their group affiliation may also be held less tightly.

Group identification and the objective and subjective features that promote such identification may co-occur and covary, but they may also be separate. For instance, pallor and white group identity can move in tandem, but the marginality of dark-skinned white people is not a function of their level of self-identification; it is more closely linked to how others see them. They are then faced with defending their group identity if they prize it. On the other hand, white individuals of any shade may assign little value to their white identity. Naomi Ellemers and Jolanda Jetten (2013) argue that marginal group members are the "'best' group members" when their identification with the group is high and the "'worst' group members" when their identification with the group is low. Nonidentifiers, after all, would not feel a need to perform or protect the identity they do not share. When they highly identify with the group, though, these marginal group members will support or perform group-protective policies and actions.

Hierarchies can evolve. For instance, there has been a historical preference for whiteness in Latin America. Some scholars argue that this pattern is shifting toward a preference for "mixedness" in some contexts or toward an emphasis on a non-white identity (Telles and Paschel 2014; Ostfeld and Yadon 2022b). That process would be slow and iterative. All members of society participate in shaping the transformation and its impacts: "People develop and enact racial and ethnic identities within social contexts" (Hitlin, Brown, and Elder 2007, 593). In the case of Israel, the relative position within the Jewish community also informs citizens' preferences and politics. Later chapters say more about marginal group membership theory as it applies to the Israeli ethnicity and religious majoritarianism (Chapter 3), support for Israeli democracy (Chapter 4), and preference for an expanded territorial state and peace with the neighbors (Chapter 5).

Ashkenormativity

A central cleavage of Israeli society and politics is the distinction between Jewish and non-Jewish people.[5] The separation between these bodies is marked and perpetuated by religious and state law; the line between the groups is bright and clear, not blurry or permeable. Operating family law (e.g., marriage and divorce) through the religious communities helps to keep the line crisp. A focus on maximal group difference would highlight the distinction between the Jewish population and the Palestinian population. The former is privileged over the latter. Focusing on this hierarchy obscures the ethnic diversity within the Jewish Israeli population by compressing it into one body. Zooming in reveals internal variety. This within-the-in-group diversity is the focus here.

Namely, the focus is on the tacit preference for Ashkenazi Jewishness. To address ethnic diversity within the Jewish Israeli population, it is necessary to understand that Jewishness encompasses "race, ethnicity, and religion," and these three categories naturally "are *interacting* categories" in Jewish communities (Gonzalez-Lesser 2020, 491). Race is often seen as more bio-logical, inherent, and rigid, although it is a social construction: "Construc-tions of racial groups often use ancestry, phenotype, stereotypes, history, identity, and racial biological definitions" (483). The racialization of Jews in Europe treated all Jews as "Semites, a category presumed to encompass the populations of the Middle East" (Alpert 2007, 82). Ethnicity reflects cultural confluences within larger racial or national categories (Gonzalez-Lesser 2020; Alpert 2007). This text uses the language of ethnicity to describe diverse origins in the Jewish community, which is more typical for contemporary Israeli discourse.[6] Ancestry can define Jewish identity; in this case, it persists even in the face of atheism or nonparticipation. Because of the ethnic di-mension (and the fact that Jewish law does not have an exit clause), indi-viduals of Jewish descent cannot opt out of being Jewish, at least ethnically.

The Jewish Israeli population can be ethnically categorized in several ways. European-origin Jews are considered Ashkenazi, while Asian/North Afri-can–origin Jews are Mizrahi. Sephardi Jews are descended from those re-moved from Iberia. Sephardi and Mizrahi labels are often merged together in political and sociological treatments.[7] For instance, the European Social Survey groups Mizrahi and Sephardi into one category. The Israeli Central Bureau of Statistics divides the population into Ashkenazi and Mizrahi on the basis of the father's continent of birth; those with Israel-born fathers are classed as Israeli-origin inhabitants (Lewin-Epstein and Cohen 2019). Ash-kenormativity normalizes the former group at the expense of the latter.

(Descendants of) immigrants from the former Soviet states can be from several groups because the Soviet states included Eastern Europe and Asia, although most identify as Ashkenazi (Lewin-Epstein and Cohen 2019). They are sometimes treated as a separate ethnic category. Jews from Ethiopia have also moved to Israel. For many analyses, all groups that are not Ashkenazi or Mizrahi/Sephardi—including those from the former Soviet states and Ethi-opians—are coded as "other."[8] Another bloc is identified as "mixed" due to intermarriage among the groups.[9] The increasing rates of intermarriage and the resulting population identified as mixed ethnicity have been put forward as an indication that ethnic distinctions no longer matter. However, the con-tinued awareness of discrimination counters that assertion.

A "proliferation of terms" has been applied to the Mizrahi/Sephardi pop-ulation: "Sephardim; non-Ashkenazic Jews; Jews of Islam; Arab Jews; Middle Eastern, west Asian, or north African Jews; Asian and African Jews; non-European Jews; Third World Jews; Levantine Jews; Jews of the Mediterra-nean; *Maghrebian* and *Mashreqian* Jews (from the western and eastern parts of the Arab world); Bnei Edot Ha Mizrah (descendants of the Eastern com-munities); *yotzei artzot arav ve-ha-Islam* (those who left Arab and Muslim countries); Blacks; Israel ha-Shniya (Second Israel); Mizrahiyim, or Mizrahim; or Iraqi Jews, Iranian Jews, Kurdish Jews, Palestinian Jews, Moroccan Jews, and so forth" (Shohat 2003, 52–53).[10] Several of these terms highlight an Arab linkage for the Mizrahim, especially references to Arab countries or the terminology Arab Jews. This positioning in proximity to the Arabs, a term often tacitly associated with Muslims, subtly otherizes this subset. That proximity to the non-Jewish Arab population undermines their in-group status. As Smadar Lavie (2018, 17) puts it, "In Israel, my phenotype always trumps my privilege." Mizrahim are Jewish, but they are not Ashkenazi.

This intertwining of religion and ethnicity complicates national identity. The state itself struggles to form policies that account for the religious character of the state, where preeminence is often afforded to Orthodox interpretation, and the uneven religiosity of the population (Yadgar 2020). The population includes the ultra-Orthodox (Haredi), the modern Orthodox (Dati), the traditional (Masorti), and the secular (Hiloni). The state, which "following the logic of mainstream Zionist ideology viewed itself as secular," was grounded in this ethno-cultural identity rather than religious regulation; it did not "focus on maintaining a sovereignty that is *Jewish*, that is, a sovereignty that dialogues with Judaism as a constituting tradition, but rather to maintain the sovereignty of *Jews*" (Yadgar 2020, 16, emphasis in the original). It nonetheless maintains a public conception as a *Jewish* state. Each individual, including waves of immigrants, must choose whether to afford Jewish or Israeli identity pride of place.

As part of the construction of a united Jewish state, including a narrative of "return," a construction of culture was undertaken. A Jewish minority community lived in Ottoman Palestine. While subject to Ottoman secular law, the religious minority communities (*millet*) could set some laws and taxes internally, such as contracts and marital law. Sephardic Jews fleeing Iberian persecution took refuge in the Ottoman Empire. In the late nineteenth century, religious persecution in Eastern Europe and economic turmoil in Yemen pushed Jews to immigrate to Ottoman Palestine (Lavie 2018). The influx of Eastern European Jews meant the Jewish community in the British Mandate period was largely Ashkenazi. A Zionist movement supplemented that population with European immigrants in response to European anti-semitism and narratives of a biblical imperative to recreate the Jewish state. This Palestinian Jewish population constituted the Sabra.

Nowadays the Sabra label can be applied to Israel-born Jews, who are an increasing segment of the population. Efforts have been made to cultivate a shared Israeli Jewish identity, rather than the ethnic identities.[11] It has not, however, eclipsed them yet.

Before 1948, the Jewish population in Mandate Palestine—approximately 600,000–650,000 individuals—was largely Ashkenazi (Sasson-Levy and Shoshana 2013; Lewin-Epstein and Cohen 2019). Lavie (2018) estimates that approximately 450,000 were Ashkenazi and 150,000 were Mizrahi. Between 1948 and 1951, Israel's population doubled, drawing in new citizens from Europe and the MENA region, especially Iraq and Yemen. In the 1950s and 1960s, Jewish communities from North African countries emigrated, largely to Israel and France. Mizrahim were about half of Israel's Jewish population into the 1980s (Mizrachi and Herzog 2012; Kalev and Maor 2015). However, approximately a million arrivals from the former Soviet Union—both Jews and their non-Jewish relatives—increased the Ashkenazi share of the population (Bagno-Moldavski 2015; Lewin-Epstein and Cohen 2019; Kalev and Maor 2015). Lavie (2018) contends that between the migration and birth rate differentials, the Sabra are heavily Mizrahi.

A Jewish community in Ethiopia, Beta Israel, sought recognition in the twentieth century. Their religious and historical legitimacy were initially questioned; however, Beta Israel was recognized for "right of return" in the 1970s (Mizrachi and Herzog 2012). Despite that recognition, this community has been subjected to racial discrimination. The largest episodes of immigration from Ethiopia, approximately 80,000–85,000 people, were facilitated by the Israeli government in the 1980s and 1990s (Lewin-Epstein and Cohen 2019; Kalev and Maor 2015). This minority is about 2 percent of the Jewish Israeli population.

In theory, all "'Diasporic Jews' had to abandon their diasporic culture" in favor of the new national Israeli culture as part of the Ingathering (Shohat 2003, 50). However, in practice, the arriving communities were not all actually abandoning their cultures of origin. Jews had been Orientalized in Europe and had historically engaged in intercommunal Orientalization in turn in the diaspora; now that continued in the treatment of the Arab Jews (Smooha 2004; Khazzoom 2008). Despite the appeals to equality, within-group discrimination persisted. Under the "rallying cry" of the "ideology of the melting pot ('mizug galuyot')," arrivals were expected to "adapt to Western codes of behaviour" (Herzog 1985, 47). For instance, the state created "organized educational interventions," such as boarding schools, to "encourage" Mizrahi Jews to replace their "oriental" "cultural capital" with a "Western," "Israeli" cultural capital (Shoshana 2016, 488). Cultural pluralism was not encouraged.

Mizrahi culture was considered "'primitive', 'traditional', 'anti-intellectual'," and threatening to "the model of the new Jew which the country's leaders were trying to imbue with the spirit of the West" (Shoshana 2016, 492). The Mizrahim were poorer and less secularized. For Jews already residing in the Middle East—Arab Jews—that gathering into Israel and attendant acculturation process "meant abandoning Arabness and acquiescing in assimilationist modernization, for 'their own good'" (Shohat 2003, 50). Rather than one large melting pot, the result was three melting pots. One melting pot amal-

gamated the Asian and North African Jews into the Mizrahim; another amal-
gamated the European Jews into the Ashkenazim. A third pot held all the
"Israelis of ethnically mixed or detached origin" (Smooha 2004, 71). The Ashkenazi melting pot melted a bit faster, with intermarriages across origin-coun-
try lines. The Mizrahim maintained the connection to their countries of origin
a bit longer. In the 1980s, though, Mizrahi activists promoted the "coalitional"
identity for ethnic unity to protect the group interest (Lavie 2018, 2).

The ongoing "persistence of ethnic cleavages within the Jewish population between the ethnic groups known today as 'Mizrahim' and 'Ashkenazim'
is typically viewed as a failure of the Jewish society to diminish cultural mark-
ers and socioeconomic attributes that differentiate Jews who emigrated from
diverse countries" (Lewin-Epstein and Cohen 2019, 2118). Sammy Smooha
(2004, 49) argues that the "cleavage" between the Ashkenazim and Mizrahim "is widely seen [in Israel] as transitional, superficial, and to a large extent
even illegitimate."[12] That supposed perception of illegitimacy has not stopped
the Ashkenazi/Mizrahi distinction from existing, persisting, as a social di-
vision.

The seeming failure of the Westernizing, homogenizing project does not
mean it had no ramifications. Ella Shohat (2003) describes the Mizrahi immigration process as traumatizing. The internal discrimination was part of
that immigration process, after all: "One could argue that by provoking the
geographical dispersal of Arab Jews, by placing them in a new situation 'on
the ground,' by attempting to reshape their identity as simply 'Israeli,' by dis-
daining and trying to uproot their Arabness, and by racializing them and
discriminating against them as a group, the Zionist project of the ingathering
of exiles itself provoked a dislocation that resulted in a series of traumatic
ruptures and exilic identity formations" (52). Even the process of integration
was tacitly otherizing.

After this acculturation process during the Ingathering, there persists a
cultural hierarchy within the Jewish Israeli population, beyond the hierarchical position over the non-Jewish population. The Ashkenazi community is
given preference over the Mizrahi/Sephardi community (Shohat 2003; Mizrachi and Weiss 2020). Although Israel is split between Ashkenazi and non-
Ashkenazi Jews, "most contemporary constructions of Jewishness are rooted in an assumption that Jews are white/Ashkenazi" (Gonzalez-Lesser 2020,
492).[13] While Mizrahim are treated as "ethnic," Ashkenazim are "neutral" or
"transparent" (Shoshana 2016, 491; see also Kalev and Maor 2015). This has
been termed Ashkenormativity.

Many of these processes were initially enacted by government figures like
soldiers, immigration officers, and teachers (Khazzoom 2008). Over time,
differential access to loans, subsidies, and tax breaks facilitated class distinction. By the 1980s, some Mizrahi families had ascended to the middle class—

or rather returned to it, as some had been middle class in their countries of origin (Selinger 2013; Lavie 2018). That did not mean, though, that they escaped the pressure for assimilation. "Arab Jews" being treated as Palestinians by security services and police continues the otherization.[14] Thus, despite the political promise of equality, these groups do not have equivalent experiences of Jewish life in Israel.

In the absence of government integrationist programs, Ashkenormativity is enforced culturally. Group stereotypes abound, and they are used to dissect behavior and identity "by classifying food, colors, spaces, characteristics, behaviors, and feelings as belonging on different sides of the Mizrahi-Ashkenazi divide" (Selinger 2013, 129). Ashkenazi and Mizrahi Jewish Israelis are not necessarily phenotypically distinguishable, but Israelis may treat them as if they are. Both Ashkenazim and Mizrahim can range from quite fair to quite tan, but people assume that darker-complected Jews are Mizrahim (Kalev and Maor 2015; Sasson-Levy 2013). Even the darker-complected Jews would not code as Black in the United States or Latin America (Sasson-Levy and Shoshana 2013). These biases are particularly likely to manifest against Mizrahim who look or act "Arab," as their peers construe that identity (Selinger 2013; Kalev and Maor 2015).* That appearance can include cheap clothes, emotionality, "bad" manners, or the "wrong" music, hairstyle, or food (Kalev and Maor 2015; Mizrachi and Herzog 2012). Manifestations of bias based on assigned "Arabness" can range from being denigrated by peers to being hassled by security services. While mixed marriages have become more common, perceived ethnicity still informs social group and familial dynamics (Sasson-Levy 2013).

In turn, those who behave the "right" way may be coded as Ashkenazi, regardless of ethnicity. Thus, researchers can distinguish "Ashkenaziness as a social category and Ashkenazim as individuals" (Sasson-Levy 2013). According to Lavie (2018, 3), "In colloquial Hebrew, when Israelis say 'Ashkenazi,' they mean" someone who is "*ḥiloni* (secular), *vatik* (old timer), socialist, and liberal," while the Ashkenazi "prefer to call themselves 'Israelis.'" The social benefits are technically assigned on the basis of how one is per-

---

* Orna Sasson-Levy (2013, 41) even quotes a subject as saying, "When I say 'Arab Jews,' I'm referring to all the Jews who come from Arab lands. Morocco, Libya, Iraq. I mean that a Sephardi [Mizrahi] Jew is not an Arab Jew, but they have the Mizrahi customs. You know, Arab Jews, they're just like Arabs. They really act like Muslim Arabs," and stating that her Mizrahi husband "really looks like a terrorist. He's very dark, he has a black beard," and she attributes his verbal abuse to being "Arab." (The bracketed text appears in the original). Another said, "Sure there can be an Ashkenazi Moroccan! An Ashkenazi Moroccan is someone who loves to eat gefilte fish, no, cholent [two traditional Ashkenazi dishes]! I see him sitting next to me at a concert, or a play, or demonstrating alongside me with the leftists, against the right wingers, and not the other way around." (The bracketed text appears in the original). Stereotypes are doing more work here than appearance.

ceived rather than what one's true heritage is.* Such biases may encourage Mizrahim to change their behavior and conceal their origins and preferences to pass as "Israeli," which is to say Ashkenazi (Selinger 2013; Sasson-Levy and Shoshana 2013). These individuals can then be mocked for trying to pass. *Mishtaknez/im* means "whitewashed Mizrachi" (Selinger 2013, 129). While Ashkenazim may be said to "perform Mizrahiness" when they adopt music or food from Mizrahi communities, the "lack of a parallel term for Ashkenazification in the opposite direction implies that such a move is not visible or desirable and indicates the normative preferability of what is referred to as 'Western culture'" (Sasson-Levy and Shoshana 2013, 456). The mere expectation of assimilation or passing itself highlights the hierarchical relationship.

Olena Bagno-Moldavski (2015, 519) compares the ethnic hierarchy to "the politically acute racial divides in the South Africa [*sic*] and the United States." This comparison, though, relies on a truncated assessment of race in Israel. If Palestinians are included, then Palestinians are the more accurate reference. Comparison of Israel to the South African apartheid is not uncommon and not uncontroversial (e.g., Amnesty International 2022). If Palestinians are included in the discussion, then they could be positioned in that space, while the Mizrahim/Sephardim would take the position of low-status white people. As Amelia R. Branigan et al. (2017, 12) describe the circumstance in the United States, "Rather than white respondents' being categorically advantaged, while minorities are differentially advantaged on the basis of their proximity to aesthetic lightness, we find black respondents to be categorically disadvantaged, while white respondents are disadvantaged differentially on the basis of their proximity to aesthetic darkness." The Palestinians are categorically disadvantaged, and the minority groups are relatively disadvantaged. This system places Mizrahi Jews in an intermediary position in the country's ethnic hierarchy overall. They are "occupying the actantial slot of both dominated and dominators; simultaneously disempowered as 'Orientals' or 'blacks' vis-à-vis 'white' Euro-Israelis and empowered as Jews in a Jewish state vis-à-vis Palestinians. In a sense, Mizrahim are both embedded in and in excess of Zionist history" (Shohat 2003, 50).

Ashkenormativity and Marginal Group Membership Theory

This book brings this hierarchy into conversation with marginal group membership theory. Marginality is not a matter of incomplete membership. Mizrahim are not considered less Jewish necessarily. In fact, insofar as they may

---

* Heritage could also be verified. After all, Lavie (2018, 39) indicates that "one of the most common questions among Israeli Jews" is "What's your origin?"

be more religiously engaged, by some metrics they could be treated as more Jewish. However, the so-called Arab Jews are less *prototypical* Jewish Israelis because they do not match the prototypical ethno-cultural background. As such, they are part of the group but not the core of it.

Several implications for Israeli social and political opinion are drawn from the confluence of Ashkenormativity and marginal group membership theory. These predictions are the substance of the following chapters. The marginality can be established in theory through the historical, sociological, and anthropological literature. It can also be empirically documented. *The non-prototypical Jewish Israelis will be more aware of the marginalization than prototypical group members are, even if the prototypical members are part of the cultural enforcement of prototypicality.* Thus, it is predicted that the Mizrahim/Sephardim will be more aware of biases and discrimination in Israel. They could also report exclusion from the political system. More is said of Ashkenormativity and its implications for experiences of discrimination and social inclusion in Chapter 2.

Marginal group members are more likely to protect group boundaries and privileges. The threat of being pushed out of the group identity means they must cling tighter to it, especially where loss of status would mean loss of privileges. In Israel, this pattern would manifest in a *stronger attachment to Jewish identity among Mizrahi/Sephardi Jewish Israelis. This link can be both for themselves and for the State of Israel.* Being Jewish matters more to their identity. In their politics, they are more likely to support enacting Jewish law, privileging Jewish Israelis, and preserving the Jewish majority in the population. That can translate into out-group derogation and unflattering downward comparisons. In Israel that means devaluing the Palestinians' standing and their desire to return. Notably, although emphasizing the Jewish identity moves the Mizrahim/Sephardim closer to the dominant group, because the prototypical Jewish Israeli is secular it does not prototypify them. Jewish identitarianism and majority-preserving preferences among the nonprototypical Jewish Israelis are demonstrated in Chapter 3.

These effects are also influential on state structural preferences. In-group majoritarianism, the prioritization of religious law, and out-group denigration are not consistent with liberal democracy. Thus, *marginal group members may be less committed democrats*, despite Israel's democratic identity, and may *prioritize Jewish law over democratic outcomes.* The implications for democracy are discussed in Chapter 4. In terms of conflict attitudes, the Mizrahim/Sephardim would experience more pressure to demonstrate a Jewish Israeli connection rather than an Arab connection, which can manifest in skepticism toward concessions or peace. *Mizrahim/Sephardim will be more supportive of expanding the Jewish state.* The implications for the Israeli-Palestinian conflict are elucidated in Chapter 5.

Bundled Identity

Race and ethnicity can be analytically challenging to study. After all, neither is amenable to experimental randomization. Furthermore, all of life occurs after birth, which is construed as assignment to "treatment." Thus, researchers might suggest that studying anything related to race involves conditioning on a post-"treatment" factor, which would corrupt analysis (Montgomery, Nyhan, and Torres 2018).

This study draws on the theory of race as a "bundle of sticks" and applies it to analysis of Jewish ethnicities in Israel (Sen and Wasow 2016). Although Maya Sen and Omar Wasow use the word *race* in titling their article, it applies to "race, ethnicity, and other seemingly immutable characteristics," such as sexuality and gender (500). This theory focuses on ethnic and racial identity as a social construct rather than merely a pattern of genetic traits. Thus, the differences are a reflection of the sociocultural, ideological, and geographical influences on the lived experience. This approach "allows race to be disaggregated into constitutive elements, some of which can be manipulated experimentally or changed through other types of interventions" (500). The sticks can include dialect, wealth and social class, religion, skin color, power relations, norms, diet, and neighborhood in addition to the more essentialist traits, such as genetics and region of ancestry. Race and ethnicity are the mixture of these forces, both those that are static and those that could change.

Researchers almost never argue that the genetic quirks that lead to curly hair, freckles, or pigmentation drive the differences among racial or ethnic groups. That is certainly not the argument here. An essentialist take on race or ethnicity might, though, leave this impression. Rather, the full social experience of living as part of a group in society is often the focus in analyzing race-associated distinctions. The social component is particularly important in considering marginal group membership theory because marginality is a social experience, including mutual (non)recognition and hierarchical structures.

The scale of the "bundle" would be problematic in examining the differences between subgroups if the difference being assessed were constitutive of the group. However, it does not seem credible that a constitutive element of the Ashkenazi population is indifference to a Jewish state or that Mizrahim are defined by an opinion on refugee resettlement. It is then possible to divide the sample ethnically, recognizing the larger experience of ethnicity, without making the answers obvious or redundant.

Some sticks in this bundle can be more important than others, especially for shaping the different beliefs or behaviors across groups. Ostfeld and Yadon (2022b) equate this to some tree roots being larger than others. Religiosity or socioeconomic status, for instance, may particularly matter for political attitudes. This does not mean they are not still part of the bundle.

It is possible to pull some sticks out of the bundle analytically. For instance, modeling strategies often include covariates for partisanship or socioeconomic status. By including this variable separately, the model effectively plucks that stick out, and the race or ethnicity variables show the effect of the remaining sticks. The ability to remove the stick analytically does not mean that the characteristic is not part of the ethnicity in that case; it just means that it is not being included in the measurement of ethnicity's relationship to the outcome then. In some cases, this is informative in its own right. Scholars may be interested to find that, even once the class, education, or religion stick has been removed, the remainder of the bundle is still significantly related. This approach could also show which facets of the ethnicity are doing a lot of the work relating ethnicity and outcome. It is a research design choice. The ethnic effect, in total, is still the full bundle of sticks.

This study is *not* asserting that primordial distinctions related to the source countries of emigration or even differences in phenotype and their underlying genetics are the causal forces. Rather, the *total social experience* of being part of this group is. In the bundle-of-sticks framework, there are sticks that are not the same between bundles, although they are includable across the bundles. For instance, Ashkenazim are seen as more secular. Mizrahim are viewed as more likely to support rightist parties, while Ashkenazim are associated with leftist parties. Mizrahim often are of a lower socioeconomic status, have fewer educational and employment opportunities, and are more traditionalist (Mizrachi and Weiss 2020; Herzog 1985; Lewin-Epstein and Cohen 2019). In fact, the partisan bents have been identified as a result of the Mizrahim marginalization (Lewin-Epstein and Cohen 2019) and the "lingering memory of painful integration" (Bagno-Moldavski 2015, 519). The predominantly lower-class status is a result of choices made by immigration officials and other state officers during the Ingathering, during which Mizrahim were relegated to lower positions because they did not fit the Western, secular ideal (Khazzoom 2008). The gatekeepers' intention was not ethnic hierarchy but rather a privileging of Westernness—"the project of Westernization, not of producing an ethnic dichotomy"—that nonetheless had that effect (e.g., by assigning occupations on the basis of cultural fit as well as technical qualification) (Khazzoom 2008, 7). The process nonetheless shaped domestic ethnic hierarchies both by drawing on between-group distinctions and by creating others as a result of their choices.

Sticks—such as education, class, or religiosity—are of varying degrees of importance depending on the context. In this case, these patterns are not being attributed to some inherent group characteristic, like "Easternness."

Rather, it is the experience of hierarchy that is thought to influence the behavior of (at least some) members of the ethnic groups.

Datasets

This manuscript draws primarily from three data sources. One is the Israel sample of the European Social Survey in Wave 8 (ESS8; September 6, 2016 to February 7, 2017) and Wave 10 (ESS10; January 1 to July 16, 2022). ESS surveys share a common battery of questions to which rotating additional topics are added. ESS8 features questions on welfare attitudes and climate change. ESS10 includes questions on understandings and evaluations of democracy and digital contacts in work and family life.

For the ESS, the sample is representative of the population fifteen years of age and older, regardless of citizenship and nationality. Participants are selected by random probability sampling for the addresses and within-household surveyed individual.[15] The survey was available in Hebrew, Arabic, and Russian. As the intention here is to focus on intra-Jewish ethnicity and group identity, the sample was subset to include only Israelis who identified themselves as Jewish ($n = 1943$, 76 percent of those surveyed in ESS8, and $n = 647$, 49.7 percent of those surveyed in ESS10[16]).

The second dataset is the Pew Research Center's Israel's Religiously Divided Society Data Set. The surveys, 5,601 face-to-face interviews with noninstitutionalized adults ages eighteen and older living in Israel, were taken between October 2014 and May 2015. The survey used a multistage stratified area probability sampling design based on national population data from Israel's Central Bureau of Statistics' 2008 census. As with the ESS dataset, this study focuses on the Jewish subset. Respondents were identified by their self-identification in response to a question of their "nationhood"—Jewish, Arab, or other.[17] The Jewish sample is 67.8 percent of the survey responses ($n = 3800$). This method includes the small number of respondents who identified as atheists on the religion question but who were from Jewish families. All the Jewish respondents took the survey in Hebrew or Russian.

The third dataset is an original survey of adult Jewish Israelis via the Israeli online panel iPanel. The sample includes 993 individuals.[18] The survey was in the field from May 18 to June 2, 2022.[19] iPanel offers quota sampling for gender, age bracket, religiosity, and region of Israel. It has been used in previous academic studies in Israel (Grossman, Manekin, and Margalit 2018; Manekin, Grossman, and Mitts 2019). The sample includes several levels of religiosity from secular (Hiloni) to ultra-Orthodox (Haredi). For information on the sample characteristics, see Appendix A. For information on variable coding for all of the surveys, see Appendix B.

This survey included a free-response space in which the survey takers could share their thoughts on the topics addressed. The question was optional, and many left it blank—open-ended responses are more cognitively taxing—wrote that they had nothing else to share, or expressed thanks for the survey and the opportunity to share their opinions. Others wrote more discursive statements. These range from short statements on particular topics to longer discussions of detailed policy preferences, political ideals, and visions for the state or the region. Their commentary is shared throughout this volume to complement the quantitative analyses. These statements demonstrate the variety of opinions circulating in Israeli popular discourse on these topics and how contradictory, impassioned, and nuanced these opinions can be. Jewish Israelis have complex thoughts on issues of identity, democracy, and conflict.

While most respondents expressed pleasure or neutrality toward being asked these questions, two were less pleased with the survey—but also chose to complete it. A 23–29-year-old vocationally trained mixed-ethnicity Dati man in the Jerusalem area wrote, "May your names be erased, troublers of Israel. This is a shockingly biased survey. The editors and initiators of the survey are a bunch of wretched cowards." "May your name be erased" is a Hebrew curse typically used for enemies of the Jewish people, such as Haman, Hitler, and Stalin, though it has been applied to lesser offenders (and, on rare occasions, said flippantly). It has also been used toward countries deemed to have persecuted Jews. That respondent had voted for Hatzionut Hadatit (Religious Zionist Party), and he supported an enlarged state with peace and a stable Jewish majority; he was opposed to liberal democracy. Evidently, he was quite displeased to be asked his opinions, though he chose to share them.

As is customary in the consent process, the respondents were told who was fielding the survey, including name, university affiliation, and contact information. Still, one respondent—a secular college-educated Sephardi man in the Sharon region, 50+ years old,—wrote at the end, "I would love to know who is behind the research? What body and for what purpose? Is it a Jew who cares about the state or one who defines himself as an Arab and promotes anti-Israeli agendas. It is easy to distort data for the sake of an argument." This book is not promoting "an agenda." The intention is to convey public opinion as relayed in these surveys, not to distort it.

As noted above, marginality is separate from group identity. All individuals in this sample are identified in these datasets as Israeli Jews. Their marginal and prototypical status occurs within that pool. Marginal group members who do not identify with the group (when such groups are exitable) may not perform their membership. Jewishness and national identity are not readily renounceable; Jewish Israelis would have to leave the country to escape the ESS Israel cluster. Ancestry and Jewish law do not offer an exit option; even atheists who renounce tenets of the faith are still within the fold in that respect. The inclusion by default of any individuals in the panel who reject these classifications on a personal level—despite their objective classification in the survey—would work against finding in-group favoring and identity-affirming patterns.

The way these subgroups are identified is important. The completeness of any person's bundle cannot be readily quantified; ancestry, though, can be taken for a strong proxy. Notably, the ESS survey for each country offers a large list of ethnicities from which respondents can choose. The questionnaire gives the option to choose an inclusive identity—Jewish or Israeli—rather than specify an ethnicity within those headings, and a large share of the respondents do just that. In ESS8, an Israeli supplemental survey identified the subgroups more specifically as Ashkenazi, Mizrahi/Sephardi, mixed, or other. Of those inclusive framings, Mizrahim were more likely to have selected Jewish than Israeli, and Ashkenazim were more likely to have selected Israeli than Jewish. Noah Lewin-Epstein and Yinon Cohen (2019, 2126) posit that this "reflect[s] the greater tendency of Mizrahim to identify with Israel via its Jewish religion and history, more than with the secular Zionist project of modern Israel." If Mizrahim see themselves as grouped by their shared religion but still excluded from social participation, then maybe the country identity deserves to be less foregrounded. In theory, this could suggest that the relative sizes of these sticks in the ethnicity bundles are different.[20] Still, Lewin-Epstein and Cohen (2019, 2130) show that there is a "strong correspondence" between Jewish Israelis' ancestral (parent and grand-parent) countries of birth—their objective group status—and their reported grouping.[21]

Because of the tendency to choose these inclusive categories, questions that do not include them are necessary to really mark the distinctions. In the iPanel study, respondents could self-identify as Ashkenazi, Mizrahi, Sephardi, mixed, or other. Those who indicated "other" were able to write in their information. Some of those respondents gave answers that actually belonged in the other categories—for instance, identifying themselves as Ashkenazi or indicating from which Arab country (e.g., Iraq or Yemen) their family derived. These responses are recoded into the correct group for analysis. The other answers (e.g., Israeli, Jewish) were coded as other.[22] Other, as a category, included groups like Ethiopian Jews as well as individuals who identified as American or Soviet. While in the latter case the large majority would be Ashkenazi, for these analyses those individuals are left in the "other" bloc. As Ethiopian migration to Israel was "met with considerable ambivalence," racial identity with the source country remains salient, even among those born in Israel (Lewin-Epstein and Cohen 2019, 2126). The Pew Research Center also offered respondents the choice of Ashkenazi, Mizrahi, Sephardi, mixed, or other.

This coding is consistent with Israel Central Bureau of Statistics (ICBS) practices.[23] For comparability across the classifications, the iPanel and Pew Research Center survey studies are coded into the four-group structure used by the ESS.[24] Ashkenazim are the reference ethnic category. A small number of ESS8 respondents ($n = 173$) volunteered an answer that was coded as "neither" or "I do not define myself according to my ethnic origin."[25] They are not included in the main analyses (Online Appendix, available at https://scholarshare.temple.edu/handle/20.500.12613/9253).

The ESS8 and iPanel surveys also offered the respondents the opportunity to self-identify as a member of a minority ethnic group. Non-Jewish Israelis were significantly more likely to report that they were members of a minority ethnic group in Israel in ESS8, but some of the Jewish Israelis identified as minorities as well. The surveys find such identifiers in each ethnic group.

There are no official statistics on the population breakdown. These several studies have slightly different proportions of each group. The ethnicity proportions are shown in Table 1.1. Other population statistics in the sample are shown in Table 1.2 to provide context for the country's demographics.[26]

This blunt classification is not meant to avoid considering the broad position of ethnicity. Sen and Wasow (2016, 502) warn that using dummy variables for race or ethnic groups can "implicitly rel[y] on essentialist ideals" if

TABLE 1.1 ETHNICITY PER SURVEY SAMPLE

Survey	Ashkenazi	Sephardi	Mizrahi	Mixed	Nonethnic	Other	Israeli	DK/NA	Minority
Pew Research Center	47.1	17.4	27.9	7.3	—	0.1	—	0.3	—
ESS8	34.8	39.4		11.0	9.1	3.7	—	2.1	3.4
ESS10	29.6	34.0		4.9	—	4.2	24.6	2.7	—
iPanel	40.3	13.1	29.8	13.5	—	2.7	—	—	4.6

TABLE 1.2 SURVEY DEMOGRAPHICS

Survey	Percent Male	Mean (SD) Age	Percent College Educated	Percent Haredi	Percent Hiloni (Secular)
Pew Research Center	49.8	43.4 (16.6)	28.2	18.6	41.7
ESS8	48.1	48.9 (19.8)	32.9	—	—
ESS10	43.0	44.2 (18.2)	40.6	—	—
iPanel[1]	42.3	—	51.2	4.3	51.2

[1] The iPanel survey used age quotas. 10.2% were 18–21, 16.8% were 22–29, 21.6% were 30–39, 18.8% were 40–49, and 32.5% were over 50.

researchers do not consider the theoretical role of race or ethnicity in the modeling strategy. In this case, the models are presented first with just ethnic group and minority identity. Additional models then pluck commonly evaluated sticks (e.g., religiosity and political ideology) from the bundles to look at those effects as well as the residuary relationship with ethnicity. Doing so shows the broadest ethnic association and accounts for major political sticks in these bundles.

Plan of the Book

The remainder of this text empirically examines Ashkenormativity and its connection to marginal group membership theory in Israel. Chapter 2 expands the discussion of Ashkenormativity and the development and perpetuation of this cultural pattern over decades. As indicated above, these tendencies derived from state policies and programs and have present-day social manifestations. Although some Israelis claim that intra-Jewish ethnicity is no longer of political importance and that "Jewish ethnicity has become more symbolic than real" (Smooha 2004, 51), recent sociological work indicates that it remains relevant. This chapter draws on data from the European Social Survey and the Pew Research Center to demonstrate the salience of ethnicity for citizens' experiences of social embeddedness. In marginal group membership theory, marginal group members can (almost paradoxically) maintain high group identity while being treated as less central to the group itself. Thus, marginal group members experience discrimination and can have stronger group attachments than prototypical group members. Mizrahi/Sephardi Jewish Israelis are more likely to recognize that non-Ashkenazi Jews in general experience discrimination in Israel. The marginal group members express greater awareness of the within-the-in-group distinctions in operation. In the face of this marginalization, the Mizrahi/Sephardi Jewish Israelis report stronger attachment to their Jewish identities than the Ashkenazim do.

Having laid this foundation, the book turns to the political implications of this within-group difference. Chapter 3 focuses on the desire for a Jewish state. It elaborates on the theory of marginal group membership, particularly its relationship to group-protective thinking and behaviors. Marginal group members have to perform group membership to secure their affiliation. Where the group receives political or social benefits, the marginal group members are incentivized to maintain those benefits, especially if, in a less hierarchical environment, they would be more likely to lose out than the prototypical group members would. In the case of Jewish Israelis, that performance manifests in the Mizrahim's endorsing and protecting the Jewish character of the state. A Jewish homeland, as promised in the Israeli Basic Law, is potentially both a religious and an ethnic phenomenon (Yadgar 2020). Protecting it has salience on both of those dimensions. The marginal group members are more likely to promote Jewish values and privileges within the state and to want the state to have a Jewish majority. Thus, Mizrahim are more likely to espouse Jewish nationalism and majoritarianism than the Ashkenazim.

This chapter uses data from the Pew Research Center, European Social Survey, and iPanel surveys to demonstrate citizens' attachment to the Jewish character of the state. The marginal group members feel more emotionally attached to Israel. They are more likely to protect Jewish privileges in Israel and to endorse the enactment of religious precepts and religious law. This protects the Jewish image of the state. They also support the Jewish majority in the state in several ways. One is by controlling entrance. The Basic Law specifically endorses the Ingathering of the Jewish diaspora. Marginal group members are open to Jewish migration, regardless of race. Their protectionism, though, makes them more skeptical and suspicious of non-Jewish immigrants, up to and including refugees, who would make the population less Jewish. Another method for maintaining a Jewish majority is controlling exit. Marginal group members are more likely to discourage Jews from emigrating. Furthermore, they are more likely to endorse expelling non-Jews from the state. In the totality of these preferences, non-Ashkenazi respondents are more invested in maintaining the Jewish national state in Israel than the prototypical group members are. Defending their majority shows their support for that group identity and attachment to the collective.

Most literature on marginal ethnic group membership focuses on race and racialized policies. Recent work, however, has argued that democratic stability in multicultural democracies is undermined by interethnic animosity and fears about relative group status (Jardina and Mickey 2022; Pérez, Robertson, and Vicuña 2023). Chapter 4 extends the consideration of marginal group membership among Israeli Jews to consider their attitudes toward Israel's democracy. Israel asserts a liberal democratic agenda, and it is coded as a democracy by most contemporary metrics. For instance, in 2022, it scored 0.72 out of 1 on V-Dem's Electoral Democracy Index, and it is rated free by Freedom House (Coppedge et al. 2022).[27] While Jewish Israelis agree that their country has the electoral institutions associated with democracy—the most minimalist definition of democracy—they are less convinced of its liberalism credentials. Israel's illiberal policies toward non-Jewish subjects in particular have been invoked to question its democratic status. Furthermore, the Mizrahim are more likely than the Ashkenazim to hold an expansive interpretation of *democracy* as a concept. In particular, they are more likely to incorporate direct democracy, anti-elitism, and socioeconomic policies into their "democracy" framework. They are taking a more maximalist interpretation.[28]

Chapter 4 unpacks Jewish Israelis' regime-type preferences. It demonstrates that the Mizrahim are marginally less confident than Ashkenazim that they are influencing the government of their democracy, although governing documents proffer equal rights. If the system does not represent all of the citizens, then the democratic caliber of the state can be called into question, irrespective of the aforementioned democracy scores. Furthermore, in any privileged group, marginal members have less reason to be liberal, as long as the illiberal policies are aimed at out-groups or the members believe that supporting the regime will make them seem more in-group. Marginal group members can, however, support majoritarianism where their group is in the majority. If they are asserting group privileges, denigrating out-group members, and trying to perform group membership to enhance inclusion, then the marginal members can be more likely to favor illiberal policies that benefit the group or restrict out-group members. For instance, discursive comments by the iPanel survey takers demonstrate some respondents' willingness to deny equal rights to non-Jewish Israelis or Palestinians. That is also consistent with the Jewish majoritarianism expressed in Chapter 3. These attitudes are not very compatible with liberal democracy, even if they could pass institutional muster.

Thus, using data from the Pew Research Center, the European Social Survey, and original surveys, the fourth chapter demonstrates that the Mizrahim place less value on having a liberal democracy in Israel. Furthermore, the Mizrahim are more likely to support a religious state at the expense of a democratic state. The marginal group members are more likely to say the state can be both a religious state and a democracy, which denies the potential conflict that exists. When push comes to shove, though, they are more willing to privilege *halakha* (Jewish law) over democratic outcomes. This is consistent with group affirmation and group (status) protectionism. Marginal group membership status then informs both overtly ethno-religious-nationalist opinions and less overtly ethnic politics—regime structural preferences.

The fifth chapter addresses the ongoing Israel-Palestine conflict and whether several related objectives—expanded territorial borders, peace, democracy, and a Jewish majority—can be united. Israel, by declaration, aims to be both a Jewish national state and a democracy. Israeli regimes purport to seek peace with the neighboring states, but several administrations have also sought to extend the boundaries of the Jewish state. Thus, there is a great tension between many desired outcomes. In truth, the policy question is not "Should there be peace?" or "Should there be equality?" but "On what terms are such ends accepted?" Jewish Israelis were asked about their preferences for expanding Israel's borders, making peace with the Arab states, forming a liberal democracy, and maintaining a Jewish majority. Marginal group members' group protectiveness and threat reactiveness predict harsher attitudes toward the Palestinians. Marginal group membership theory would also predict a greater willingness to defend the group's interest and conduct compared to prototypical members. That propensity marshals for a larger state, for a Jewish majority, and maybe even against peace.

For instance, marginal group members were more likely to believe that Jewish settlements in the Occupied Territories enhance security. From a practical standpoint, settlements and security are not concordant; however, the settlements promote group dominance. Those who prioritize that outcome may adopt a contradictory belief in its service (Oren 2019). The marginal Jewish Israelis demonstrate less support for retrenching to the Green Line borders.[29] This is even evident in the discursive responses the survey takers provided. While many respondents supported peace as a notion, even the most important one, others insisted that maintaining a Jewish majority or extending the boundaries of the state was decisive for their conception of Israel. Diverging preferences and preference hierarchies on these points demonstrate the difficulty of resolving these contradictions in Israeli politics.

In addition to asking for respondents' direct preferences on these points, the survey also included a conjoint experiment asking citizens to rate potential futures for Israel along these dimensions. It builds on Michal Shamir and Jacob Shamir's (1995) study during the First Intifada; in that time of conflict, Jewish Israelis valued peace and a Jewish-majority state. Democracy was an afterthought. This chapter demonstrates that segments of the Jewish Israeli population have strongly held but contrary preferences on these issues. In the recent results, these groups express similar average relative ratings to each other; they are largely not behaving differently in the conjoint. When it comes to balancing these features against each other, Ashkenazim place lower relative weight on maintaining a liberal democracy in Israel. Secular Israelis—whether defined by self-identification or by nonparticipation—place greater relative weight on enlarging the state and maintaining a durable Jewish majority. They are more tolerant of nondemocracy. The population is divided on the most important features for the state's future, and not everyone supports liberal democracy (especially not as the most important part).

Taken together, these results show just some of the domains in which Jewish ethnicity continues to influence the politics of Israel, a Jewish ethno-religious state. The conclusion considers the implications of the continuation of Ashkenormativity and of social biases for attitudes toward a Jewish-majority state. For instance, eradicating bias is a normative good. However, not all parties favor reducing popular interest in the Jewish majority. They may be philosophically committed, or they may see this belief as a political advantage. The conclusion also considers the intersection of Jewish and Arab identity as it links to the ultimate out-group in Israeli society, the non-Jewish minority. The developing demographic threat to Israel's Jewish majority will then increase the out-group threat and could shape in untold ways attitudes toward these nonprototypical in-group members. The Ingathering of Jewish diaspora will have to include non-Ashkenazim, increasing the ethnic diversity of the state, which will challenge the Westernizing and homogenizing project. Intra-Jewish ethnic diversity constitutes, then, a source of perpetuation and discord for Israel's Jewish identity. Understanding that discord and its political implications starts with recognizing the existing biases in Israeli society.

These findings also point to the need for greater consideration of race and ethnicity in comparative politics. Although the discussion here is focused on the majority ethno-religious community in Israel, there are other elements of ethnic politics that should continue to be explored. Relative group positions reveal the loci of power within countries. Which groups have sway, and, within the major players, are there strata of authority? The fusion and rupture of ethnicity, religion, and nation are animating political discourses in many countries around the world. Other countries, particularly those that would appeal to ethno-nationalism, grapple with prototypical and marginal group members. In countries that centralize religion, schismatics and immigrants can pose a similar dilemma. Enhancing the understanding of the confluence of ethnicity, religion, and politics will require globalizing the analyses.

2

EXPERIENCES OF DISCRIMINATION AND ALIENATION

Substantial work has already documented the culturally constructed disparities between ethnic groups within Israel's Jewish population. European-origin Israelis benefited from their assumed Westernness and the goal of establishing Israel as a Western state (Khazzoom 2008). This pattern evolved into a continuing socioeconomic disparity between European-origin Israelis (Ashkenazim) and the Orientalized Asian/North African–origin Israelis (Mizrahim/Sephardim).

It is easy to imagine individuals who benefit from social privilege—either in a broad hierarchical sense or by being prototypical group members within a community—not recognizing that advantage. Peggy McIntosh (1989) described white privilege as an "invisible package of unearned assets" to which people were "'meant' to remain oblivious": "White privilege is like an invisible weightless knapsack of special provisions, maps, passports, codebooks, visas, clothes, tools and blank checks." Being Jewish in Israel operates that way— both metaphorically and at literal checkpoints. Members of a group—especially if the group identity has been linked to experiences of discrimination— may be reticent to see even prototypicality as a privilege.[1]

It is harder to imagine that victims of discrimination do not see it. However, it happens. American ethnic groups, for instance, disagree within and across groups about the extent to which racism exists in American society and whether it is driven by institutional forces or personal choices (Schaeffer and Edwards 2022). Members of racial, ethnic, and religious minorities can, however, also be acutely aware of their position and its implications

(Daniller 2021; Dawson 1994). Their political awareness and practices would be shaped by their lived experiences and by what they are taught about the state around them. This social subordination or othering and the awareness thereof, rather than any innate differences between the groups, drives political differences.

This chapter focuses on that awareness. In particular, the discussion demonstrates that nonprototypical Jewish Israelis are aware of the marginalization of the non-Ashkenazim living in Israel. Even if they themselves have not experienced ethno-racial bias (or rather think that they have not), they are aware that group-based distinctions are made. Nevertheless, these nonprototypical Jewish Israelis are still strong group identifiers—even stronger Jewish identifiers than the prototypical group members are.

From Marginality to Marginalization

The most obvious domain of ethnicized difference in Israeli politics is the schism between the Jewish Israeli population and the Palestinian population. While there are Palestinian citizens of Israel and they are promised equal rights in the Declaration of Independence, they are separate from the religious national claim. Palestinian noncitizens are further removed. The challenges of that out-group in the Israeli framework have been traversed elsewhere. Within the Jewish population—also promised equal rights in this national state—intragroup ethnic distinctions have been reified. As is noted in subsequent chapters, recognizing these in-group dynamics contributes to our understanding of out-group policy preferences. First, though, it is necessary to unpack the nature of these within-group distinctions.

As part of the development of a new Jewish state, including a narrative of "return," a construction of culture was undertaken. Most, but not all, Mandatory Palestine Jews were connected to Eastern Europe (Shoshana 2016). It was this Ashkenazi-predominant population that would establish the norms for integration of the next generation of immigrants. The population rapidly increased in the early years of the new state, drawing in new Israelis from more than twenty countries, including Europe and the Middle East and North Africa (Sasson-Levey 2013). This was followed by more Jews from the Middle East in the 1950s and 1960s, as Jewish communities exited the postcolonial Arab states (Bagno-Moldavski 2015; Lewin-Epstein and Cohen 2019). In those decades, then, the balance shifted toward the Mizrahim. Another influx came from the former Soviet Union and Ethiopia in the 1980s and 1990s (Lewin-Epstein and Cohen 2019; Kalev and Maor 2015). These arrivals enlarged the Ashkenazi population. When individuals are gathered with "no interpersonal relationship with any individual group members, they are motivated to sustain a psychological representation of a cohesive, well-defined, and normatively legitimated group" (Marques et al. 1998, 976). In the case of Israel, that formulated group identity was based on European-inflected Jewish norms.

During this process of Ingathering, proto-Israelis were processed by government officials, often veterans of the initial conflicts with the Arab states; many of these officials were Ashkenazim who had migrated from Eastern Europe during the Mandate period. Aziza Khazzoom (2008) describes how the immigrating populations were dispersed somewhat haphazardly throughout the country to populate it with Jews. The government agents could influence access to housing, government employment, or state subsidies. Thus, "the system's all-encompassing grip left new citizens with no alternative but complete reliance on the bureaucratic infrastructure" (Lavie 2018, 19).

In that infrastructure, choices were made that would promote an ethnic hierarchy in Israel. For instance, new arrivals were processed upon arrival, distributed throughout the claimed territory, granted access to benefits systems, and assigned or admitted to occupations.[2] In theory, this would be an egalitarian process; however, "resources were eventually distributed by the Mizrahi/Ashkenazi distinction" (Khazzoom 2008, 7). State gatekeepers gave privileges to the European populations as part of a concerted effort to make Israel into a Western state, so "in a case in which class and ethnicity were not initially fully correlated, this modern industrialized society distributed occupations along ethnic lines directly" (5).

It was not an immediate process; rather, it developed over several years. As noted above, the melting pots did not immediately convert Poles and Russians into Ashkenazim and Yemenis and Iraqis into Mizrahim. The subversion of these origin communities, though, was facilitated by intermarriage and by others' reification of those distinctions.

In fact, initially, some high-skilled Mizrahim were able to access privileges. These were typically Eastern migrants who could signal Westernization. For instance, Iraqi Jews were more likely than Yemeni or Moroccan Jews to have lived in urban areas and to have Western educations, and more of the community and its leaders moved to Israel in a short burst and brought some wealth with them; that made the Iraqi community better able to act as a group. While Moroccan Jews had access to European education, many immigrated to France, and migration to Israel was spread over more time. Yemeni Jews were more likely to have received a religious education than a European one (Khazzoom 2008). Eastern migrants who could signal Westernization (e.g., through knowledge of European languages or secular education) could receive some access to privileged positions. Cultural bias meant that qualifications, such as education and source-country occupation, could offset some of the statistical discrimination that these "Arab Jews" experienced: "Gatekeepers did not exclude Mizrahim but rather excluded Mizrahim who could not prove westernness" (Khazzoom 2008, 156). However, the statistical discrimination still worked in favor of the Ashkenazim, and the benefits of European language and secular education would accrue to them at a greater rate. Thus, even a fuzzy application in the beginning could congeal over time.

The contemporaneous memory of these early biases demonstrates that they were eventually discerned—although now some argue that they were only a phenomenon of the past. It is possible in the initial period that the new immigrants were not as aware. This introduces the possibility of an integration paradox phenomenon (Schaeffer and Kas 2023; Lajevardi et al. 2020). In that case, the more educated immigrants and those with a better command of languages used by the Ashkenazi community (e.g., languages from Europe) would be better able to perceive the discrimination they were experiencing. This cannot be assessed with contemporary public opinion data—most current Jewish residents of Israel are native-born Israelis and capable Hebrew speakers. However, it is an area that can be explored in future research.

This bifurcation was increased in the subsequent generation. Children of the Mizrahim who had achieved higher-status employment were still Mizrahim in the Israeli education system. Schoolteachers—often Ashkenazim who obtained their positions in the ethnicized assignment of occupations—served as gatekeepers in the subsequent generations, reducing the Mizrahim's ability to turn their own surpassing of bias into gains among their offspring. Even in families that had demonstrated Westernness in the prior generation—performing Ashkenaziness, to use Sasson-Levy's (2013) language—were likely to see their children "'became Mizrahim,' in a resource distribution sense" (Khazzoom 2008, 185). Over time, the Ashkenazim who were tacitly benefiting from the Orientalist bias would have an economic incentive not to question the disparity or to even see it as a bias. Ultimately, the "problem of class distinction [did] not derive directly from ethnic differences but from differences in the opportunities structure" as a result of these practices and policies (Herzog 1985, 47).

Thus, state policies encouraged an ethnic bifurcation: "In Israel, the moral question of gatekeeper culpability for discrimination against Mizrahim remains a potent political and emotional one. Moreover, because Ashkenazim and Mizrahim were supposed to be 'brothers,' discrimination against Mizrahim is often perceived as less legitimate than discrimination against Palestinians" (Khazzoom 2008, 155). Nonetheless, discrimination occurs. Discrimination against marginal group members can be a way for prototypical members to assert their prototypicality (Hogg and Reid 2006) and enforce group norms (Marques et al. 1998). Ongoing derogation of the nonprototypical group members, however, will remind them of their marginality. Thus, the social inequality between ethnic groups "endures in the second, third and even fourth generation" (Mizrachi and Herzog 2012). Nativity and the erasure of ethnic classification on census forms—these citizens being Sabra now legally—have not, it seems, done the work.

In theory, all "'Diasporic Jews' had to abandon their diasporic culture" (Shohat 2003, 50). In practice, the "Oriental"-seeming immigrants were meant to shuck their culture in favor of a Western image that was more readily adopted by Western immigrants. A melting-pot ideology, rather than pluralist ideology, aimed to remove the Eastern culture in favor of an Ashkenazi cultural pattern (Herzog 1985; Bagno-Moldavski 2015; Yadgar 2020). The cultural diversity in successive waves of immigration was seen as "a threat to national unity" (Yadgar 2020, 27). Mizrahi culture was considered "'primitive', 'traditional', 'anti-intellectual',," and threatening to "the model of the new Jew which the country's leaders were trying to imbue with the spirit of the West" (Shoshana 2016, 492). This West was also secular. Being perceived as extra religious led to a double hit for the Eastern Jews:

> Orthodox Mizrahi Jews were the quintessential "unfit," a group requiring secularisation and modernisation, whereas the Arab Muslims were the quintessential "other." That is, whereas religious Jews in general were regarded as unfit for the Zionist enterprise of establishing a modern Jewish state, the Mizrahi ultra-Orthodox working class were (and still are among many liberal secular Jews) regarded as needing cultural adaptation to modernity. (Mizrachi and Weiss 2020, 176)

For Jews already residing in the Middle East—Arab Jews—that gathering into Israel and the attendant acculturation process "meant abandoning Arabness and acquiescing in assimilationist modernization, for 'their own good'" (Shohat 2003, 50). Lavie (2018, 61) cites one Mizrahi woman's approval of that differentiation: "'They hate us alright, but they advanced us' said Sigal. 'We're no longer 'Aravim.'"* She sees her community's change toward Ashkenazi-inflected culture as an improvement as a differentiation from the Arabs. That the ultimate Other was also Arab would only compound the stigmatization of Arab identity.

This circumstance creates a double bind. Religious participation can increase citizens' sense of religious-group-linked fate, which would in turn likely inform political preferences (Donnelly 2021). In particular, it would highlight their hierarchical social position. These individuals must be Jewish

---

* The same speaker also argued against unity with the Arab population because she did not think it would be reciprocated. She favored Jewish nationalism and a hard line: "Why do you speak in favor of the 'Aravim? It's over with. Do you really love them? When the time comes, and they slaughter us, you won't get a pass because you call yourself an 'Arab Jew' and think you're one of them. They are the enemy" (72).

to separate themselves from the Palestinians, but they must be secular to be Western. They can be pulled into the group and marginalized within it by the same action.

This ethnic formation and the cultivated distinction led, over not even very much time, to economic disparities between the two groups. There is a socioeconomic gap between "Jews of African and Asian origin" and "those of European and North American origin" wherein "people from Asian and African countries suffer low social esteem and status" (Herzog 1985, 47). This is reflected in educational and employment inequality (Lewin-Epstein and Cohen 2019). In time the word "'Oriental' in Israel has become synonymous with the lower class" (Herzog 1985, 48).[3]

How crucial these patterns are to the overall ethnic bundle is debatable:

> An individual may identify with one ethnoracial category and have some "sticks" (such as religion or skin color) that appear inconsistent with the prototypes associated with that category, yet have other "sticks" (such as region of ancestry or dialect) that appear quite consistent . . . the degree to which any of these components of ethnoracial identity persist as a basis of enduring stratification or division has been linked to their relative stickiness and their visibility. (Ostfeld and Yadon 2022b, 53, 59)

Ancestry is not shiftable, and skin pigment can only be changed so much. Ancestry and color would be harder to remove from the bundle or to conceal. Accents and language choices have been strategically developed among Jewish Israelis to signal integration and group membership (Khazzoom 2008). These sticks may not be out of the bundle, but they can be concealed. For example, almost every Jewish Israeli in these samples took the surveys in Hebrew or Russian. The marginal group members experience "the competing pressures embodied in the dynamic: the desire to distance oneself from adversity versus the desire to embrace the 'essential mother' of one's own community" (Ostfeld and Yadon 2022b, 65). The more durable and more visible sticks are most likely to be used to "maintain social divisions and stratifications" (60).

Class dynamics do not have to exist into perpetuity, and theoretically a state would want to ameliorate educational disadvantage in the population. These sticks, then, could be removed from the ethnic bundle or equalized across these bundles over time. That process would require social cooperation. In keeping with the bundle-of-sticks theory of ethnicity, these sticks are included in the overall Mizrahim bundle for now (Sen and Wasow 2016).

The role of the skin-color stick in these ethnic bundles is complicated. Recall that Mizrahim are sometimes called Jews of color or Black Jews. That does not mean that they are necessarily or always visually distinguishable.

Researchers sometimes "offhandedly refer to Mizrahi Jews as a group with relatively dark skin, without offering systematic analysis" (Kalev and Maor 2015, 15).[4] Although they are "associated with" darker complexions, "the skin color of Mizrahim ranges from very light (like north Europeans) to light-dark skin (like Hispanics or Arabs), to very dark (like that of Africans)" (Kalev and Maor 2015, 16). As both Ashkenazi and Mizrahi Jews "range from very light to very dark," "it is often impossible to discern a person's ethnic identity based solely on his or her phenotype" (Sasson-Levy 2013, 37). Even the darker-complected would not code as Black in the United States or Latin America (Sasson-Levy and Shoshana 2013). Instead of skin color, "class and habitus (e.g., accent, 'look,' phenotype (among Yemenites) and names)" contribute to the perceived ethnicity and "the term 'black' . . . was used primarily as an ethnic epithet, conflated with orientalism" (Mizrachi and Herzog 2012, 421). Although the appearances may objectively overlap substantially, a socially constructed notion of visual distinction has ramifications, at least for those on the far ends of the spectrum, because it will affect their classification by others— their "street race"—and thus their treatment. While color and the associated colorism are not singularly at work here, they are not absent from the story.

It is possible that intragroup dynamics are obscured among members of a group that enjoys social privilege. For instance, white Americans may be less cognizant of the disparate outcomes that darker-skinned whites experience, like increased likelihood of prosecution and lower levels of education: "A lack of attention to skin color dynamics among White people makes Whiteness appear to be relatively uniform, stable, and essentialized compared to what happens within other ethnoracial categories, thus falsely positioning Whites as unaffected by or uninvolved with this dimension of American racial dynamics" (Ostfeld and Yadon 2022b, 80). This could obscure Jewish Israelis' awareness of differential outcomes within the Jewish community.

There are, though, objective differences, whether or not all white Americans choose to notice them. As Branigan et al. (2017, 12) describe that circumstance in the United States, "Rather than white respondents' being categorically advantaged, while minorities are differentially advantaged on the basis of their proximity to aesthetic lightness, we find black respondents to be categorically disadvantaged, while white respondents are disadvantaged differentially on the basis of their proximity to aesthetic darkness."[5] Maintaining the parallel, the Palestinians are categorically disadvantaged, and the intra-Jewish groups are experiencing relative disadvantage.

The experience of marginality can be highly salient. Nonprototypical group members may feel isolated or invisible within their identity groups or from those observing their group (Ostfeld and Yadon 2022b). They can experience stress, ego depletion, mental distraction, and impaired cognitive ability due to stress (Ellemers and Jetten 2013). Over time, they can become particularly attuned to the biases in the structure and perceive negative interactions in that lens: "Somebody who aligns himself with structurally discriminated groups might perceive mistreatment that may or may not have occurred" (Hitlin, Brown, and Elder 2007, 596). Other victims of discrimination may downplay that experience for self-protection (Napier, Suppes, and Bettinsoli 2020). How they adapt is a personal and a situational choice.

Where a group is generally disfavored, the negative experiences among the marginal group members could manifest in seeking to leave the group or to avoid being identified with it. Experiences of discrimination may cause marginal group members to have negative feelings about their group (Ostfeld and Yadon 2022b). Historically, some individuals who were able to pass as white chose to do so to avoid the social, economic, and political costs of membership in a minority group. In the case of the Jewish community, some Mizrahim adopt Ashkenazi habitus (Selinger 2013; Kalev and Maor 2015). "In Israel, the phenomenon of ethnic passing is known as *hishtaknezut* (loosely translated as 'Ashkenazification')" (Sasson-Levy and Shoshana 2013, 448). These individuals—the *mishtaknez/im*—would be at risk of discovery and, subsequently, mockery or social sanction. Not all individuals, though, were able to make a strategic choice on this point, even if they were willing to do so.

Where individuals are marginal members of a dominant group, though, they are less likely to seek exit. Rather they would seek affirmation and connection. A stronger sense of group identity could form, especially if it offered social benefits. In this case, they would not seek to exit Jewish identity on this basis—even those trying to blend in with the Ashkenazim are still asserting membership in the macro-group. That they may desire to perpetuate that group's privileges is discussed more in the following chapter. Although individuals may try to strategically position themselves closer to one group or

TABLE 2.1 DEPENDENT VARIABLES AND DATASETS FOR CHAPTER 2			
Outcome Variable	Dataset	Table Number	Difference between Ashkenazim and Mizrahim/Sephardim
Group Discrimination	European Social Survey 8/10	2.2/2.3	–/–
Ethnic Discrimination	European Social Survey 8/10	2.2/2.3	–/#
Racial Discrimination	European Social Survey 8/10	2.2/2.3	–/#
Ethiopians Experience Discrimination	Pew Research Center	2.4	*
Mizrahim Experience Discrimination	Pew Research Center	2.4	*
Have a Say in Government	European Social Survey 10	2.5	–
Influence on Politics	European Social Survey 10	2.5	*
*p<0.10; *p<0.05			

another to gain access to privilege or to group protection, "ambiguity does not enable" individuals "to fully control how they are seen or treated" by others (Ostfeld and Yadon 2022b, 117). Prototypical members may still treat the marginal members with disfavor. This chapter addresses the extent to which these marginal group members identify and experience discrimination in Israel. Table 2.1 summarizes the variables and datasets used.

Discrimination in Israel

Recent Israeli public opinion surveys shed light on these issues of marginalization. Being part of the macro-group does not mean that one would necessarily be unaware of within-group differences in treatment and experiences. Despite the assertions of equality—both in the governing documents and by some members of the public—Jewish Israelis report that there is discrimination in their country.

In the Pew Research Center (2014–2015) study, 21.4 percent of Jewish Israelis stated that "there is a lot of discrimination" against Mizrahim in Israel. 75.9 percent indicated that there was "not a lot of discrimination." Discrimination against Ethiopian Jews was more readily admitted: 36.2 percent of Jewish Israelis reported extensive discrimination against Ethiopian Jews. 59.8 percent stated that there was not a lot of discrimination. Ethiopian-origin Jews in Israel are racially distinguished, and their immigration was initially fraught because of questions about their Jewish heritage and practice. Muslim and Christian respondents reported similar rates of discrimination for the two groups respectively. For comparison, 20.6 percent of Jewish Israelis said that Muslims experienced discrimination, while 74.9 percent said there was not a lot of anti-Muslim discrimination;[6] 20.6 percent identified antigay discrimination, while 74.9 did not, and 24.3 percent reported discrimination against women, while 73.6 percent did not. Disagreements about what constitutes *a lot of discrimination* could lead to an underreporting of social bias. Agreement by ethnic group is shown in Figures 2.1 and 2.2; the lighter bar represents the proportion perceiving discrimination, and the darker bar represents not perceiving it. (NB: Because of the small number of "other" identifiers in the Pew sample, that column is highly skewed for all figures using this dataset.) The report rates are higher among the marginal Jewish Israelis.

To a lesser extent, Jewish Israelis also mark themselves as experiencing discrimination. The European Social Survey asked respondents first broadly whether they self-identified as part of a group that is discriminated against in Israel. Those who reported identifying with a discriminated-against group were asked the form of the discrimination (race, ethnicity, religion, sexuality, disability, nationality, language, age, gender, other). In ESS8, 11.9 percent of Jewish Israeli respondents reported such identification: 1.6 percent of the

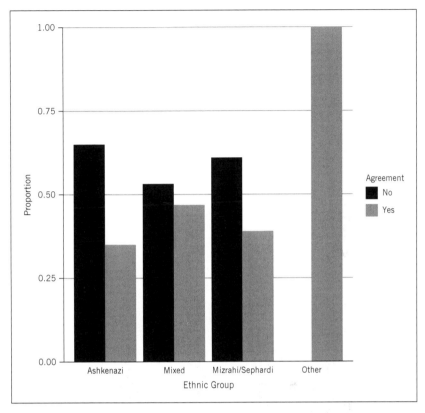

Figure 2.1 Ethnic Group Proportion Discrimination against Ethiopians *(Pew Research Center)*

Jewish respondents reported racial discrimination, and 1.1 percent reported ethnic discrimination. In ESS10, 28.0 percent of Jewish Israeli respondents reported experiencing discrimination:[7] 3.4 percent of the Jewish respondents reported racial discrimination, and 3.1 percent reported ethnic discrimination. It is possible that respondents incorporated their experiences outside of Israel in their thought processes; however, all the respondents live in Israel and likely spend most of their time there. Reported identification with ethnic discrimination by group is shown in Figure 2.3. The lighter bar indicates discrimination identification. The Mizrahi/Sephardi rate is slightly higher.

These survey questions asked respondents whether they identify as part of a group experiencing discrimination. This phrasing introduces noise into the data, which likely makes the Pew Research Center questions better indicators of social discrimination. Individuals can be hesitant to take on the identity of a victim of discrimination, preferring to blame other factors for particular incidents of bias. This rationalizing behavior has been document-

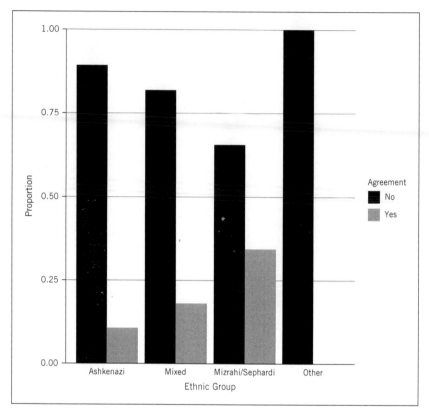

Figure 2.2 Ethnic Group Proportion Discrimination against Mizrahim *(Pew Research Center)*

ed in American women (Napier, Suppes, and Bettinsoli 2020). Nissim Mizrachi and Hanna Herzog (2012, 427) found that Mizrahi and Ethiopian Jewish Israelis "avoid using the first person" when discussing ethnic or racial discrimination and instead "most of our Mizrahi informants prefer to narrate such events as if experienced by friends and family." Admitting to that experience might legitimize ethnicity as a basis of social distinction. They may also see it as perpetuating the idea of otherization. They "deny the history of discrimination that they and their parents experienced in order to fit into the Ashkenazi middle-class mainstream, that is, to embody 'Israeliness'" (Lavie 2018, 88). Reporting that discrimination occurs to others may be less psychologically burdensome on the respondents. As such, these ESS results likely undercount the experiences of ethno-racial discrimination.[8]

Individuals who do not want to think of themselves as victims may underreport instances of discrimination (Foster 2000; Napier, Suppes, and Bettinsoli 2020). Failure to identify the macro problem and cooperate against it

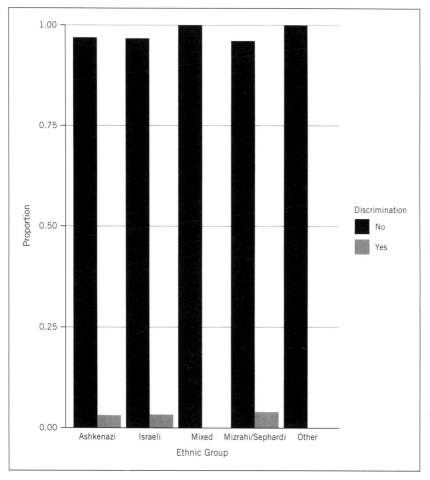

Figure 2.3 Ethnic Group Proportion Reporting Experiencing Ethnic Discrimination
(European Social Survey 10)

reduces the possibility for change. A countervailing assertion is that "some-body who aligns himself with structurally discriminated groups might perceive mistreatment that may or may not have occurred" (Hitlin, Brown, and Elder 2007, 596). That view would postulate that some reports are unwittingly erroneous. However, that principle acknowledges a larger, extant discriminatory pattern.

Logistic regression models assess identification with group discrimination (Table 2.2 and Table 2.3).[9] In each case, the table first shows the ethnicity variable by itself; the model is repeated with covariates. Some of these covariates pull sticks like religiosity and higher education out of the ethnic bundle. These models also include a binary indicator for identifying as a member of an ethnic minority group in the country, in ESS8, and for being born outside Israel. Religiosity is a self-identification of how religious the respondent is, from not at all religious (0) to very religious (10). Life and economic satisfaction rate from extremely dissatisfied (0) to extremely satisfied (10). Others are binary variables.

In the ESS8 data, compared to Ashkenazim, Mizrahim were not more likely to report discrimination generally, racially, or ethnically. Individuals self-identified as "other" were more likely to report racial discrimination. This likely reflects bias against Ethiopian Jews, who are Black and thus racially othered. Not only are they not prototypical within the Jewish community but they are racially distinct from the European-origin and Arab-country-origin communities, which exposes them to discrimination on that dimension as well. Those who identified as ethnic minorities were more likely to report experiencing discrimination, including ethnic discrimination.

In ESS10, compared to Ashkenazim, Mizrahim were not more likely to report general discrimination. However, they were marginally more likely to report experiencing racial ($p = 0.08$) and ethnic discrimination ($p = 0.08$), even when religiosity and class sticks were pulled from the ethnic bundles. The "other" group includes Ethiopian Jews as well as descendants of Latin American and Soviet immigrants. While some are then racially othered, others likely are or pass for Ashkenazi, which would affect their relative experiences of discrimination.

Not identifying discrimination against oneself could be a self-fulfilling prophecy. These individuals may wish to believe that their experiences are

TABLE 2.2 EXPERIENCES OF DISCRIMINATION (EUROPEAN SOCIAL SURVEY 8)

	Any Discrimination		Racial Discrimination		Ethnic Discrimination	
(Intercept)	−1.79***	−51.87*	−4.92***	−76.82	−4.28***	−42.92
	(0.24)	(21.19)	(1.00)	(39.38)	(0.73)	(45.32)
Mizrahi/Sephardi	−0.46	−0.72	1.51	1.24	−0.27	0.11
	(0.34)	(0.38)	(1.07)	(0.91)	(0.99)	(0.91)
Mixed	−0.16	−0.44	0.60	0.37	0.16	0.40
	(0.46)	(0.49)	(1.51)	(1.28)	(1.26)	(1.10)
Other	0.08	−0.07	3.03*	2.47*	1.04	1.11
	(0.65)	(0.69)	(1.19)	(1.05)	(1.36)	(1.26)
Covariates	No	Yes	No	Yes	No	Yes
AIC	102.98	117.01	40.34	59.83	11.46	30.25
N	1,722	1,623	1,726	1,627	1,726	1,627

Source: European Social Survey 8 (2016–2017), models 1–2: binary logistic regression; models 3–6: rare events logistic regression model.
*$p<0.05$; **$p<0.01$; ***$p<0.001$

not attributable to their ethnic bloc. This would parallel Herzog's (1985, 55) finding that "there is a strong tendency among people of Asian and African origin to deny the attribution of ethnic meaning to their political behavior." It could lead to underreporting bias incidents or to misattributing the cause.

Not personally experiencing discrimination, at least consciously, could also reflect de facto segregation. At least some segments of the public report that there are problematic levels of discrimination in Israel. If, however, people have a social network structured largely within their social group, then they could avert some *personal* experiences of bias. It would not truly be an absence of bias *in general*. Such isolationism would not speak well of the macrocultural element though. As the social networks were not addressed in these surveys, such analyses must be left to future research.

Even if one has avoided personal cases of anti-group bias, one can be aware that bias exists in the overall society, as noted in the aforementioned Pew data. Perception of societal bias is examined with logistic regression models. In each case, the table first shows the ethnicity variable by itself; the model is repeated with covariates. Again, some of these covariates pull sticks like religiosity and higher education out of the ethnic bundle. Being from the former Soviet Union, being an immigrant, being college educated, being employed, being satisfied with the way things are in Israel, and being male are binary variables. Religious group is included as a factor variable; Hiloni (secular/not religious) is the reference category. While many studies include re-

TABLE 2.3 EXPERIENCES OF DISCRIMINATION (EUROPEAN SOCIAL SURVEY 10)

	Any Discrimination		Racial Discrimination		Ethnic Discrimination	
(Intercept)	−0.82***	−22.74	−4.47***	−38.02	−4.03***	−70.37
	(0.22)	(15.70)	(0.98)	(33.74)	(0.79)	(39.76)
Israeli	−0.21	−0.60	0.02	−0.55	0.92	0.73
	(0.33)	(0.38)	(1.40)	(1.27)	(0.95)	(0.91)
Mixed	−2.29*	−3.35	0.72	0.62	0.27	0.11
	(1.10)	(1.77)	(1.76)	(1.59)	(1.66)	(1.54)
Mizrahi/Sephardi	0.20	0.16	1.92	1.62	1.18	1.45
	(0.29)	(0.32)	(1.03)	(0.91)	(0.87)	(0.82)
Other	−1.67	−2.13	1.26	1.03	0.56	0.57
	(0.98)	(1.24)	(1.64)	(1.52)	(1.68)	(1.62)
Covariates	No	Yes	No	Yes	No	Yes
AIC	314.64	298.07	72.11	76.17	90.71	88.73
N	628	550	633	551	633	551

Source: European Social Survey 10 (2022), models 1–2: binary logistic regression; models 3–6: rare events logistic regression model.
*$p<0.05$; **$p<0.01$; ***$p<0.001$

ligious bloc as a scale from secular to ultra-Orthodox, the blocs do not necessarily perform linearly when it comes to issue preferences (Yuchtman-Yaar, Alkalay, and Aival 2018); for this book they are treated as nominal groups rather than ordered groups. Those who identify as Hiloni may still participate in elements of Judaism, so they identify as not religious but not necessarily anti-religion (Yadgar 2020). Religion's importance in the respondents' lives is included as a binary marker for very or somewhat important compared to not too important or not at all important. Economic condition is a binary indicator for whether their personal economic circumstances are very or somewhat good as opposed to very or somewhat bad.

Non-Ashkenazim are more likely to report that Ethiopian Jews experience discrimination in Israel (Table 2.4). The difference between the Mizrahi/Sephardi and the Ashkenazi in the likelihood of identifying anti-Ethiopian discrimination decreases when the educational, economic, and religious sticks are pulled from the bundle. This suggests that these components of the ethnic bundles in Israel are doing some of the work in forming that difference in perception.

The Mizrahi/Sephardi Israelis, compared to the Ashkenazi Israelis, are also more likely to perceive discrimination against the Mizrahim. This effect persists even after some of the sticks are pulled from the ethnicity bundle. Thus, while these elements may be doing some of the work, the residuum of the ethnic bundle still has explanatory power. Notably, the marginal group members are not uniformly more likely to report that discrimination exists in society; they are less likely, even once the religion stick is removed from the bundle, to report that "a lot of discrimination" against Muslims occurs in Israel. Thus, they are more likely, as marginal group members, to see the

TABLE 2.4 DISCRIMINATION AGAINST ETHNIC GROUPS				
	Discrimination against Ethiopian Jews		Discrimination against Mizrahi Jews	
(Intercept)	−0.60***	0.20	−2.20***	−1.18***
	(0.05)	(0.14)	(0.07)	(0.17)
Mixed	0.35**	0.07	0.65***	0.30
	(0.13)	(0.14)	(0.17)	(0.18)
Mizrahi/Sephardi	0.16*	−0.01	1.52***	1.20***
	(0.07)	(0.08)	(0.09)	(0.10)
Other	12.15	12.09	−9.35	−9.80
	(198.96)	(198.96)	(198.96)	(198.96)
Covariates	No	Yes	No	Yes
AIC	5,572.59	5,053.69	4,110.17	3,747.50
N	3,638	3,412	3,685	3,454

Source: Pew Research Center (2014–2015), binary logistic regression models.
*p<0.05; **p<0.01; ***p<0.001

discrimination within the group but not necessarily more likely to recognize discrimination outside the group.

Respondents from the former USSR, older respondents, and those who are satisfied with Israel are less likely to report the existence of discrimination against either group. The college educated and unemployed are more likely to recognize anti-Ethiopian discrimination. Those who state that their personal economic circumstances are good are more likely to say that there is anti-Ethiopian discrimination and less likely to report anti-Mizrahi bias. Foreign-born and religious respondents are more likely to identify anti-Mizrahi bias in Israeli society.

Political Marginalization

This sense of social alienation, to a lesser extent, translates to the political realm. The ESS10 data show a sense of political alienation. Respondents reported whether Israel's political system "allows people like you to have a say in what the government does" and "allows people like you to have an influence on politics," on a scale from not at all (1) to a great deal (5). This is a blunt metric because the respondents could interpret "people like you" in many ways.[10] Even with the noise that the nonspecific phrasing introduces into the data, the results still show that Mizrahi and Sephardi Jewish Israelis, compared to Ashkenazi Jewish Israelis, are less likely to say that the system allows people "like them" to influence politics. This is some indication of their relative sense of political alienation from the Israeli system.

TABLE 2.5 INFLUENCE ON POLITICS				
	Have a Say in Government		Influence on Politics	
(Intercept)	2.05***	5.09	2.06***	−0.43
	(0.07)	(4.41)	(0.07)	(4.18)
Israeli	−0.14	−0.01	−0.18	−0.12
	(0.10)	(0.11)	(0.09)	(0.11)
Mixed	0.28	0.43*	0.10	0.18
	(0.16)	(0.17)	(0.15)	(0.16)
Mizrahi/Sephardi	−0.07	0.03	−0.24**	−0.16
	(0.09)	(0.10)	(0.08)	(0.09)
Other	0.04	0.24	0.23	0.35
	(0.18)	(0.20)	(0.17)	(0.19)
Covariates	No	Yes	No	Yes
R^2	0.01	0.10	0.03	0.08
Adj. R^2	0.01	0.08	0.02	0.06
N	632	551	632	551

Source: European Social Survey 10 (2022), OLS regression models.
*$p<0.05$; **$p<0.01$; ***$p<0.001$

Marginality and Group Identity in Israel

Despite these experiences of discrimination and alienation, marginal group members can be quite identified with their group. They want to feel included by others, to experience identity concordance, and to access the privileges attendant on membership in a dominant group. This heightened sense of group identification is evident in citizens' expressed attitudes.

The Pew Research Center survey addresses group identification in several ways. Respondents could indicate how important being Jewish is in their lives: 90.9 percent said it is very or somewhat important; 8.7 percent said that it was not too important or not at all important. They were also asked if they are proud to be Jewish: 94.5 percent agreed that they were, while 3.4 percent disagreed. Respondents indicated whether they had a strong sense of belonging to the Jewish people: 88.5 percent agreed that they do, while 9.5 percent said that they do not. Figures 2.4 and 2.5 visualize the response patterns across ethnic blocs; the lighter bar indicates the percentage saying that being Jewish is important and saying that they feel responsible for other Jews. Identification was more common among the Mizrahim/Sephardim.

While these statements were largely met with agreement, not all sense of group sentiment was as widely shared. Pew also asked respondents whether they agreed that they have "a special responsibility to take care of [Jews] in need around the world." Israel's governing documents promote this claim, and many link the state to survival. That said, they may expect the Jews in need to relocate to Israel for that protection. Only 56.5 percent of the respondents agreed with this statement; 36 percent disagreed. Group solidarity does not extend as far as group belonging overall.

The 2018 Basic Law in Israel asserts this connection between Israel, Israeli Jews, and diasporic Jews. It states that "the State shall act in the Diaspora, to strengthen the affinity between the State and members of the Jewish People" and that "the State shall act to preserve the cultural, historical, and religious heritage of the Jewish People among Jews of the Diaspora." In turn, Israeli politicians regularly treat the diaspora as a security benefit to and assumed ally for Israel (Abramson 2024). In asserting this globalized connection, then, these citizens are consistent with the Knesset's own mandate for the state. Those who opposed the survey statement were moving against the Basic Law statement.

The marginal group members were more likely to say that being Jewish is important in their lives (Model 1). This effect persisted after parts of the ethnicity bundle, including the religiosity sticks, were disaggregated (Model 2). Mizrahim/Sephardim were more likely to be proud to be Jewish (Models 3 and 4) and to have a strong sense of group belonging (Model 5), though this effect diminished when religious and socioeconomic sticks were pulled

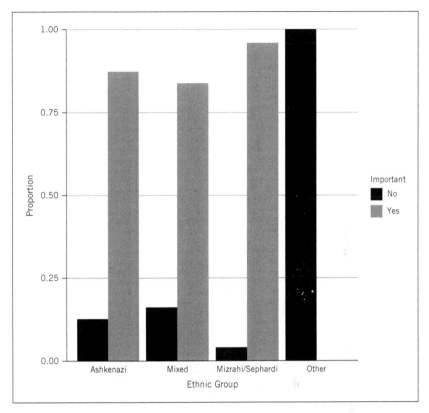

Figure 2.4 Ethnic Group Proportion Believing Being Jewish Is Important to Identity *(Pew Research Center)*

out (Model 6). The Mizrahim/Sephardim were more likely than the Ashke-nazim to identify a sense of group responsibility (Model 7). The residual sticks, after the religious and socioeconomic pieces of the bundle were removed, were not significantly different from the Ashkenazim residual bundles. These results are consistent with marginal group membership theory.

Unsurprisingly, individuals who identified as more religious were more likely to affirm these statements. This was particularly evident in terms of group belonging and responsibility. It was also true of older people and those satisfied with Israel. Immigrants, especially from the former USSR, were less likely to have strong group sensibilities.

Discussion and Conclusions

Marginal group members are both part of and peripheral to their social identity group. In the case of Jewish Israelis, these marginal group members—

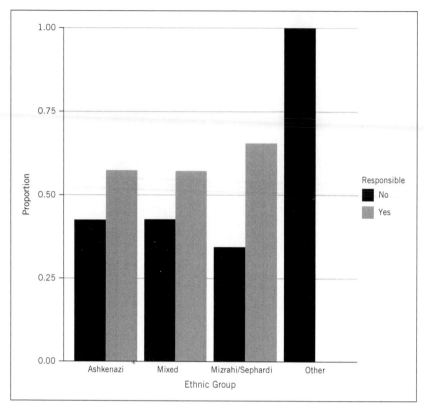

Figure 2.5 Ethnic Group Proportion Feeling Responsible for Other Jews *(Pew Research Center)*

the non-Ashkenazim—"are both embedded in and in excess of Zionist history" because they are Jewish, which fits the religious identity of the state, but they also come from Asian and African states, which does not comport with the preference to construct Israel as a Western state (Shohat 2003, 50). As marginal group members, they are more likely to experience cognitive identity discordance and a lack of social identity affirmation. This disparity between group membership and social recognition can be mentally and emotionally taxing for marginal group members. The Jewish Israeli marginal group members have also been disfavored in Israeli social construction, to their economic and status detriment. This disparate treatment opposes the governing documents' assertions of equality.

These patterns of marginality and membership play out in the survey respondents' lived experiences in Israel. Jewish Israelis recognize to some degree that nonprototypical Jewish Israelis are subject to discrimination. Although

TABLE 2.6 JEWISH GROUP IDENTIFICATION

	Important in Life		Proud to Be		Belonging		Responsibility	
(Intercept)	1.64***	-0.03	2.51***	1.57***	1.89***	0.67**	0.16***	-0.51***
	(0.06)	(0.21)	(0.09)	(0.31)	(0.07)	(0.21)	(0.05)	(0.14)
Mixed	0.08	0.12	-0.31	-0.53*	0.19	0.08	0.09	0.01
	(0.17)	(0.19)	(0.21)	(0.24)	(0.19)	(0.21)	(0.13)	(0.14)
Mizrahi/Sephardi	1.49***	0.80***	2.41***	1.51***	0.62***	-0.00	0.48***	-0.01
	(0.12)	(0.15)	(0.27)	(0.29)	(0.11)	(0.13)	(0.07)	(0.08)
Other	-14.20	-19.18	11.05	17.54	-1.90	-1.10	-12.71	-12.36
	(231.67)	(4,633.37)	(381.96)	(7,669.52)	(1.44)	(1.45)	(231.67)	(230.11)
Covariates	No	Yes	No	Yes	No	Yes	No	Yes
AIC	2,812.85	2,088.95	1,455.72	1,230.14	2,867.88	2,447.37	5,446.81	4,761.16
N	3,789	3,550	3,707	3,479	3,710	3,482	3,504	3,290

Source: Pew Research Center (2014–2015), binary logistic regression models.
*p<0.05; **p<0.01; ***p<0.001

only a minority acknowledged the bias in the surveys, the discrimination-recognition rates outstrip those of the well-documented discrimination against religious minorities. As such, it is not particularly surprising that discrimination could be overlooked by the majority of respondents.

The marginal-prototypical divide informs Jewish Israelis' recognition of these social biases. Although marginal group members may not report experiencing ethnic discrimination on a personal basis at higher rates than the Ashkenazim do, compared to prototypical group members, they are more likely to be aware that marginal group members experience discrimination. They are more likely than Ashkenazim to report that discrimination occurs against both Mizrahi Jews and Ethiopian Jews. They also feel relatively disempowered in the Israeli political system. Arguably, these factors would reinforce their awareness of group marginality, while the prototypical group members, if they can ignore the discrimination at work, would be less cognizant of it. In that way, the divergences could become stronger over time.

Despite (or even because of) being marginal group members, these individuals report a strong sense of group connectedness. The Mizrahi and Sephardim are still strong group identifiers—more so than the Ashkenazim. They are proud to be Jewish, being Jewish is important in their lives, and they feel connected to other Jews in the world. This group-identification pattern is consistent with marginal group member theory. The heightened group identity is a link to the more privileged part of the cross forces, Jewish in-group and Arab out-group. By viewing themselves as part of the global and Israeli Jewish community, they are affirming their position. Unfortunately for them, that does not necessarily mean that they will be viewed that way by others in return (Ostfeld and Yadon 2022b).

Given the role that group membership, including ethnic and religious group membership, is already understood to play in politics on many fronts, it makes sense to anticipate political ramifications from marginal group membership. For instance, strong group identifiers are more aware of and responsive to threats to the group (Pérez 2015). Their identification primes them for group-defensive behaviors and political preferences. Marginal group members also feel called on to perform their group connectedness to increase prototypical group members' affirmation of their inclusion and to maintain their group's relative status (Yadon and Ostfeld 2020). They can do that with their political behavior. Having empirically validated the historical and anthropological studies identifying Ashkenormativity in Israel, it is now possible to examine the effect of the resulting marginal group membership on Mizrahi/Sephardi Jewish Israelis' political preferences, which will be the substance of the subsequent chapters. The first of these will consider their preferences for a Jewish-majority state.

3

Marginal Group Membership and the Jewish State

The Basic Law of Israel of 2018 defines Israel as "the nation state of the Jewish People in which it realizes its natural, cultural, religious and historical right to self-determination" and states that the "right to national self-determination in the State of Israel is exclusive to the Jewish people." It affirms the same tenets of Ingathering and "Jewish immigration" espoused by the Declaration of Independence. This document, however, does not make the same assertions of freedom and equality for non-Jewish Israelis that the Declaration makes. In these documents, the assertion of a Jewish state identity is evident. Having "Israel as a Jewish state is a central theme" of the Israeli ethos, "a goal or value with 'transcendental significance'" (Oren 2019, 5).

Since the early days of Israel, there has been a demographic threat to the idea of a Jewish state. The Jewish majority had to be constructed and maintained. Aliyah, the "return" of diasporic Jews, helped build a Jewish state in former Mandatory Palestine. However, Mizrahi immigration created a "cultural problem" by being from the wrong culture according to the "ruling political elite in Israel (largely Jews from Eastern Europe)" (Shoshana 2016, 492). This ethno-religious majoritarian agenda thus required some compromise. Part of that compromise was, as discussed in the previous chapter, the formation of a hierarchy that benefited those who served both the Jewish and Western objectives of the new state. For Jews already residing in the Middle East—Arab Jews—that gathering into Israel and attendant acculturation process "meant abandoning Arabness and acquiescing in assimilationist modernization, for 'their own good'" (Shohat 2003, 50). These inhabitants would then reasonably be especially aware of Israel as a Jewish nationalist state and most pressed upon to distinguish themselves from the non-Jewish Arab population.

This chapter focuses on the implications of that constructed hierarchy for political attitudes toward the state and its identity. The Mizrahim are non-prototypical Jewish Israelis because they are not in the Western mold of the Ashkenazim. Thus, although they are members of the macro in-group, they are not in the in-group for each context. As was shown in Chapter 2, the marginal group members—the Mizrahim/Sephardim—have a stronger Jewish identity than the prototypical group members—the Ashkenazim. This chapter demonstrates that the effects of (non)prototypicality extend as well to their political sentiments.

Marginal group members have a great incentive to maintain their group' status when it is a dominant position (Hornsey 2008; Pérez 2015). They access a higher-status position than they would otherwise hold by maintaining the status of the group as a whole. Breaking apart their identity group or deprioritizing that group's benefits could cost them social standing and privileges. The marginal group members can also affirm their group identity to the prototypical group members and other observers by defending the group, which would earn them group approbation (Marques et al. 1998; Ellemers and Jetten 2013). In the case of Israel, then, the marginal group members would reasonably benefit from perpetuating a Jewish state and the identification of the state with Judaism.[1]

Marginalization and the Jewish State

Marginal members belong to a group while being peripheral to it. That leaves them less room to deviate from group norms without being perceived as abandoning the group. They may even adhere to norms above and beyond the performance of prototypical group members to demonstrate their belonging (Ostfeld and Yadon 2022b). Among Jewish Israelis, that assertive performance can manifest in the norms of Jewish identity. It can even become a feedback loop: "Jews who are more traditionally religious often exhibit stronger connections to a specifically ethnic Jewish identity than those with little to no religious practice or involvement," with some religious practices being linked to ethnic identity (Gonzalez-Lesser 2020, 488). For instance, those who follow Sephardic liturgical traditions could be especially aware of their subgroup because of their distinct practice (Mizrachi and Weiss 2020). Chapter 2 showed that they are more likely to view themselves as part of that identity. Affirming group identity among the Mizrahim includes "setting themselves apart from those who share their phenotype and regional heritage, but who are not

Jewish—the Palestinians and the citizens of neighboring Muslim states" (Lavie 2018, 28). The perceived overlap of culture and phenotype risks costing them status if they do not set themselves apart.

Ashkenormativity places the nonprototypical Jewish Israelis in a bind. Marginal group members must affirm a group membership to access the associated social and economic privileges (Hitlin, Brown, and Elder 2007) and to promote cognitive identity concordance (Saperstein and Penner 2014). Performing Jewishness, though, makes them (appear) more religious—a trait associated with the Mizrahim rather than with the secular, Western ideal. Israel, "following the logic of mainstream Zionist ideology viewed itself as secular" and did not "focus on maintaining a sovereignty that is *Jewish*, that is, a sovereignty that dialogues with Judaism as a constituting tradition, but rather to maintain the sovereignty of *Jews*" (Yadgar 2020, 16). Thus, there is pressure to conform to Jewish norms to be Jewish, rather than non-Jewish Arab, but they cannot by doing so be made prototypical.

Asserting identity (if not prototypicality) can also be done by adopting prejudices against out-groups or low-status groups. For instance, Latinos may adopt anti-Black attitudes to signal Americanness or to counter the impression that they are un-American (Pérez, Robertson, and Vicuña 2023). Among Eastern Europeans, this practice is seen in the "desire to be among the beneficiaries and not among the victims of white privilege [which] goes a long way toward explaining the success of racist rhetoric among many Central Europeans" (Kalmar 2022, 197). In the case of Israel, this would manifest in defending Jewish privilege against the equality claims of liberal democracy and the other inhabitants. The marginal group members would be incentivized to defend the inequality as part of affirming their in-group status.

Nonprototypicality can manifest in attempting to cognitively subordinate an ethno-religious identity to the macro identity. Studies have identified that "Asian and African origin" students "refer much significance to the identification with the Jewish people, with the nation, and the State of Israel" at the expense of their identification with their ethnic group (Herzog 1985, 55). The Jewishness of the state is part of that superordinating identity—Israeli. That overlapping set of requirements means that the superordinating identity is narrower than it might otherwise be, because Israel does not have to be a Jewish state. Israeli as an identity has a greater potential for being an encompassing identity. When the European Social Survey allowed respondents to self-identify as Jewish or Israeli instead of with their ethnic group, Lewin-Epstein and Cohen (2019) found that Mizrahi Jews are more likely than Ashkenazim to indicate Jewish rather than Israeli. They attribute this to "the greater tendency of Mizrahim to identify with Israel via its Jewish religion and history, more than with the secular Zionist project of modern Israel" (2126). Thus, these individuals are identifying with a macro-class. However, they favor a grouping around religion over a grouping based on general citizenship.

Marginal group member theory predicts that marginal members will be more aware of and responsive to threats to the group or to its position in society. Where members of any majority group feel that their group is threatened with a loss of social status, they are more likely to take conservative political positions on both "race-related and more race-neutral issues" (Craig and Richeson 2014, 952), especially on issues whereby they can increase the privilege gap between their group and those who are not in the group (Ostfeld and Yadon 2022b). Plus, group members who feel that their group is being devalued will act politically to protect it (Pérez 2015). This pattern would be heightened among group members whose status would decline most with the decline of group privileges. "Among those who are identified with an ethnoracial category with high levels of historical privilege and group boundaries that are blurring (for example, [American] Whites)," the marginal group members "feel the greatest sense of racialized threat and will consequently be most likely to embrace conservative views on racialized political issues" (Ostfeld and Yadon 2022b, 35). The blurry edge around the Jewish group is this ethnic dimension rather than a religiosity dimension. The role of religion in the state takes the space of the aforementioned racialized political issue. Following the logic of marginal group member theory here, then, they would be expected to defend the Jewish character of the state more than prototypical group members would. They have the most reason to imagine that deprioritizing the Jewish character of the state would undercut their limited access to privilege.[2]

The presence of the Palestinian population is itself a continual impetus to assert the connection between Judaism and the state:

> From the perspective of members of the country's majority religion, the presence of minority religious groups is sufficient to activate the majority's desire to reinforce their high group status in the nation. Conflict may not necessarily ensue, but the majority religious group will seek to maintain its belief in its legitimate intertwinement with the nation-state and its moral superiority, an aspect of identity that scholars have linked to expressions of nationalism. (Shady 2022, 748)

That the "Arab Jews" could be rendered more similar to Palestinian populations by the collapsing of the social hierarchy would make this fact more salient to them. As is discussed further in Chapter 5, decades of public opinion studies have proposed that the Mizrahim take a harder line on the Palestinian population and, as a result, on policy preferences related to the conflict (Yuchtman-Yaar, Alkalay, and Aival 2018). Lower-status group members are psychologically incentivized by a desire for a "positive social identity" to "mak[e] downward intergroup comparisons that are more flattering to the ingroup," which, in this case, works against the Palestinians (Hornsey 2008, 207). As is shown here, the Mizrahim and Sephardim are also more likely to support policies that are aggressive about removing Palestinians from Israel.

High group identifiers are more reactive to group threats, are more ethnocentric, and evince greater in-group pride (Pérez 2015). As Chapter 2 demonstrates, Mizrahim are more likely than the Ashkenazim to be high group identifiers. They would then be motivated to protect the group boundary against the perceived threat to the demographics or from renewed conflict.

This need not be about particular intergroup animus. Ryan D. Enos and Noam Gidron (2018) do not find that Mizrahi/Sephardi Israelis have a greater desire for social distance from Palestinians than Ashkenazi Israelis do. They do not report a stronger objection to having Palestinian neighbors or coworkers. This would suggest that a distinct ethnic preference for the state, which would subordinate Palestinians, is not necessarily personal. It is political.

Nonetheless, asserting and promoting the Jewish character of the state would come at the Palestinians' expense. The marginal group members would be more likely, then, to express exclusionary attitudes toward the non-Jewish populations in Israel as well as toward would-be Palestinian returners and non-Jewish immigrants. Prior work has found that "levels of exclusionary attitudes [toward Palestinian Citizens of Israel] are high" generally, and they are "highest among low-status Jews (the relatively poor and uneducated ultra-Orthodox population)" (Enos and Gidron 2018, 743). The Mizrahim and Sephardim are relatively lower status. They are also more exclusionary.

Jewish Nationalism in Israel

It is hardly surprising that Jewish nationalism permeates the Israeli public. All manner of governing documents proclaim it the Jewish state. There is not one meaning to the phrase *Jewish state*. It could be a state meant to be the homeland of the Jewish people and open to their immigration, a state in which "the public life . . . will conform to the Jewish tradition," or a state that has a Jewish majority (Oren 2019, 27). Nonetheless, this is an important social and political identity. "On a broader political scale, in Israel, unlike the situation in many liberal democracies where citizenship is universal and the state is assumed to be neutral, the polity is formally and culturally Jewish, with the vast majority of Jewish Israelis viewing the state as the manifestation of the Jewish national entity" (Mizrachi and Weiss 2020, 176). For instance, in the iPanel survey, a secular Mizrahi man in his forties with vocational training from the central area wrote, "There is no way for the State of Israel to exist without a Jewish majority." The 2018 Basic Law of Israel reminds the world that the Israeli government means the state to manifest just that identity, even at the expense of more inclusive possible identities. Each formulation referenced by Neta Oren (2019), though, appears in the responses.

Religion for many countries has played an important role in shaping or reinforcing national identity. Studies on European countries have found that the "weaker the tie a particular religion has to the historical development of the nation and the majority of its population, the less the members of the religion can construct a narrative that binds adherence to the religion and belonging to the nation" (Shady 2022, 748). Judaism has been intensely and intentionally linked to the creation and defense of Israel as a contemporary state. It would be hard to argue that any current state has a larger role for religion—especially for an ethno-religion—in forming the "imagined community" (Anderson 2006) and the mutual memory and forgetting of nation formation than Israel has (Renan 1882).

Just as Israel's governing documents appeal to a Jewish national identity, so do members of the public. Some of the iPanel respondents demonstrated this with an explicitly religious appeal. A 50+-year-old Dati (modern Orthodox) Mizrahi woman with a secondary education from the north area wrote, "The Land of Israel was given to the Jewish people." It was given by God and the international community in various histories. A Haredi Ashkenazi man in his forties from the Jerusalem area with an advanced degree described this belief in more detail: "The State of Israel is the State of the Jews. There is no other option. We don't have another country. We received it with God's promise, and it will remain so with His help. We will continue to pray for our complete redemption and that the people of Israel will preserve their Torah in their land, which will preserve it most of all. Our Torah—our preservation as it is said in this week's *parshat* [Torah portion] of the upcoming Shabbat 'if in my laws you will walk you will live safely in your land.'" The passage he is referencing is Leviticus 25:18. Not all Israeli Jews, though, feel as strongly about following Jewish law. There is a sense of popular connectedness, complete with a popular history, and an assertion that it is linked to a state claim.

Israel is even framed as singular in this feat. The lack of alternative Jewish states was echoed by several respondents. An 18–22-year-old Masorti Mizrahi woman from the south area with a secondary education wrote, "The State of Israel will always have a Jewish majority! This is the Jewish state and there is no other." Majority status, security, and uniqueness are merged in some popular conceptions. Not only should it be a homeland for Jews but it must be, by these lights, inhabited largely—or only—by them as well.

If Jews become a minority population in Israel, it could, despite that history, lose the popular identity as a Jewish state. So many respondents made this assertion in the free-response section of the iPanel survey that only a sampling are included here. A 50+-year-old secular Mizrahi woman from the central area with a secondary education stated, "The Jews must not be a minority in our country! Everything else, we will manage." She did not clarify the scope of "everything" or the method of management. Her words would imply, though, that security, human rights, democracy, and conflict are secondary considerations. A 50+-year-old secular Ashkenazi man from the central area with vocational training wrote, "If there is no Jewish majority there will be no Jewish state!" A 50+-year-old secular mixed-ethnicity man from the Jerusalem area with vocational training used almost the same phrasing: "Once the Jewish people don't have a majority there will be no Jewish state." A 50+-year-old Masorti Sephardi woman from the north area with vocational education stated, "Israel must have a Jewish majority." Although older respondents generated these comments, it is not only the elders who believe that a Jewish majority is necessary. As is discussed, that belief is widespread.

Multiple domains in which this preference for the Jewish character of the state could be demonstrated are considered in this chapter. Some pertain to the enactment of religious law or customs. Others address access to social privileges. Marginal group members are expected to support Jewish religious majoritarianism and privileges. The Jewish character of the state can also be affected by citizens' behavior. For instance, Jews moving out of Israel would undercut the Jewish majority. Similarly, Jews marrying outside the Jewish community could dilute the Jewish population or signal a deprioritization of Jewishness. Marginal group members would reasonably discourage these practices. The potential exclusion of non-Jewish populations from Israel is a counterpart policy to the former proposals for keeping a Jewish majority. Table 3.1 summarizes the variables and datasets used in this chapter.

These dependent variables are all binary or nominal variables, so binary or multinomial logistic regressions are used. In each case, after the model with just ethnicity, models with covariates are also shown. Some of these will remove components from the ethnic bundle of sticks. Being from the former Soviet Union, being an immigrant, having a college education, being employed, being satisfied with the way things are in Israel, and being male are binary variables. Religious group is included as a factor variable; Hiloni (secular) is the reference category. While many studies include religious bloc as a scale from secular to ultra-Orthodox, the blocs do not necessarily perform linearly with respect to issue preferences because the groups also have differences with respect to domains like Zionism (Yuchtman-Yaar, Alkalay, and Aival 2018). They are treated as nominal groups rather than ordered groups. Religion's importance in the respondents' lives is included as a binary marker for very or somewhat important compared to not too important or not at all important. Economic condition is a binary indicator for very or somewhat good personal economic circumstances as opposed to very or somewhat bad.[3]

TABLE 3.1 DEPENDENT VARIABLES AND DATASETS FOR CHAPTER 3			
Outcome Variable	Dataset	Table Number	Difference between Ashkenazim and Mizrahim/Sephardim
Emotional Attachment to Israel	European Social Survey 10	3.2	*
Jewish First Israeli Second	Pew Research Center	3.3	*
Jews Deserve Preferential Treatment	Pew Research Center	3.4	*
Government Should Promote Jewish Values	Pew Research Center	3.4	*
Make Halakha Israeli Law	Pew Research Center	3.4	*
Prefer Jewish Majority	iPanel	3.5	*
Restrict European Christian Immigration	iPanel	3.5	*
Restrict Ethiopian Jewish Immigration	iPanel	3.5	—
Government Interpretation of Refugee Applications	European Social Survey 8	3.6	*
Refugee Petitions Are Honest	European Social Survey 8	3.6	*
Expel Arabs from Israel	Pew Research Center	3.7	*
Jews Can Support Palestinian Right of Return	Pew Research Center	3.7	*
Non-Orthodox Conversions Are Acceptable	Pew Research Center	3.8	*
Uncomfortable with Children Marrying Christians	Pew Research Center	3.9	*
Uncomfortable with Children Marrying Muslims	Pew Research Center	3.9	*
Jewish Israelis Should Stay in Israel	Pew Research Center	3.10	*
Israel Is Necessary for Jews' Survival	Pew Research Center	3.10	*
$^{+}p<0.10; *p<0.05$			

Some scholars have suggested that ethnicity is of declining importance in Israel. For instance, Ephraim Yuchtman-Yaar, Yasmin Alkalay, and Tom Aival (2018, 3) write, "Regarding the ethnic factor, it appears that there are relatively small gaps between the effects of the Ashkenazim and Mizrahim on political attitudes and voting preferences." Similarly, Bagno-Moldavski (2015) proposes that ethnic voting is declining in Israel. She finds that "in the 2000s, political attitudes were less sensitive to ethnic, ideological, and class differences than to variation across religious groups" (530). In some cases, this claim reflects optimism; as noted already, administrations have sought to minimize the popular sense of within-group difference. In other cases, it is a methodological illusion. These studies reach these conclusions by removing big sticks, like religiosity and class, from the bundles entirely, rather than treating them as part of the ethnic bundles, as they should be. If the political salience of ethnicity has truly faded, although these groups may be cognizant of their social experiences—as is shown in Chapter 2—Ashkenazi-Mizrahi/Sephardi differences on these political questions should be minimal to nonexistent. The results here show otherwise.

Note that political ideology is excluded from the models shown here. This is because it is difficult to know if political affiliation is the cause or consequence of some of these opinions. Political affiliation is ethnically linked in Israel, which could make it a stick in the ethnic bundle, and scholars have attributed a causal nature to that pattern. Historically liberal parties were associated with "the intellectual and literal offspring of the secular Ashkenazi founders of the state" rather than the "working-class, traditionalist Mizrahim as well as other religious and Orthodox groups" (Mizrachi and Weiss 2020, 175). Mizrahim, despite their economic circumstances, are accused of supporting Likud or Shas in rejection of Labor's link to the Ashkenazim. "Labor embraced the universal discourse of equal rights while sidelining the Mizrahim," and it was "elitist, exclusionary, and detached from their socioeconomic woes," so they favored the "right's ethno-national discourse" (Yuchtman-Yaar, Alkalay, and Aival 2018, 3). They may also support right-wing parties because they favor hawkish and Jewish nationalist positions (Lavie 2018). Notably, the Likud leadership is not Mizrahi (e.g., Benjamin Netanyahu is Ashkenazi), while the Shas leadership is. Models including partisan leanings are shown in the Online Appendix (available at https://scholarshare.temple.edu/handle/20.500.12613/9253).

There are many ways for citizens to express their affiliation. The ESS10 asks citizens "how emotionally attached" they feel to their country on a scale from no emotional attachment (0) to very emotionally attached (10). This question taps into the affective dimension of national identity (Shady 2022). It identifies whether they are expressing an emotional connection to Israel.

The Mizrahim/Sephardim exhibit higher levels of emotional attachment to Israel (Model 1). The "other" group—a group with many immigrants and Ethiopian-heritage Israelis—are less likely to feel emotionally invested in Israel. The religiosity stick of the ethnic bundle seems to be doing substantial work here; the more religious are more emotionally attached (Model 2). This is consistent with the prior finding that Mizrahim/Sephardim feel connected to the state by religious affiliation rather than by the secular Zionist move-

TABLE 3.2 EMOTIONAL ATTACHMENT		
	Model 1	Model 2
(Intercept)	8.53***	64.37***
	(0.16)	(9.74)
Israeli	−0.09	0.21
	(0.23)	(0.25)
Mixed	0.26	0.51
	(0.37)	(0.38)
Mizrahi/Sephardi	0.48*	0.32
	(0.21)	(0.21)
Other	−1.27**	−0.43
	(0.42)	(0.45)
Covariates	No	Yes
R^2	0.04	0.12
Adj. R^2	0.03	0.10
N	632	550

Source: European Social Survey 10 (2022), OLS regression model.
*$p<0.05$; **$p<0.01$; ***$p<0.001$

ment. Older respondents report greater attachment, as do those who are sat-isfied with their lives in Israel.

As was noted previously, the Mizrahim are in a double bind for being Jewish and Israeli. Yoav Peled (1998, 105) critiques their decision, as if they were being willful "against the modernizing Israeli establishment" when they "failed . . . to become satisfactorily absorbed" into the "universalistic compo-nent of the Zionist ideology": "To emphasize their connection to the domi-nant Ashkenazi majority, they have clung, rather, to the Jewish component of Zionism, reviving, in many cases, some of their own religious traditions which had already been eroded."[4] This would suggest that they are more likely to identify with Judaism than with the secular state structure. That is, after all, their greater claim to social privilege.

This manifests in the public opinion. In 2014–2015, Jewish Israelis were also asked whether they consider themselves Jewish first or Israeli first: 29.0 percent characterized themselves as Israeli first; 51.5 percent characterized themselves as Jewish first.[5] The proportion identifying themselves as Jewish first, unsure, or Israeli first for each group is shown in Figure 3.1. The gray bar indicates Jewish first, while the dark bar is Israeli first. The Mizrahi/Sephardi Jewish Israelis are more likely to consider themselves Jewish first rather than Israeli first (Model 1). The religiosity sticks in the ethnic bundle seem to be doing a lot of work in shaping this pattern (Model 2). Older respondents and foreign-born respondents are more likely to identify as Jewish first, while college-educated respondents are more likely to identify with Israel first.

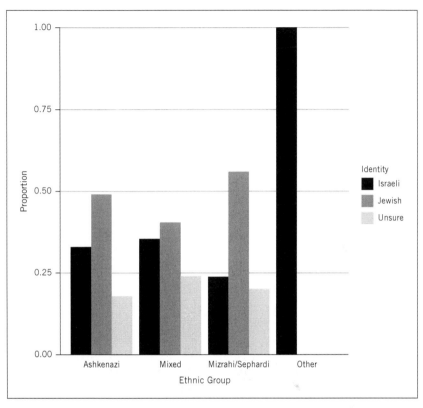

Figure 3.1 Ethnic Group Proportion Identifying as Jewish First or Israeli First *(Pew Research Center)*

TABLE 3.3 JEWISH FIRST		
	Model 1	**Model 2**
(Intercept)	−0.06	−1.82***
	(0.05)	(0.20)
Mixed	−0.04	0.14
	(0.14)	(0.19)
Mizrahi/Sephardi	0.73***	0.02
	(0.07)	(0.12)
Other	−12.49	−10.98
	(231.67)	(231.53)
Covariates	No	Yes
AIC	4,748.13	2,912.12
N	3,055	2,851

Source: Pew Research Center (2014–2015), binary logistic regression models.
*p<0.05; **p<0.01; ***p<0.001

Prioritizing the Jewish State

An overt expression of Jewish nationalism would be the assertion of privileged status for Jewish people and Jewish traditions in Israel. The 2018 Basic Law declares Israel the national homeland for Jewish individuals and proclaims a religious right to self-determination. Some public opinion favors substantially blending the religion and nation. Because members of subordinated groups can adopt negative attitudes toward (other) low-status groups to affirm or generate a privileged status—which in turn manifests in support for anti-out-group policies (Pérez, Robertson, and Vicuña 2023)—it is expected that the Mizrahim are more likely to support privileging the Jewish community in Israel over non-Jews.

Respondents were asked whether "Jews deserve preferential treatment in Israel." 81.9 percent agreed that they did, while 17.1 percent stated that they did not. Mizrahi/Sephardi Jews are more likely than Ashkenazi Jews to agree that Jews deserve preferential treatment (Model 1 in Table 3.4). While the effect is diminished by removing the religious stick from the ethnic bundle, the residuum is still significant (Model 2). College-educated, foreign-born, and economically precarious respondents were less likely to agree. Conversely, when the respondents indicated whether "religion should be kept separate from government policies" or whether "government policies should promote religious values and beliefs in our country," 51.8 percent endorsed the former view, and 43.5 percent stated that the latter was closer to their beliefs Mizrahi/Sephardi Jews are more likely than Ashkenazi Jews to favor promoting religious values in Israel (Model 3 in Table 3.4). Again, the religiosity stick appears to be doing substantial work here. College-educated respondents were less likely to hold this belief, while immigrants were more supportive.

Some of the respondents overtly felt that Jewish values were superior. A 50+-year-old Masorti mixed-ethnicity woman from the north area with a vocational education wrote a detailed summary:

> I don't believe in Muhammad's people. He was not a prophet, and they are not righteous. Their words and actions are not in line with the truth, of those whose souls desire peace and a peaceful life, fruitfulness and faith in free love, and I am talking about the people of Israel, my dear and gentle people who have never longed for war and never, in all human history, never went on murderous missionary journeys, as Christianity and Islam did to this day and unfortunately maybe forever, and I write this for the Jews who are being murdered on the streets of Israel every day.

Islam and Christianity are the most common religions in the world and in the Palestinian population. Although Judaism allows conversions, missionizing is not customary. The mention of missionaries highlights the idea that these groups are threats to the Jewish community. The invocation of murder also suggests that these groups are ethically inferior. When questioned about the future of Israel, the respondent expressed a preference for a *not*-liberal democratic regime.

The respondents could also indicate whether they favored enacting Jewish law, making "halakha the state law for Jews in Israel." 37.7 percent favored that idea; 55.2 percent were opposed. The proportion of each group that supported establishing Jewish law in Israel is shown in Figure 3.2. The lighter bar shows the proportion who supported enacting halakha. A majority in each case opposed the idea. Nonetheless, Mizrahi/Sephardi Jews are more likely than Ashkenazi Jews to favor enacting halakha (Model 5 in Table 3.4), an effect that persists even after the religiosity sticks are removed from the

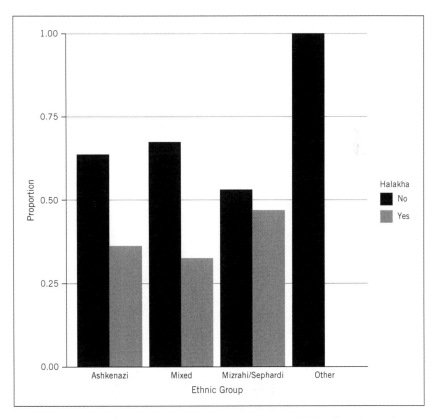

Figure 3.2 Ethnic Group Proportion Supporting Enacting Halakha *(Pew Research Center)*

TABLE 3.4 JEWISH PRIVILEGES, VALUES, AND LAW

	Preferential Treatment		Promote Values		Enact Halakha	
(Intercept)	1.10***	0.76***	−1.01***	−2.29***	−1.28***	−2.65***
	(0.05)	(0.18)	(0.05)	(0.19)	(0.06)	(0.22)
Mixed	−0.03	0.00	0.39**	0.41*	0.17	0.39
	(0.14)	(0.16)	(0.13)	(0.18)	(0.15)	(0.21)
Mizrahi/Sephardi	0.71***	0.35***	0.96***	0.05	0.90***	0.25*
	(0.08)	(0.10)	(0.07)	(0.11)	(0.07)	(0.12)
Other	11.45	11.48	1.02	2.21	−11.28	−9.91
	(231.67)	(229.24)	(1.44)	(1.45)	(231.67)	(230.34)
Yes	No	Yes	No	Yes	No	Yes
AIC	4,310.95	3,538.17	5,331.26	3,298.95	4,778.80	2,758.13
N	3,751	3,514	3,611	3,382	3,524	3,307

Source: Pew Research Center (2014–2015), binary logistic regression models.
*p<0.05; **p<0.01; ***p<0.001

bundle (Model 6). Male and foreign-born respondents were more likely to support enacting halakha, while those from the former Soviet Union and the college educated were less likely to do so. Not only does this belief endorse a majority religion but it would make the state an agent of religious law enforcement. State policies that enforce religious law can increase popular compliance (Ridge 2019). However, the regulation of religion does not necessarily make the public more devout (Ridge 2020; Ruiter and van Tubergen 2009).

Unsurprisingly, more-religious respondents were more likely to favor all of these policy proposals. College-educated respondents and those in better economic circumstances were less favorable toward these principles. This is consistent with the argument that lower socioeconomic status would make Jewish Israelis defensive about incorporating Palestinians, a source of cheaper labor (Peled 1998). Peled (1998) even argues that the socioeconomic status stick of the ethnic bundle did a lot of the work in predicting support for exclusionary politician Rabbi Meir Kahane. Those satisfied with Israel's current condition supported Jews having privileges in the state, but they opposed further entwining religious authority and the government.

A Jewish Population

Promoting Israel as a Jewish state also manifests in controlling who lives in it. As noted above, a non-Jewish majority would be a demographic threat to that identity. As a secular Mizrahi woman in her thirties in the Jerusalem area with a secondary education put it, "My opinion is clear. The State of Israel belongs only to the Jewish people." This language is exclusionary. It expressly dispossesses non-Jewish inhabitants. Another respondent—a Haredi Mizrahi woman in her thirties in the north area with a university education—echoed this sentiment: "The State of Israel belongs to the people of Israel! To the Jewish people." This phrasing similarly denies possession by non-Jewish Israelis, despite their residence or citizenship.

Israeli Jewish nationalism then appears as a preference for maintaining a Jewish majority population and for religion-related immigration and refugee policy preferences. The European Social Survey regularly asks members of the public the degree to which they would support or oppose immigration by groups from a different race or ethnicity than the majority of their country. This question is difficult to interpret in the case of Israel, since it is not clear whom the respondents consider the majority and what ethnic groups they would think of in formulating their answers. Also, in prior surveys, some members of every ethnic group classified themselves as in the minority in Israel, which could skew their interpretation of this question.

Furthermore, for the purposes of Jewish nationalism, not all ethnic or racial out-group members are created equal. Some could be coreligionists. Would Jewish Israelis accept racial out-group Jews moving into the state? What about European non-Jews? These individuals would share the historical source countries of the Ashkenazim but not the religion. The nationalist logic, developed out of Zionism, "demands, of course, the national exclusion of the 'significant Other,' but it is also . . . wary of those 'other Others,' non-Jews/non-Arabs, who do not fall inside the primary friend-enemy binary" (Yadgar 2020, 55). These differences were incorporated in the iPanel survey. Of that sample, 56.4 percent favored restricting immigration by European Christians, while 43.6 percent would not heavily restrict that population. That question was juxtaposed with a question about immigration by Jews from Ethiopia. These individuals would be coreligionists from another racial group. Only 9.6 percent of respondents wanted to restrict their immigration; 90.4 percent did not. Religious affinity then supersedes racial difference for immigration policy preferences. The proportion, across ethnic groups, who supported restricting Christian European migration is shown in Figure 3.3. The lighter bar is the proportion endorsing restrictions. Mizrahim/Sephardim are more likely to support restrictions.

The iPanel survey also asked respondents how they felt about the scope of the Jewish population. They could indicate whether they favored the state's having a sizable Jewish majority that would continue into the future or a Jewish majority that could become a minority in the future. While the ability to construct a Jewish-majority state will depend somewhat on where the borders are drawn and what is done with the non-Jewish population, it is not surprising that the vast majority of the respondents preferred a strong, stable majority (97.1 percent) to a potential future minority (2.9 percent). The distribution across ethnic groups is depicted in Figure 3.4. The lighter bar in-

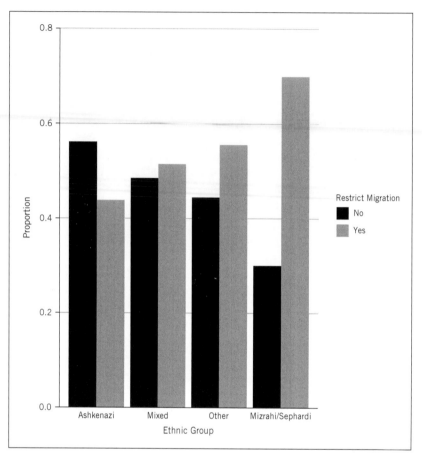

Figure 3.3 Ethnic Group Proportion Supporting Christian Migration Restrictions *(iPanel)*

dicates support for a stable Jewish majority. Ashkenazim are more likely to be tolerant of a weak majority or possible minority, but it is overall an uncommon view.

Israeli policies are designed to encourage and facilitate "returning" to Israel. Jews outside of Israel are treated as diasporic, which presumes a natural connection to the country although the connection is temporally remote. In the meantime, politicians' rhetoric spins the diaspora into a security asset and promotes a sense of ideational membership (Abramson 2024).

After being presented with all the questions about the political structure, demographics, and potential for war in Israel's future, many respondents endorsed a Jewish-majority state. A Haredi Mizrahi man in his twenties from the central area with a secondary education responded, "What I care about most is that there will be a Jewish religious country." That is consistent with

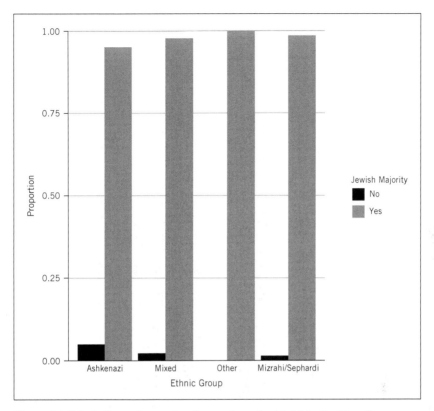

Figure 3.4 Ethnic Group Proportion Supporting a Jewish Majority *(iPanel)*

the large majority who chose that option, although they may not share his truly religious aspirations. As for the few who chose the weak-majority option, they were not necessarily without trepidation. A secular Mizrahi woman in her forties from the central area with a university education stated, "I have a concern that we will be a minority and about the future of the country. There is no strong and cohesive leadership today, and this is a very significant Achilles heel for the country." She also wanted the state to stay within the Green Line and pursue democracy but not sign peace agreements. She may have concluded that with sufficient leadership and cohesion, a weaker majority would not pose the same worry she was currently expressing.

Mizrahi and Sephardi Jewish Israelis, compared to the Ashkenazi respondents, were more likely to favor maintaining a Jewish majority in Israel (Model 1). The desire to maintain a Jewish majority also manifests in attitudes toward migration. The Mizrahi and Sephardi respondents were more likely than the Ashkenazi respondents to support restrictions on Christian European immigration (Model 3). In both cases, the effect persists even when

TABLE 3.5 JEWISH MAJORITY AND MIGRATION

	Stable Jewish Majority		Restrict Christian Immigration		Restrict Ethiopian Immigration	
(Intercept)	3.03***	17.17	−0.28**	−0.21	−2.13***	−0.36
	(0.24)	(1,592.95)	(0.10)	(0.69)	(0.16)	(0.87)
Identify as an Ethnic Minority	−1.04	−1.03	0.65	0.29	−0.09	−0.52
	(0.64)	(0.68)	(0.34)	(0.37)	(0.54)	(0.56)
Mixed	0.81	0.65	0.31	0.40	−0.93*	−0.80
	(0.63)	(0.66)	(0.20)	(0.22)	(0.45)	(0.47)
Other	14.80	15.88	0.39	0.55	−0.38	−0.67
	(750.99)	(1,207.06)	(0.40)	(0.43)	(0.76)	(0.78)
Mizrahi/Sephardi	1.47**	1.23*	1.10***	0.88***	−0.05	0.18
	(0.51)	(0.57)	(0.15)	(0.18)	(0.23)	(0.28)
Covariates	No	Yes	No	Yes	No	Yes
AIC	250.39	260.09	1,303.20	1,157.38	625.89	611.00
N	991	988	991	988	991	988

Source: iPanel, binary logistic regression models.
*$p<0.05$; **$p<0.01$; ***$p<0.001$

the economic and religious sticks are removed from the bundle. On the flip side, when it comes to immigration that would not threaten the Jewish character of the state—such as immigration by Jews from Ethiopia—the ethnic groups are not significantly different in their expressed preferences (Model 6). This is not to say that there is no bias against the Ethiopian Jewish population. It is just that the Ashkenazi Jewish Israelis and the Mizrahi/Sephardi Jewish Israelis did not express different preferences from each other with respect to regulating Ethiopian Jewish immigration.

Attitudes toward immigrants can be distinguished from attitudes toward refugees with respect to Jewish majoritarianism. As part of the principle of Ingathering, Israeli immigration law features a right of "return" for Jewish individuals—including the children and grandchildren of a Jewish person—as well as their families. Individuals making a refugee petition, then, are people who could not simply avail themselves of the right of return. That means they are not Jewish. Marginal group members would then approach these would-be immigrants with more skepticism and less openness.

ESS8 asked individuals about refugee applicants, describing them as follows: "Some people come to this country and apply for refugee status on the grounds that they fear persecution in their own country." They responded to the following sentences: (1) "The government should be generous in judging people's applications for refugee status," and (2) "Most applicants for refugee status aren't in real fear of persecution in their own countries." Respondents could respond with choices from strongly agree (1) to strongly disagree (5).

TABLE 3.6 REFUGEE ATTITUDES				
	Judge Conservatively		True Fear	
(Intercept)	3.30***	15.97***	2.99***	−1.55
	(0.05)	(2.94)	(0.05)	(3.31)
Mizrahi/Sephardi	0.41***	0.31***	−0.25***	−0.25***
	(0.06)	(0.07)	(0.07)	(0.08)
Mixed	0.10	0.12	0.01	−0.02
	(0.09)	(0.09)	(0.10)	(0.10)
Other	0.31*	0.27	−0.33*	−0.38*
	(0.13)	(0.14)	(0.15)	(0.15)
Covariates	No	Yes	No	Yes
R^2	0.03	0.07	0.01	0.03
Adj. R^2	0.03	0.06	0.01	0.02
N	1,652	1,565	1,494	1,427

Source: European Social Survey 8 (2016–2017), OLS regression models.
*$p<0.05$; **$p<0.01$; ***$p<0.001$

In the former case, disagreement opposes non-Jewish immigration. In the latter case, disagreement favors non-Jewish immigration. Linear regression models are used to analyze the responses.

The models also contain binary indicators for self-identification as a member of a minority ethnic group, college education, gender, and employment. Religiosity is included with the respondents' self-rating on a scale from not at all religious (0) to very religious (10). Life and economic satisfaction are rated from extremely dissatisfied (0) to extremely satisfied (10). Age is marked by the year of birth.

Mizrahi/Sephardi respondents are more likely to believe that the government should evaluate refugee petitions conservatively (Model 1). This effect remains even when the religiosity and economic precarity sticks are removed (Model 2).[6] They are more likely to claim that refugees have made a false assertion of fear of persecution (Model 3). This effect also persists when the religious and economic sticks are removed (Model 4). These patterns indicate that they are less welcoming toward non-Jewish migration, which is to say immigration that would undermine the Jewish character of the state. Religious individuals move in a similar pattern. Those identifying as minorities are less likely to think that refugee petitions are disingenuous.

Another inverse to bringing more Jews to the state would be bringing in Palestinians, the population behind the supposed demographic threat. The Pew Research Center asked Jewish Israelis whether they thought one could be Jewish and support "the Palestinians' right of return."[7] 57.0 percent agreed, while 34.6 percent disagreed. Opposing a right of return would deny those removed from the state and their descendants the opportunity to come back;

Israeli governments have opposed the return of Palestinian refugees since 1948, occasionally violently repelling or killing returners (Pearlman and Atzili 2018). Notably, this assertion counterpoises a law of return granting Jews around the world—or any person with a practicing Jewish grandparent or married to a Jewish person—the right to move to Israel and claim citizenship.

That survey also asked whether respondents agreed that "Arabs should be expelled or transferred from Israel." This is a more extreme mechanism for achieving and maintaining a Jewish majority. Among respondents, 49.6 percent supported expelling Arabs from Israel; 44.8 percent did not agree with that proposition. The question did not specify to where they should be expelled. Many states, including Jordan, Syria, and Lebanon, host refugee populations. During the 2023–2024 Gaza War, the government proposed driving them into the Sinai desert in Egypt. Marginal group members are expected to support a Jewish majority for the state as part of the group-protective behavior. Clearer boundaries between the Jewish and non-Jewish populations would benefit them by distinguishing them more clearly from the Palestinians (Pérez, Roberson, and Vicuña 2023). As such, they are expected to be more likely to oppose the right of return claim and to endorse expelling the Palestinians.

The Mizrahi and Sephardi respondents were more likely than the Ashkenazi respondents to support expelling the Arabs from Israel (Model 1). The effects held even when the religious and economic sticks were removed (Model 2). Similarly, the Mizrahi and Sephardi respondents are less likely to believe individuals can be Jewish and support a Palestinian right of return to Israel (Models 3 and 4). Those from the former USSR and the religious are more likely to support a Jewish majority against the Palestinians. The college

TABLE 3.7 TREATMENT OF PALESTINIAN POPULATION				
	Expel Arabs		Palestinian Right of Return	
(Intercept)	−0.28***	−0.72***	0.42***	0.75***
	(0.05)	(0.14)	(0.05)	(0.14)
Mixed	−0.08	0.12	−0.09	−0.22
	(0.13)	(0.14)	(0.13)	(0.14)
Mizrahi/Sephardi	0.65***	0.49***	−0.34***	−0.27**
	(0.06)	(0.08)	(0.07)	(0.08)
Other	12.83	13.31	12.13	11.90
	(231.67)	(231.48)	(231.67)	(231.60)
Covariates	No	Yes	No	Yes
AIC	5,642.98	4,863.51	5,458.61	4,845.99
N	3,579	3,354	3,473	3,253

Source: Pew Research Center (2014–2015), binary logistic regression models.
*p<0.05; **p<0.01; ***p<0.001

educated are less likely to support expelling the Arabs and are more likely to believe in a right to return, while men are more likely to support expelling Arabs. In both cases, then, the marginal group members are more likely to endorse a reduced Palestinian population.

Some of the survey respondents overtly favored ethnicity-based removals. This even extended into homicidal invocations. A secular Mizrahi man in his thirties from the Jerusalem area with a vocational education wrote, "Death to the Arabs." He favored an enlarged state with a Jewish majority, but he was less favorable toward democracy or peace. The mass murder of the Palestinians would resolve the demographic threat posed by such a one-state solution, but it is antithetical to peace; the mass violence would be necessary to make his policy preferences viable. To that extent, his deathly agenda is internally consistent.

He was not the only respondent to advocate killing the Arabs in Israel. A Dati Ashkenazi man, 18–22 years old, from the Jerusalem area with a secondary education, described the following:

> The state of the Jews is the state of Israel and it includes the territories of Judea and Samaria, and the entire West Bank. If it does not suit the Arabs, no one forced them to stay here and lie to the world that the Israelis are murderers. There is not and will not be a Palestinian state on the settlements!!!
> Forgiving terrorists is God's job,
> Our job is to bring them together!!!!!

The tacit assertion here is that Palestinians are terrorists who misrepresent the actions of the Israeli police and military. Notably, some people apply the term *terrorist* liberally to Palestinian citizens. The respondent advocates killing them to move them toward God's judgment. The reliance on death to remove the Palestinians is consistent with the assertion of the expanded state claim. After all, he would leave no Palestinian state into which they could move. He also denies a validity to the idea of Palestinian towns, although the current Israeli state establishes settlements in the Palestinian Territories. Killing the Palestinians resolves his dilemma. At the same time, he professes to support peace with the Arab states. There are already substantial Palestinian populations living in some of these states after fleeing Israel. He may expect the remainder to relocate as well. It would be a political and logistical hurdle though.

A similar view was implied by another respondent. The 50+-year-old secular Ashkenazi woman from the central area with secondary education broke her commentary into three points:

The State of Israel is the only Jewish state.
All the other citizens
    1) the Arabs especially belong in the sea
    2) the rest of the citizens can vote for the Knesset
    3) I'm left-wing.

She wields her support for a left-wing party as a defense for opposing liberal democracy and seeking to force out the—presumably non-Jewish—Arab population. This language of pushing a population into the sea has a mirror in the response of some foreign regimes (e.g., Iranian leaders) to the creation of Israel. This homicidal language, including one-Israel-from-the-river-to-the-sea, was employed widely, especially by right-wing politicians, during the 2023–2024 Gaza War.

Other respondents were willing to take a nuanced stance on the Arab expulsion. A Dati mixed-ethnicity man in his thirties from the north area with vocational training responded, "Okay, I think there should be a state of Israel and that the Arabs who hate Israel should leave and the Arabs who love Israel want to live in peace, so they will stay here." In that case, he would not necessarily expel all the Arabs, but he is certainly open to removing at least some of them. The standard for *loving Israel*, however, is ill-defined. Presumably it would involve not challenging the Jewish character of the state. That would be a problem if their existence itself were seen as the challenge.

Alternatively, non-Jewish individuals might be allowed to remain in Israel if they changed their tune. A secular Ashkenazi man in his twenties in the Sharon area with a university education described his views:

> In my opinion, the country needs a very significant change that will be made by electing public representatives who do not sit in the government who will be involved in what is happening.[8]
>
> In addition, I would do more explaining to the Israeli Arabs about the fact that they chose to live here and they should be thankful for such a day because in other Arab countries in the vicinity the situation is bad.

Be the circumstances in Israel however much against the Arab inhabitants' wishes, this Israeli thought they should prefer Israel to another situation. His stance, though, takes the view that they are only allowed in Israel on sufferance. It also omits Israel's being created around the extant population rather than their having moved into it.

Not everyone was so exclusionary. A Masorti Mizrahi man in his twenties in the south area with a university education expressed a nearly opposite view:

We must understand that we do not live here alone in this country.

You can't throw everyone into the sea, and we must live here in peace with each other.

We are fighting over such a small country and territories instead of trying to settle down and preserve the status quo.

Israel is a Jewish state, the only state that this nation has, and it is important to preserve and protect it not only from a security point of view, but also from the point of view of citizens, to maintain honor and the unity of the people, and not to divide and incite it.

It will destroy us later.

With all due respect, this country is not just land and an army and wars.

There are many things that are beyond [that], and I don't think the average citizen is interested in what is happening with Iran or what is in Sheikh Jarrah.[9]

All in all, they want to live and make a living with dignity.

You do everything but what you really need [to do].[10]

A 50+-year-old Masorti Sephardi woman from the north region with vocational training stated, "I believe in the fact of live and let live. I really don't mind the matter of living with Muslims and Christians in Israel, only the wars and all the trouble in Israel." She does not question their existence or discuss them as a threat to the state. This seems like a rare position for a Likud supporter to hold.

Another—a Dati Mizrahi man in his thirties in the Jerusalem area with a university education—wrote, "The land of Israel belongs to the people of Israel. We are a nation state that allows the residents of our country to live in peace and harmony with us. Whoever rejects the above idea is not entitled to equality because he endangers the entire ideal of equality and the state of the Jewish nation." This viewpoint opposes those who would oppress the Palestinians, although they are not part of the nation. It is still technically illiberal.

These negative attitudes—to the point of violence—to the presence of an ethnic out-group have become a point of international contention. They are often juxtaposed with the historical experiences of antisemitism in Europe: "In fact, it became increasingly common for international actors to comment how the victims had now become the victimisers, and the Palestinians were now the Jews of the Middle East" (Vandermaas-Peeler, Subotic, and Barnett 2024, 179).[11] This statement relies on the premise of "Jews as a permanent victim" (179).[12] At the same time, official Israeli narratives draw on histories of persecution to frame many issues, including justifying the state and state-sanctioned violence. As a result, Israel is a "complex victim, simultaneously victim and perpetrator" (179).

Personal Life Majoritarianism

Marginal group members need not only express exclusionary attitudes toward the most overt out-group members. They may also aggressively police the boundary of in-group membership. Boundary policing can include being exclusionary of potential group members. Consider for instance those in the United States "closest to the perimeter of the skin color boundaries that have exerted so much influence over Americans' conceptualization of Whiteness" (Ostfeld and Yadon 2022b, 247). Marginal Jewish Israelis may be more conservative in interpreting who has *become* Jewish. Jewish law passes membership matrilineally. Israel has struggled to flex the rules of inclusion into religious or cultural Judaism, such as for the non-Jewish families of Jewish immigrants (e.g., those from the former Soviet states) (Yadgar 2020). Additional controversy exists over the inclusion of those who were not converted traditionally to Judaism. The Chief Rabbinate is Orthodox, but Israeli law recognizes Reformed and Conservative conversions that are performed outside of Israel. The Pew Research Center shows that 33.5 percent of respondents said that individuals converted by a non-Orthodox rabbi were really Jewish; 59.8 percent said that such individuals were not really Jewish.

Mizrahi and Sephardi Jewish Israelis were less likely than the Ashkenazi Jewish Israelis to say that these individuals count as Jewish (Model 1). This is true even when respondents' religiosity is accounted for (Model 2). More-religious individuals were less likely to accept the non-Orthodox conversions. Those from the former Soviet Union were more likely to accept these individuals as Jewish. This befits the history in which individuals from the foreign Soviet Union were more likely to be from mixed-religion families and

TABLE 3.8 NON-ORTHODOX CONVERSIONS ARE VALID		
	Model 1	Model 2
(Intercept)	0.16***	1.14***
	(0.05)	(0.16)
Mixed	0.54***	0.74***
	(0.13)	(0.16)
Mizrahi/Sephardi	−1.19***	−0.68***
	(0.07)	(0.09)
Other	−0.17	−0.59
	(1.44)	(1.49)
Covariates	No	Yes
AIC	5,192.77	4,013.78
N	3,534	3,312

Source: Pew Research Center (2014–2015), binary logistic regression models.
*p<0.05; **p<0.01; ***p<0.001

of patrilineal descent that would not meet the Orthodox standards for inclusion. They were *"zera Yisrael"* (seed of Israel). This was deemed enough connection to permit migration. As part of immigration to Israel, they were (quasi-)converted to Judaism to facilitate the Ingathering (Yadgar 2020). The politics of inclusions are complex and historically freighted.

A demographic threat to the Jewish national state could also be triggered by out-marriage or out-migration among the Jewish population. Either of these behaviors by Jewish Israelis could compromise the Jewish character of that family and of the state. Out-migration would literally reduce the Jewish population, which also undermines the Jewish–non-Jewish population ratios. Some Middle Eastern countries attempt to control out-migration (Tsourapas 2020) and securitize emigrants differently from the rest of the diaspora (Abramson 2024). Israel does not prohibit emigration, but citizens may still disapprove of it because it reduces the Jewish population and because emigrants may lose their Israeli culture. Israel does place limits on interfaith marriages. As Israeli family law is based on religious community, interfaith marriages cannot be contracted in Israel.[13] Out-marriage could signal that a citizen has deprioritized his own Jewish identity or that of the community. It poses the risk that children would not be raised Jewish or that the citizen would seek to bring non-Jewish family into the state. This has been highlighted particularly with respect to Jews from the former Soviet territories. Some politicians have sought to alter the right of return to prevent such marriages from diluting the state's Jewish population.

Attitudes toward out-marriage are considered first. Since Jewishness is passed matrilineally, out-marriage is an overt threat to the perpetuation of the group. Some families will act as if a child who marries outside the faith has died. In the story *Fiddler on the Roof*, for instance, one of the daughters is shunned for marrying a Russian Christian, a fictional depiction of real-world occurrences. Some Israeli figures, including Orthodox rabbis, have controversially compared out-marriage to a "second Holocaust" (Lebovic 2019). The Pew Research Center asked respondents how comfortable they would be if their child married a Christian or a Muslim: 90.2 percent said they would be uncomfortable if their child married a Christian; only 5.9 percent would be comfortable. The aversion was stronger toward Muslims: 97.3 percent were not comfortable with their child marrying a Muslim. Less than 1 percent (0.8) would be comfortable with it.

Mizrahi and Sephardi Israelis are much more likely than Ashkenazi Israelis to report that they would oppose their children marrying out of the faith, either to a Christian (Model 1) or a Muslim (Model 3). These between-group differences continue even when the religiosity sticks have been extracted (Models 2 and 4). This represents two mechanisms for performing group identity. First, they are discouraging a future with non-Jewish descen-

TABLE 3.9 OPPOSITION TO OUT-MARRIAGE				
	Christian Marriage		Muslim Marriage	
(Intercept)	1.89***	0.69**	4.13***	2.62***
	(0.07)	(0.25)	(0.18)	(0.69)
Mixed	0.45*	0.09	−0.17	0.23
	(0.22)	(0.25)	(0.46)	(0.55)
Mizrahi/Sephardi	2.21***	1.15***	2.02***	1.53**
	(0.18)	(0.22)	(0.50)	(0.53)
Other	−1.88	−1.41	10.43	17.05
	(1.44)	(1.46)	(629.75)	(12,604.23)
Covariates	No	Yes	No	Yes
AIC	2,033.18	1,592.81	446.76	386.59
N	3,643	3,415	3,720	3,485

Source: Pew Research Center (2014–2015), binary logistic regression models.
*p<0.05; **p<0.01; ***p<0.001

dants by discouraging out-marriage. Second, being seen to enforce a group norm can earn approbation from other group members (Marques et al. 1998). Traditionalist marriage norms, then, can be a way both to signal group norm enforcement and to perpetuate the group's numbers.

That individuals from the former Soviet states are less opposed to intermarriage with Christians could reflect that that was more common in the Soviet Empire; they are, however, more likely than Israelis unconnected to the former Soviet Union to oppose marriage to a Muslim. More-religious respondents are more likely to oppose marriage to a Christian. Older respondents are more likely to oppose out-marriage in both cases. These results are consistent with greater traditionalism among older and more religious demographics.

Attitudes toward migration out of Israel are considered second. Israeli politicians have treated emigration as unpatriotic, treacherous, and cowardly (Oren 2019). Marginal group members would also be more skeptical of Jewish out-migration, which undermines the Jewish character of the state and the narrative of its international necessity. The Pew Research Center asked whether respondents felt that "Jews in Israel should feel free to pursue the good life anywhere in the world, even if it means leaving Israel" or that "Jews in Israel should remain in Israel, even if it means giving up the good life elsewhere." This is an appeal to linked fate; it posits that the respondent should do what is good for the group, which they believe is to secure a Jewish state, rather than what suits that individual in isolation (Dawson 1994). 42.5 percent thought Israeli Jews should move if it suited them, while 49.0 percent thought that they should remain anyway. If Israel is the natural homeland for the

Jewish people or is necessary for the Jewish people's survival, then personal interest is less important. Emigration could even undermine that claim.

Respondents highlighted the fact that Israel is the only Jewish-majority state. They felt that Jews should be in that state both to maintain the Jewish majority and to take advantage of that security. A 50+-year-old Dati Ashkenazi woman from the south area with a vocational education stated, "There is no equality between people. And Israel should remain the state of the Jews with a large majority forever and ever. Arabs and Christians have many countries in which they can live and Jews have only one country. Israel forever and ever. Israel is alive and well." When presented with options for Israel's future, she preferred that Israel be a Jewish-majority state and not a liberal democracy.

Mizrahi and Sephardi Israelis are more likely than the Ashkenazi Israelis to say that Jews should remain in Israel, even at the expense of a good life abroad (Model 1). This is true even when the religiosity and economic factors are removed (Model 2). Older, male, and more religious respondents are more likely to think that Jews should remain in Israel. The unemployed were more amenable to out-migration.

In the same vein, marginal group members would be more likely to believe that Israel is itself necessary to avert group threats. Israeli administrations, especially under Likud leadership, have promoted the view that "because the world's antisemitism was an unchangeable fact, Israel would always be the victim. . . . This interpretation of Jewish history defined Jews as a permanent victim—if Jews allowed themselves to be vulnerable" (Vandermaas-Peeler, Subotic, and Barnett 2024, 179). Respondents were asked whether "a Jewish state is necessary for the long-term survival of the Jewish people, or not?" 87.2 percent stated that it is; only 11.0 percent said that it is not. The proportion, per ethnic group, indicating that Israel is necessary for the survival of the Jewish people is shown in Figure 3.5. The lighter bar represents those who see Israel as necessary. Mizrahim/Sephardim are more likely to say Israel is necessary for the survival of the Jewish people.

Some of the respondents in the iPanel survey were explicit on this point. A Masorti Mizrahi woman in the northern area in her thirties with a university education wrote, "The State of Israel was established because the Jewish people were persecuted and destroyed in the Holocaust in the most shocking way possible. The state should first and foremost be the state of the Jews and thus maintain the orientation according to which it was established. I strongly oppose any situation where the majority in the country is not Jewish—simply because I don't want to be afraid to walk down the street." For her, a Jewish state is inextricably linked to her own safety as well as the continuation of the community. This appeal to the Holocaust is particularly noteworthy because this respondent was Mizrahi. North African states' experi-

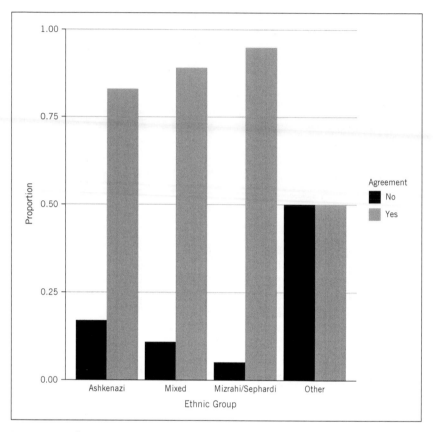

Figure 3.5 Ethnic Group Proportion Believing Israel Is Necessary for Survival *(Pew Research Center)*

ences are less commonly discussed. North African communities experienced occupation by German, Italian, and Vichy forces, including denials of citizenship, expropriation, and sometimes internment. Yad Vashem describes this as the "*looming* Holocaust," as the mass extermination campaigns were not implemented before the Axis powers' defeat in North Africa (Metzger 2023).[14]

The Holocaust is a focal point in Israel, especially because of its connection to the founding of the state.[15] Political usage could account for the woman's reference. A generalized potential for persecution based on Jewish history is also salient. Another respondent—a Masorti Mizrahi woman in her thirties in the central area with a vocational education—stated, "The Jewish people went through hardships and torture for years just because they were Jews! And thanks to them we are here in a Jewish country!" The current state's existence is framed by these respondents in the context of past suffering. The state is the answer to that history of violence.

TABLE 3.10 MAINTAINING ISRAEL				
	Remain in Israel		Israel Is Necessary	
(Intercept)	−0.31***	−1.77***	2.19***	1.53***
	(0.05)	(0.15)	(0.07)	(0.26)
Mixed	−0.27*	−0.35*	0.15	0.22
	(0.13)	(0.15)	(0.21)	(0.24)
Mizrahi/Sephardi	0.64***	0.21*	1.05***	1.14***
	(0.06)	(0.08)	(0.14)	(0.16)
Other	12.87	13.84	−2.19	−1.92
	(231.67)	(231.66)	(1.44)	(1.45)
Covariates	No	Yes	No	Yes
AIC	5,573.35	4,696.81	2,087.55	1,703.25
N	3,467	3,254	3,720	3,486

Source: Pew Research Center (2014–2015), binary logistic regression models.
$^*p<0.05$; $^{**}p<0.01$; $^{***}p<0.001$

Mizrahi and Sephardi Israelis are more likely than the Ashkenazi Israelis to say that a Jewish state is necessary for the survival of the Jewish people (Model 3). This between-group difference remains when the religiosity stick is removed from the ethnic bundle (Model 4). This could reflect the relative prevalence of antisemitism in the MENA region as compared to contemporary Europe (Fox and Topor 2021); former inhabitants of those states may feel a greater survival threat.[16] Older respondents are more likely to say that Israel is necessary, as are more religious respondents and those satisfied with Israel as it currently is. Men are less likely to agree. Marginal group members are more likely to be invested in Israel as a Jewish state.

Discussion and Conclusions

Marginal members of a dominant social group have tremendous reason to promote that group's interests and place in society. It gives them access to social privileges that they might lose if that group lost power. They also can use the act of defending the group's position to assert their membership in it. In the face of threats to the group, marginal group members are more likely to be aware of and responsive to those threats.

These forces compound in the case of Jews in Israel. The country purports to exist as a space *for the group*. Defending that space and the privileged position of the group in it gives nonprototypical Jewish Israelis access to privilege in their society. In particular, being seen as "Arab Jews" means that they can be almost assured of a status loss with the collapse of the privilege hierarchy. If being Jewish offered no cachet, then they would just be subject to Orientalism (see Chapter 2). Furthermore, the ongoing conflict makes the threat to the group salient. In this context, it is hardly surprising that non-prototypical Jewish Israelis support the idea of a Jewish state and the perpetuation of the Jewish community there.

That is seen in these several surveys. Marginal Jewish Israelis are more likely to support the fusion of religion and the state by giving Jews special status in Israel, enacting Jewish law, and promoting Jewish values. They also promote a Jewish majority in the population. Quite a corpus of opinions comes together to defend the majority. There is an overt expressed preference for a strong, stable majority plus influence on attitudes toward immigration and refugees. Immigrants are acceptable if they are coreligionists; the marginal group members and prototypicals were not distinguished in their racial migration attitudes, only their religious attitudes. Marginal Jewish Israelis are more skeptical of refugee applicants—non-Jews who would move into the country—and less welcoming. They also hold a tighter line on converts; they are less likely to accept a non-Orthodox conversion. They expect newcomers to be seriously, rather than casually, Jewish.

The marginal group members would even defend the Jewish majority against some of their fellow citizens' personal choices that might undermine it. They are less tolerant of out-marriage—marriages less likely to perpetuate the group. This kind of question is often taken as a mark of social distance from the targeted groups. The opposition to exogamy could indicate far less social willingness to be connected to religious minorities. Marginal group members also oppose out-migration in pursuit of personal benefit. At the time the Pew Research Center survey was being conducted, 2014–2015, newspapers like the *Jerusalem Post* were running articles discussing (or lambasting) the willingness of Israeli youth to move to countries like Germany for a lower cost of living (Rudoren 2014; Turner 2014). These sentiments have recently recurred (Weiss 2022; Klein 2022). Such an emigration for personal gain would be in defiance of the principle of linked fate and a denial of the group utility heuristic (Dawson 1994). Marginal group members, who are more invested in the perpetuation of the state as a Jewish national state, see that out-migration as a threat. Marginal group members were also, after all, more likely to assert that a Jewish national state is necessary for the long-term survival of the Jewish people. Willing out-migration undermines that assertion.

The nonprototypical Jewish Israelis benefit from Israel's stepwise social structure, which privileges all Jews above all non-Jews. They can shore up the bright line that places them in the in-group rather than the out-group. This is consistent with the racially conservative preferences avowed by darker-skinned white people in the United States. By promoting the Jewish community and subverting the Palestinian population, the marginal group members would be preserving access to greater privilege, although they may experience intracommunal bias.

Consistent, then, with substantial literature on race and ethnic politics, ethnicity matters for citizens' attitudes on racialized political domains—in this case an ethno-religious policy space. One can stretch the bounds a bit more, though, to examine ethnicity and marginality's effect on less racialized domains. This study turns next to citizens' attitudes toward Israeli democracy. Can Israel be both the Jewish national state sought here and a liberal democracy? Is that what the people want?

4

Marginal Group Membership
and Israeli Democracy

I srael is sometimes held out as a democratic island in the Middle East. It has been rated as a democracy by Polity for decades (Marshall and Gurr 2020), and Freedom House (2022) marks it as a free country. Democracy, particularly liberal democracy, would be consistent with the assertions of equality and freedom espoused in Israel's Declaration of Independence. Although the most recent Basic Law of Israel—enacted in 2018—does not describe Israel as a democracy, prior iterations (e.g., the Basic Laws enacted in 1992 and 1994) have.

The (liberal) democratic nature of the state, however, has been called into question because of the sociopolitical inequalities at work and because of the religious-nationalist profile. Oren (2019, 90) notes that the promotion of "a single ethnopolitical group in a multinational setting" makes it a "hegemonic state" and, at best, a "flawed" democracy, rather than a liberal one. Dean Mchenry Jr. and Abdel-Fattah Hady (2006, 261), for instance, note that the traditional democratic classification requires ignoring the circumstances in the Palestinian Territories and that the Israeli Arab population "has been kept from sharing fully in Israeli democracy" through discriminatory policies and restrictions on political participation, civic organization, and political speech.[1] While Jonathan Fox and Jonathan Rynhold (2008, 508) argue that Israel's extensive "government involvement in religion (GIR)" does not "undermine democracy,"[2] Baruch Kimmerling (2001) argues that Israel is not a democracy; rather, it is an ethno-state that gives privileges to one group.

More to the point, elite and popular support for democracy has also been questioned. Liberal democracy would actualize the promise of equal rights for the Jewish minorities and even for the non-Jewish residents. It could permit citizens to act against halakha. Democracy may well be something they value, something to which they ascribe a normative good. However, it would come with costs. Is (liberal) democracy worth it if democracy requires integrating the outsider or sacrificing the Jewish character of the state?

This chapter focuses on public support for democracy in Israel. More specifically, it considers whether that support varies on the basis of Ashkenormativity. On one hand, individuals who are at a lower social stratum arguably stand to gain from equalization in society. On the other hand, the same process of equalization could lift those below them. In that case, the marginal group members may prefer to sacrifice that move toward equality in favor of maintaining some relative group status. The non-Ashkenazi population could show less investment than the Ashkenazi Jewish Israelis in developing or perpetuating a democratic state structure in Israel. As is shown in Chapter 3, the Mizrahim/Sephardim are more likely to be interested in maintaining the Jewish character of Israel. That preference could even override interest in a democratic regime.

Marginal Group Membership and Democracy

In anticipating a relationship between marginal group membership and democratic commitment, this study is extending the usual scope of marginal group membership literature, which focuses on racialized policies (e.g., welfare spending). However, as Israel is operating as an ethno-state, democracy is arguably a racialized policy in this case. Furthermore, it is not new to speculate on a relationship between racial identity and democratic attitudes. When members of a majority group see that their racial group's status is threatened, they "express greater political conservatism on race-related and more race-neutral issues" (Craig and Richeson 2014, 952). Maureen A. Craig and Jennifer A. Richeson studied white Americans', who have historically enjoyed cultural advantage in the United States, response to learning about the impending majority-minority population demographics in the United States. For those concerned about racial identity or group hierarchies, this would parallel the demographic threat narrative in Israel about non-Jewish populations. Notably, this conservatism manifests *only when doing so can heighten the privilege differential between themselves and non-Whites* (Ostfeld and Yadon 2022b, 250, emphasis in the original). Where the conservative position would reduce their status within the group, they need not adopt it.

For some white people, this threat to group power can open the door to authoritarian institutional support. Kalmar (2022, 15)[3] notes that "illiberalism appeals strongly to white groups with precarious, partial privilege" to explicate the rise of illiberal movements in Central Europe as part of the response to exclusion by Western Europeans, who treat Eastern Europe as "white but not quite." Ashley Jardina and Robert Mickey (2022) speculate that a threat to white racial status in a multiracial democracy leads strong white identifiers to be more tolerant of authoritarian politics. This effect occurs among those with white "racial consciousness"—white Americans with "a sense of solidarity defined by a psychological attachment to their racial group, grievance about the relative status of this group, and a belief that their group should work collectively on behalf of its interest" (84). They are more susceptible to authoritarian claims, "particularly [claims] relevant to securing their power and status" (85). Their group identity and sense of group preservation then drive their willingness to sacrifice democratic opportunity for group benefit.

Threats to group standing can drive all members to defend the group's interest, even if it is not a normatively justifiable interest. Marginal group members are more likely to be strong group identifiers and to engage in group-protective thinking. Thus, among the dominant social group—a group that could already be willing to prioritize group benefits and identity over democracy, particularly the *liberal* elements associated with democracy—they could be more likely to engage in illiberalism.

Threat response to the demographic shift is not guaranteed. Access to privilege is a key component in that process though. For instance, Craig and Richeson (2014) demonstrate that telling members of the current dominant group that they would continue to enjoy social privileges, even in the face of demographic change, makes them less likely to exhibit a threat reaction in favor of conservative policies. If this pattern translates to the Israeli context, then maintaining Jewish privilege in Israel, even in the face of demographic change, could reduce the adoption of political conservativism. Maintaining that privilege—which nonprototypical Jewish Israelis were more likely than prototypicals to favor in Chapter 3—can be difficult to square with democracy. This propensity introduces the question of whether the prototypical and nonprototypical Jewish Israelis will favor democracy over the Jewish character of Israel, treat them as equal factors, or privilege Jewish nationalism.

Israelis do not necessarily see these positions as in contest. In the Pew Research Center study (2014–2015), 72.8 percent of Jewish Israelis thought the state could be both a Jewish state and a democracy; 23.2 percent disagreed. When confronted with tension in core beliefs, citizens and states can turn to denial and information avoidance rather than confront values dissonance (Oren 2019). For reference, only 30.0 percent of Muslim Israelis and 24.7 percent of Christian Israelis thought the state could fulfill both metrics, while 63.8 and 67.9 disagreed, respectively. This chapter unpacks the disparities by

| | | | Difference between |
| | | Table | Ashkenazim and |
Outcome Variable	Dataset	Number	Mizrahim/Sephardim
Prefer Liberal Democracy	iPanel	4.2	*
Living in a Democracy Is Important	European Social Survey 10	4.3	–
Strong Leader Is Acceptable for Israel	European Social Survey 10	4.3	–
Israel Can Be a Democracy and a Jewish State	Pew Research Center	4.4	*
Prioritize Halakha over Democracy	Pew Research Center	4.5	*

TABLE 4.1 DEPENDENT VARIABLES AND DATASETS FOR CHAPTER 4

ᵖp<0.10; *p<0.05

prototypicality. Table 4.1 summarizes the variables and datasets used in this chapter.

Democracy in Israel

Israel's citizens would naturally have opinions on the democratic caliber of the state and its continuation. After all, the "combination of socioeconomic deprivation, ethnic animosity, and a protracted national conflict may still lead to serious challenges to the democratic arrangements prevailing in Israel" (Peled 1998, 104). That opinion is the focus of this chapter. In particular, the chapter addresses the precarious privilege of the Mizrahim in the Jewish community. It draws on several survey questions that tap into Israel's democratic condition. Such questions are commonly asked in national and cross-national panels. First, questions about interest in democracy are introduced, as well as authoritarian openness. The final element is the relative preferencing of the democratic and Jewish characters of the state.

These dependent variables are all binary, nominal, or numerical-integral variables, so binary or multinomial logistic or ordinary least squares (OLS) regression models are used. In each case, after the model with just ethnicity is presented, models with covariates are also shown. Some of these will be removing elements from the ethnic bundle of sticks. Being from the former Soviet Union, being an immigrant, having a college education, being employed, being satisfied with the way things are in Israel, and being male are binary variables. Religious group is included as a factor variable; Hiloni (secular) is the reference category. Religious blocs from secular (Hiloni) to ultra-Orthodox (Haredi) are treated as nominal groups rather than ordered groups (Yuchtman-Yaar, Alkalay, and Aival 2018). Religion's importance in the respondents' lives is included as a binary marker for very or somewhat important compared to not too important or not at all important: "Previous studies have found that religious identity and ethnicity have been the most salient socio-demographic variables affecting the political attitudes and voting preferences of the Israeli-Jewish electorate" (Yuchtman-Yaar, Alkalay, and Aival 2018, 2). Economic condition is a binary indicator for very or somewhat good personal economic circumstances as opposed to very or somewhat bad.[4]

The iPanel survey asked respondents directly for their state structural preferences. When considering "some scenarios regarding the future of the State of Israel," they could indicate whether their preference was "a democratic state with equal political rights to all residents, regardless of religion, race, or sex" or "a non-democratic state, denying political rights, such as voting, to non-Jewish residents residing in the state." Notably, this phrasing refers specifically to a *liberal* democracy; not only would there be electoral institutions but the system would offer equality among the citizens. With a Jewish majority, a religion- or ethnicity-linked illiberal democracy would be possible—and thus potentially imagined by the survey respondents—under a purely democratic question formation. This liberal qualification means equality for the non-Jewish residents of the state, including rights for the Palestinians.

Not all of the respondents were pleased with the specification of liberal democracy. A mixed-ethnicity Haredi man in his thirties from the central area with secondary education wrote, "The questions are blatantly worded for a weak and non-objective leftist view, for example calling Israel a non-democratic state if the government decides to deny the right to vote to *enemies* (not to citizens of any religion, of course) etc. etc." He supported a Jewish-majority state within the Green Line borders that would not be a liberal democracy. He reported voting for Shas, a conservative Sephardi party. Another respondent—a 50+-year-old Haredi Sephardi man from the central area with vocational education—used the free-response space to simply state, "Israel is a democratic country." He still voted against the liberal democracy option. Another—a Dati Mizrahi woman in her thirties from the central area with a university education—said, "The State of Israel is a Jewish and democratic state and should remain so for generations." Supporting democracy and belief in Israel as a democracy are apparently distinct propositions.

Of the provided options, 83.5 percent preferred the liberal democracy. A secular Ashkenazi woman in her forties in the north area with a university education wrote that she "oppose[s] any option in which Israel would be a non-democratic state." Another commenter, a 50+-year-old secular Ashkenazi woman from the north area with a university education wrote, "We want to live in a democratic Israel."[5] By contrast, 16.5 percent of the respondents indicated a preference for the alternative. This could reflect an opposition to equality, an opposition to democratic institutions themselves, or both.

For instance, one respondent seemed to accept democracy but not liberalism. The 18–22-year-old Masorti Ashkenazi woman from the south area with a vocational education wrote, "The State of Israel should not be a non-democratic country. It is simply necessary to take away ID and rights from the Arabs." By that exclusion, she is insisting on illiberal democracy for her state. She even chose the not-liberal democracy option when given the choice. The *overall* rate of expressed support for liberal democracy, though, is quite high.[6] The proportion of support by ethnic groups is shown in Figure 4.1. The light bar indicates the proportion supporting liberal democracy. In each case, the majority of respondents preferred liberal democracy.

Mizrahi/Sephardi respondents were less likely to indicate a preference for liberal democracy (Model 1). The religiosity stick in the bundle seems to have done important work here, as the residuum is not significant, although it is negative (Model 2). The more religious respondents were less likely than

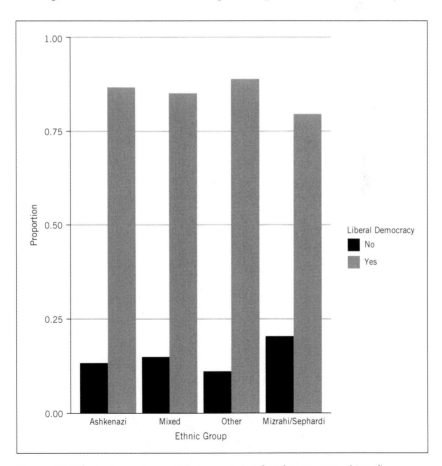

Figure 4.1 Ethnic Group Proportion Supporting Liberal Democracy *(iPanel)*

TABLE 4.2 PREFERENCE FOR LIBERAL DEMOCRACY

	Model 1	Model 2
(Intercept)	1.86***	0.22
	(0.15)	(0.70)
Identify as an Ethnic Minority	0.25	0.75
	(0.45)	(0.47)
Mixed	−0.13	−0.28
	(0.28)	(0.31)
Other	0.17	0.24
	(0.63)	(0.65)
Mizrahi/Sephardi	−0.51**	−0.30
	(0.19)	(0.23)
Covariates	No	Yes
AIC	887.45	829.17
N	991	988

Source: iPanel, binary logistic regression model.
*$p<0.05$; **$p<0.01$; ***$p<0.001$

the Hiloni respondents to express democratic commitment. That women are significantly more likely to favor a liberal democracy is consistent with the specification of women's rights in that option.[7]

ESS10 also asked respondents about the relative importance of democracy: "How important is it for you to live in a country that is governed democratically?" They could rate it from not at all important (0) to extremely important (10). In this case the liberalness of the democracy is not explicitly built into the question. It could be an illiberal majoritarian regime.

The respondents were asked how important several potential state features are "for democracy in general."[8] The Mizrahim are more likely to be operating under a *maximalist* conception of democracy. The Mizrahim and Ashkenazim did not report significantly different levels of importance for the most minimal element of democracy, free and fair elections. They also did not assign significantly different ratings for media freedom or the rule of law. The Mizrahim, however, assigned more importance to direct democracy and citizens' ability to influence the government by referendum, and they were slightly less likely to assume that democracy protects minorities' rights. They assigned more importance to economic policies and outcomes than the Ashkenazim did. For instance, they assigned more importance to the government's fighting poverty and reducing income inequality. They also gave marginally higher ratings to populism, the will of the people triumphing over the will of elites. In total, they seem to think of democracy more in terms of the voice of the people than the Ashkenazim do.

They were also asked to rate the extent to which these features were present in Israel currently. On average, they rated elections highly (7.39) but did not rate civil liberties as highly (minority rights, 5.54; rule of law, 4.54; freedom of the press, 7.23). The Mizrahim/Sephardim were less likely to say Israel runs free and fair elections—the sine qua non of democracy—but they were similar to the Ashkenazim in rating most other features. Other-identifying respondents were less impressed with Israeli democracy. They were less likely to say the state runs free and fair elections, protects minority rights, or fights economic inequality and poverty.

Most Jewish Israelis said that living in a "democracy" was very important to them. On the 0 to 10 scale, 89.3 percent rated it 7 or higher. The Mizrahim/Sephardim and Ashkenazim do not give significantly different ratings. The more religious respondents place less weight on living in a democracy, whereas those who are more satisfied with their lives are more likely to assign importance to it. Recall that the Mizrahim/Sephardim were less likely to endorse a liberal democracy. That they endorse this "democracy," which is not specifically liberal, likely reflects the difference in meaning they are assigning to the term. They favor a regime that has elections and the rule of law *and* fights economic inequality. Ridge (2023a) demonstrates that citizens assigning maximalist definitions to democracy may overreport their interest in actual democracy—choosing their government by election—because they are reporting their interest in an assumed economic outcome. Since the Mizrahim are more likely to be in a financially precarious position, if that is how they are interpreting the question, then their support is consistent with their social marginalization. While the Mizrahim were not less likely to say a democracy should protect minority rights, the question's specification that it would include equal rights regardless of race or religion (e.g., for the Palestinians) may have reduced the support. Future work should follow up on these diverse construals of democracy and examine the implications of more specific questions about support for democracy.

In turn, the marginal members of a dominant group may show more tolerance for a nondemocratic leader if they anticipate that he or she will act in the group's interest. If democratic commitment can be threatened by the thought of power sharing and the loss of status, then these conditions could be protected by the *right kind* of authoritarian structure. ESS10 addressed one kind of nondemocratic regime. The same respondents were asked to rate "How acceptable for you would it be for Israel to have a strong leader who is above the law?" from not at all acceptable (0) to completely acceptable (10). Jewish Israelis were not likely to say it was acceptable; only 13.9 percent rated it 7 or higher. The Mizrahim/Sephardim did not rate it significantly differently from the Ashkenazim. The more religious respondents were more likely to

TABLE 4.3 REGIME-TYPE PREFERENCES				
	Important to Live in Democracy		Strong Leader Acceptable	
(Intercept)	9.22***	23.74*	2.34***	−16.37
	(0.15)	(9.67)	(0.26)	(16.09)
Israeli	−0.39	−0.27	−0.08	−0.52
	(0.22)	(0.24)	(0.38)	(0.41)
Mixed	0.22	0,17	−0.41	−0.50
	(0.36)	(0.38)	(0.60)	(0.63)
Mizrahi/Sephardi	0.02	0.12	0.03	−0.49
	(0.20)	(0.21)	(0.34)	(0.35)
Other	−0.52	−0.38	−0.78	−1.22
	(0.41)	(0.45)	(0.68)	(0.74)
Covariates	No	Yes	No	Yes
R^2	0.01	0.05	0.00	0.11
Adj. R^2	0.00	0.03	−0.00	0.09
N	627	548	622	547

Source: European Social Survey 10 (2022), OLS regression models.
*$p<0.05$; **$p<0.01$; ***$p<0.001$

say it would be acceptable, while those satisfied with their current lives and the college educated were less interested in a strongman government. Future research should consider additional nondemocratic alternatives to find the boundaries of popular support. For instance, it could consider military, religious, or ethnic regimes.

The prior chapter showed that these nonprototypical group members are more likely to be committed to the Jewish character of the state. How does that stack up against their democratic commitment? As noted above, many Jewish Israelis believe that Israel can be both a Jewish state and a democracy. The proportion across the ethnic groups who hold this belief is shown in Figure 4.2. A majority of respondents believed this in each case. The lighter bar indicates the proportion believing that the state can fulfill both objectives simultaneously. (NB: The small number of "other" identifies in the Pew Research Center sample skews that column).

The Mizrahim/Sephardim are more likely than the Ashkenazim to espouse this belief (Model 1). The religiosity stick is again doing a lot of work in this pattern (Model 2). Former residents of the USSR, men, and the college educated are less likely to endorse this potential duality.

Just because the public believes that Israel can be a Jewish state and a democracy—even granting that it could be the case—does not ensure that no conflict could ensue. Democracies, particularly regimes celebrating freedom as Israel's Declaration of Independence does, may lead to individuals' enjoying some freedoms and regimes' enacting some policies that other citizens

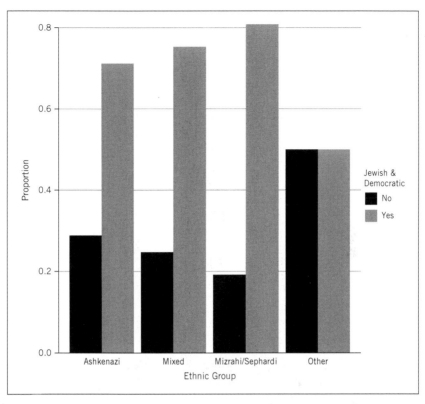

Figure 4.2 Ethnic Group Proportion for Jewish and Democratic State *(Pew Research Center)*

TABLE 4.4 DEMOCRACY AND JEWISH STATE		
	Model 1	Model 2
(Intercept)	1.07***	1.58***
	(0.05)	(0.17)
Mixed	0.16	−0.20
	(0.15)	(0.16)
Mizrahi/Sephardi	0.51***	0.14
	(0.08)	(0.10)
Other	−1.06	−1.51
	(1.44)	(1.44)
Covariates	No	Yes
AIC	4,317.80	3,957.50
N	3,640	3,412

Source: Pew Research Center (2014–2015), binary logistic regression models.
*$p<0.05$; **$p<0.01$; ***$p<0.001$

wish they would not. For instance, for all the discussion about Israel's openness to LGBTQ individuals and LGBTQ rights, homosexuality is not condoned by all citizens. In ESS8, 14.9 percent of Jewish Israelis disagreed with the statement that "gay men and lesbians should be free to live their own life as they wish," and 21.8 percent would be ashamed of a gay family member. In ESS10, it was 13.9 percent and 13.4 percent, respectively. The democratic system would allow the government, even of a "Jewish state," to enact laws that conflict with halakha, Jewish law. In the event of such conflict, the favorability toward the Jewish character of the state—as discussed in Chapter 3—would lead to privileging halakha over democracy.

The Pew Research Center study asked respondents to make that choice: "If there is a contradiction between halakhah and democratic principles, should the state of Israel give preference to democratic principles or halakhah?" 52.0 percent of Jewish Israelis favored privileging democracy, 34.1 percent favored Jewish law, and 11.9 percent said it depended on the case. Unsurprisingly, 83.0 percent of Muslim Israelis and 91.5 percent of Christian Israelis would give preference to democracy, while 8.7 percent and 2.0 percent preferred religious law respectively.[9] The ethnic distribution among the Jewish respondents is shown in Figure 4.3. The dark bar shows the proportion that favor privileging democracy over halakha. A majority in each group supported privileging democracy, though it was a bare majority for the Mizrahim (50.1 percent).

Consistent with the results seen so far, Mizrahi/Sephardi Jewish Israelis are significantly less likely than Ashkenazim to give the preference to democracy over Jewish law (Model 2). They are even less likely to say "it depends" (Model 1). More-religious individuals are more likely to give the preference to religious law or to believe it depends (Models 3 and 4). The residuum of the ethnic bundle is not significantly less likely to privilege democracy once the religiosity stick has been removed, suggesting that that stick is doing a lot of work. The educated and those satisfied with the current circumstances in Israel are more likely to privilege democracy over halakha.

Discussion and Conclusions

Marginal members of a dominant group benefit from that group's relative social superiority. The equality-based nature of democracy, especially a liberal democracy, could naturally threaten that position. Therefore, the marginal group members already have less reason to be committed democrats. When democracy occurs in comparison to perpetuated privilege, democracy's relative value can suffer in comparison. This is consistent with Oren's (2019, 90) description of Israel as a "hegemonic state."

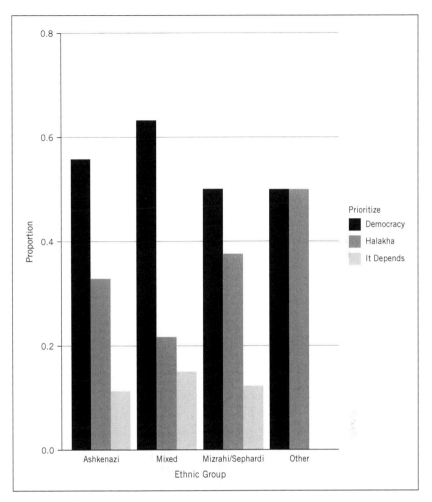

Figure 4.3 Ethnic Group Proportion Supporting Halakha or Democracy *(Pew Research Center)*

Israel's founding documents make reference both to a system of equality and a system of social privilege. The prior chapters have shown the marginal Jewish Israelis to be invested both in their group identity and in its privileges. This chapter has shown that democracy does not receive the same backing—at least relative to the prototypical group members—if it subordinates Judaism. Although Jewish Israelis on the whole express support for democracy, prototypicals can be significantly more likely to support liberal democracy.

The Jewish Israeli population wants to believe that the country can be a religious ethno-national state *and* a democracy. The marginal group members

TABLE 4.5 JEWISH LAW VERSUS DEMOCRACY

	Dependent Variable:			
	It Depends	Privilege Democracy	It Depends	Privilege Democracy
	(1)	(2)	(3)	(4)
Constant	−0.341***	1.349***	3.177***	5.238***
	(0.081)	(0.059)	(0.386)	(0.371)
Mixed	0.382	0.338	0.210	0.128
	(0.232)	(0.179)	(0.287)	(0.280)
Mizrahi/Sephardi	−0.567**	−0.777***	−0.337**	−0.151
	(0.109)	(0.076)	(0.151)	(0.145)
Other	−3.966	−1.418	−13.361***	−5.023***
	(8.680)	(1.442)	(0.00004)	(1.486)
Covariates	No	Yes	No	Yes
AIC	7,878.59	7,878.59	4,644.68	4,644.68
N	3,719	3,719	3,486	3,486

Source: Pew Research Center (2014–2015), multinomial logistic regression models.
*$p<0.1$; **$p<0.05$; ***$p<0.01$

hold to this point even more so. Nonetheless, when the rubber meets the road in the juxtaposition, the intragroup diversity continues to manifest. These citizens who are more often faced with asserting and maintaining their connection to the dominant group (Chapter 3) are more likely to privilege religious law over democracy. Democracy's popularity does not extend to allowing it to challenge or undermine religious law, at least for some of the citizenry. Those who must defend their in-group status can manifest their group affiliation by supporting such prioritization as well.

This demonstrates the multiple directions in which these citizens can be pulled. The state is to be a Jewish state—a state for a particular ethno-religious community. Being more religious and supporting the religious character of the state is consistent with that. The state is also supposed to be secular and Western. Such a state could have an official religion and an ethnic majority. However, supporting religious law over democracy is not consistent with that goal. These ethnic blocs are, on balance, weighing these parameters differently.

As the expectations of liberalism and progressivism grow, the policy domains in which religious law and democratic outcome conflict are likely to increase in number, not decrease. The rules of marriage and divorce (Cortellessa 2015; Weil 2019), who counts as Jewish (Gross 2022), and working on the Sabbath are contemporary debates in Israel (TOI 2022; Lis 2018). Many more can be imagined. This question of democracy and religious nationalism will then only grow more prominent.

The most salient policy domain in Israel—the Israeli-Palestinian conflict—however, remains to be discussed here. Ethno-nationalism and liberal democracy play a role in these engagements; however, security concerns matter as well. Marginality has shaped citizens' preferences on these other domains. Does it affect their attitudes toward the conflict or the peace process? This question is addressed in the following chapter.

5

Marginal Group Membership
and Conflict

This chapter turns to "the major cleavage dimension in Israeli politics"—the "Israeli-Arab conflict" (Shamir and Shamir 1995, 110). This moniker is itself pertinent to the ethnic dimension of Israeli politics. The label *Arab-Israeli conflict* overtly refers to tensions between Israel and the nearby Arab-majority states; it implicitly also suggests that Arabs are entirely separate from the Jewish population in Israel. The "Arab Jews"—even more than the Palestinian Citizens of Israel—put paid to that idea. This chapter focuses on how the ethnic diversity in the Israeli Jewish population shapes public opinion on the conflict.[1]

On one hand, peace would seem nearly universally popular, so examining conflict attitudes may seem frivolous. However, public buy-in is necessary for durable conflict settlements (Tellez 2019), and a sense of perpetual threat and conflict preparedness is part of the Israeli ethos (Oren 2019). In keeping with that fact, there is a long history of polling Israelis on their conflict-resolution attitudes (Shamir, Ziskind, and Blum-Kulka 1999; Bagno-Moldavski 2015; Yakter and Tessler 2023).

It has already been demonstrated that these marginal group members are more likely to be protective of the Jewish character of the state (Chapter 3). Despite discrimination against non-Ashkenazi groups—potentially even because of it—the Mizrahi and Sephardi Jewish Israelis are more likely than the Ashkenazi Jewish Israelis to feel a strong connection to Jewish identity and seek to protect Jewish privilege in Israel (Chapter 2). They are even more willing than the Ashkenazim to protect it at the expense of democracy (Chapter 4).

How then do these marginal group members address this conflict and the potential for peace with their non-Jewish neighbors? This analysis builds on the finding that marginal group members are more reactive to threats and more likely to engage in group-protective behavior. In this case, they are expected to be more responsive to the conflict and more aggressive with respect to Israel's position of dominance.

Marginal Jewish Israelis and the Conflict

Marginality and prototypicality are particularly relevant in times of conflict. At these times, when the group may be at risk, marginal members will be "call[ed] on to display their loyalty" (Ellemers and Jetten 2013, 13). This can manifest in group membership performance and in defensiveness. This fact would be particularly salient for individuals from the Arab states and their proximal descendants. After all, they are faced with asserting their connection to the Jewish state. The idea that Arabness is antithetical to Jewishness requires them to perform their group membership choice as a signal to the in-group. This propensity to be even more connected to the Jewish identity and the world Jewish community is discussed in Chapter 2. The marginal group members would be aware that "external threat increases the risk that they raise distrust or are cast out as scapegoats," and they need to head this off (Ellemers and Jetten 2013, 13). Seeming threats to Israel's security can be handled sharply, an incentive not to be perceived as a threat, which the out-group members tacitly are perceived to be. The conflict keeps salient the value of having the in-group claim and signaling that group identity.

Marginal members are more likely to be aware of threats to their group, and they are more reactive to them (Pérez 2015; Ellemers and Jetten 2013). Recall that the Mizrahim/Sephardim were more likely than the Ashkenazim to say that Israel is necessary for the survival of the Jewish people; most Jewish Israelis expressed that belief, but the marginal group members were even more prone to do so (Table 3.9). They perceive the world in general as more dangerous to Jewish people and Israel as more important for security. When responding to a perceived threat, marginal group members will "work harder on behalf of the group and adopt more extreme attitudes and behaviors than prototypical group members" (Yadon and Ostfeld 2020, 1375–1376). These extreme positions can take the form of personal practices or of the policies that the marginal group members support. For instance, marginal white Americans might support building a wall to keep out immigrants or making English the national language. In the case of marginal Jewish Israelis, this propensity can manifest in a more hawkish approach to the conflict, which keeps the macro in-group/out-group distinction salient and affirms their group membership. Recall, for instance, that marginal group members evinced a greater willingness to expel Palestinians (Chapter 3).

Beyond the threat, another factor could amplify this pattern. If marginal Jewish Israelis were concerned about being socially collapsed into the Arab stratum and must perform their in-group status, that itself provides a reason not to sue for peace, at least not any more than the prototypicals do. To do so might expose them to assertions of divided loyalties or laxity toward the out-group. Thus, the social order incentivizes an aggressive posture toward the out-group.

This propensity is arguably constrained to high group identifiers, because those who do not identify strongly with the group may slip from its bounds in times of crisis. However, residents of Israel cannot readily opt out of the conflict or of being assigned a side by observers; also, all individuals in these surveys identified themselves as Israeli and Jewish, which indicates at least some group sense. Any nonreactive weak identifiers still included in the sample, though, would ultimately work against finding any effects.

The heightened threat response often turns individuals to relative political conservatism (Craig and Richeson 2014). This is especially true among those from high-status groups for which the group-identity boundary is blurring; they will adopt conservative positions that ensure their macro-group's status relative to others (Ostfeld and Yadon 2022b). It has already been noted that Mizrahim and Sephardim have been described as voting Likud *at* Labor because of Labor's perceived ties to the Ashkenazim. Another reason for them to support right-wing parties is the conflict; the Mizrahim's nationalism and "security stances were closer to Likud's hawkish policy than to Labor's dovish policy" (Yuchtman-Yaar, Alkalay, and Aival 2018, 3).[2] These stances are considered here.

Marginal Jewish Israelis and Conflict Attitudes

Israeli citizens are regularly asked about their attitudes toward the conflict. How this issue is addressed in public opinion work is an evolving area: "Over time we find fewer references to 'true peace,' 'full and final peace,' 'enduring peace' and more to a 'peace agreement'" in the survey questions asked in Israel (Shamir, Ziskind, and Blum-Kulka 1999, 367). One iPanel respondent—a secular Ashkenazi man in his forties in the north area with an advanced degree—questioned the utility of asking about peace: "Everyone wants peace, this is not a question that you can really learn anything from. The questions should be more formative in my opinion. Why[,] the way to produce peace/negotiations/agreements[,] and how much the individual 'trusts' that there

TABLE 5.1 DEPENDENT VARIABLES AND DATASETS FOR CHAPTER 5			
Outcome Variable	Dataset	Table Number	Difference between Ashkenazim and Mizrahim/Sephardim
Prefer a Lasting Peace	iPanel	5.2	#
Prefer Borders beyond the Green Line Borders	iPanel	5.2	*
Israeli Government Is Making a Sincere Effort for Peace	Pew Research Center	5.3	*
Palestinian Leadership Is Making a Sincere Effort for Peace	Pew Research Center	5.3	*
Building Settlements Improves Israel's Security	Pew Research Center	5.4	*
#p<0.10; *p<0.05			

is a return for giving up territories, or if the future demographic risk will indeed be a weight on the subject." Even this citizen sees a role for demography in public opinion. As is discussed here, "everyone wants peace" is an overly rosy picture of the current situation. Recent surveys have probed citizens' attitudes toward whether or not to integrate the non-Jewish population or what kinds of concessions to make for peace. Table 5.1 summarizes the variables and datasets used in this chapter.

The necessity for concessions makes peace negotiations more challenging. If participants do not agree on the crux of the matter, then they can negotiate past one another. While Palestinians are more likely to construe the conflict as religious, Jewish Israelis are more likely to frame it as "a *nationalist* conflict between two ethnic peoples striving for political self-determination" (Canetti et al. 2019, 740). Thus, control over the material space is also tied to issues of identity. The marginal group members, who must assert identity, are also religionizing that nationalist proposition. Thus, to the extent that "religious grievances are likely to be more deeply held," in conjunction with the other factors, the Mizrahim may feel less able to make concessions (Canetti et al. 2019, 740).

As in the prior chapters, this public opinion data can be probed with binary and multinomial logistic regression models. In each case, the table first shows the ethnicity variable by itself; the model is then repeated with covariates. Some of these covariates pull sticks like religiosity and higher education out of the ethnic bundle. Being from the former Soviet Union, being an immigrant, being college educated, being employed, being satisfied with the way things are in Israel, and being male are binary variables.[3] Religious group is included as a factor variable; Hiloni (secular) is the reference category. Religion's importance in the respondents' lives is included as a binary marker for very or somewhat important compared to not too important or not at all important. Religious identity is part of the conflict; Bagno-Moldavski (2015) finds that the more religious blocs were less likely than the secular to support a political solution to the conflict and less likely to oppose state inducement for Palestinians to emigrate. Furthermore, "the political stances of the Orthodox public have been more hawkish than those of the secular public, particularly since the Six-Day War" (Yuchtman-Yaar, Alkalay, and Aival 2018, 13). Economic condition is a binary indicator for whether the respondent's personal economic circumstances are very or somewhat good as opposed to very or somewhat bad. Finding these effects indicates that, although recent work has argued that religiosity matters but that the effect of ethnicity has declined, ethnicity is still a factor to consider.

There seems to be little public interest in resolving the conflict with the Palestinians at the expense of the Jewish-majority state. A 50+-year-old Dati Mizrahi woman in the north area with a university education stated, "The most important to me is the Jewish majority, everything else is less important to me." In the binary choices, she endorsed an expanded state, was permissive toward future conflict, and preferred the non-liberal-democracy option. An 18–22-year-old Dati Ashkenazi woman from the central area with a secondary education proclaimed that "the State of Israel is the state of the Jewish people." She preferred the enlarged state, Jewish majority, peace, and democracy. Recall from Chapter 3 that 87.2 percent of the respondents in the Pew Research Center survey believed that "a Jewish state is necessary for the long-term survival of the Jewish people." Only 11.0 percent said that it is not. Support for peace would reasonably be conditioned by this sentiment. Pertinently for this discussion, Mizrahi and Sephardi Jewish Israelis are more likely than the Ashkenazi Israelis to say that a Jewish state is necessary for Jewish survival. This pattern is consistent with the abovementioned reactivity to threat.

The threat reaction also manifested in an increased likelihood to believe that "Arabs should be expelled or transferred from Israel." A willingness to do just that was expressed by many respondents. A 50+-year-old secular Ashkenazi man from the central area with a university degree expressed this belief bluntly: "Get rid of the Arabs." He favored a Jewish-majority state and preferred the state not give equal political rights to all residents. Nearly half of the Jewish Israelis surveyed by the Pew Research Center agreed with this point, and the Mizrahi and Sephardi respondents were more likely than the Ashkenazi respondents to support expelling the Arabs (Table 3.7). While it would affirm the Jewish character of the state, expelling the non-Jewish population would antagonize the targeted communities and likely inflame tensions with the neighboring states. This was evident in the 2023–2024 Gaza War, when expulsion to Egypt was proposed; Israel undertook large-scale attacks on Palestinian civilians.

In a direct question on the iPanel survey, respondents were generally favorable toward peace. An 18–22-year-old mixed-ethnicity Masorti woman from the central area with vocational training wrote, "I'm in favor of peace. We don't need wars. It causes fear, a lack of normal behavior, and everyone should always be considered." Consistent with that, she favored peace and liberal democracy in the direct questions. A secular Ashkenazi man in his twenties in the central area with an advanced degree reported that "peace with Arab countries is more important in my opinion than a clear and stable majority of Jews." In direct questions, he favored both, but he was able to identify a preference between the two factors. Clearly others do not share his views. Similarly, a 50+-year-old secular Ashkenazi woman from the north area with a university education said, "Peace, democracy and economic prosperity are what matters." She did not rank-order these items. They would, though, seem to rank higher than the features not included in her list. Likewise, a 50+-year-old Masorti Mizrahi woman from the central area with a secondary education stated, "I want a Jewish majority, a democratic state, [and] peace with all peoples." Again, by exclusion, it would seem that these factors rate higher than an enlarged state, but she does not specify how they rank against one another. That is in direct contrast to respondents like the 23–29-year-old Masorti Mizrahi woman in the south area with a secondary education who wrote, "The most important thing is that Jews are not a minority." That means peace is less important.

When offered a choice of possible futures, 92.4 percent preferred "a lasting peace with Arab countries, and the chances of war with these countries will be low." The across-group distribution is shown in Figure 5.1. The lighter bar indicates support for durable peace. A supermajority in each bloc supported peace. Only 7.6 percent preferred that "Israel will not reach peace agreements with Arab countries and the chances of war with other countries will be high." Granted, "compromise is easier to support when it is vague than when it is specific" (Canetti et al. 2019, 745). Maybe people are overstating their pacifism, but peace is also alluring. Given that fact, preferring the option for conflict is an intense choice. This 7.6 percent minority is seemingly strongly committed to the martial position. It could be a desire for the fight. They may have strong out-group animosity, a desire for revenge, or a desire for land. They may think that Israel would win any future wars. Alternatively, they may see peace as a challenge to the siege and security ethos or see the perpetual small risk during peace as more anxiety inducing than war (Oren 2019).

These numbers may have shifted away from peace with the 2023–2024 Gaza War. A survey by the Israel Democracy Institute in October 2023 showed that most Jewish Israelis opposed considerations of international humanitarian law or civilian welfare in Israel's military strategy: 83.4 percent said

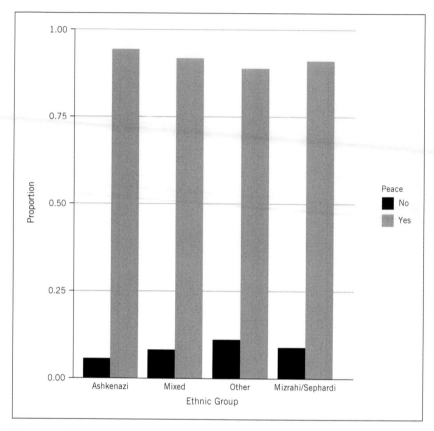

Figure 5.1 Ethnic Group Proportion Supporting a Stable Peace *(iPanel)*

civilians' suffering should be considered not at all or not so much, while 12.9 percent would consider it quite a lot or very much. Only 47.9 percent strongly or somewhat agreed that "the IDF [Israel Defense Forces] should ensure that it is not breaking international laws and rules of war," while 45.6 percent did not want the rules of war considered.[4] Such beliefs do not augur well for peace or international law. Israeli leaders were subsequently investigated for violations of humanitarian law.

The marginal group members were less likely to endorse peace, if not significantly so ($p<0.10$) (Models 1 and 2 in Table 5.1). The constrained effect may reflect the fact that peace is so universally desirable on its face that pulling against that is a very heavy lift for any other social force, even the perpetuation of group privilege. If the groups are collapsed to an Ashkenazi/non-Ashkenazi binary, the difference is significant. This negative relationship is consistent with the principle that marginal group members are more threat reactive and more determined to hold on to the religio-nationalist

TABLE 5.2 PREFERENCES FOR PEACE AND BORDERS

	Lasting Peace		Green Line Borders	
(Intercept)	2.83***	16.67	0.09	−0.54
	(0.22)	(628.96)	(0.10)	(0.69)
Identify as an Ethnic Minority	−0.41	−0.20	−0.48	0.01
	(0.50)	(0.51)	(0.33)	(0.37)
Mixed	−0.40	−0.64	0.05	0.19
	(0.38)	(0.40)	(0.20)	(0.23)
Other	−0.67	−0.69	−0.70	−0.83
	(0.66)	(0.67)	(0.42)	(0.46)
Mizrahi/Sephardi	−0.47	−0.59	−0.75***	−0.25
	(0.28)	(0.31)	(0.14)	(0.18)
Covariates	No	Yes	No	Yes
AIC	532.17	536.07	1,331.85	1,132.40
N	991	988	991	988

Source: iPanel, binary logistic regression model.
*$p<0.05$; **$p<0.01$; ***$p<0.001$

conflict agenda against the Arab population with which they are sometimes elided. That the Haredi are less likely to endorse peace or the Green Line borders could reflect the fact that the ultra-Orthodox can take exemptions from the mandatory military service; this could relatively isolate the community from the costs of perpetuating and expanding the conflict.

Although peace is desirable, some respondents expressed doubts that it would come to pass. One respondent—a 50+-year-old secular Ashkenazi woman in the south area with a university education—wrote, "Unfortunately [there are] not partners in peace." She favored peace, democracy, and a Jewish majority within the Green Line. An 18–22-year-old Masorti Mizrahi woman from the central area with a secondary education stated, "There must be a Jewish majority. There will always be war because Arab countries are not interested in peace."[5] She favored peace, when given the choice, but not liberal democracy. Alon Yakter and Mark Tessler (2023) dub Israelis who support territorial compromises in principle but who are skeptical of the viability or durability of a peace with the Palestinians or Arabs in practice the Doubtful Doves.

The public peace support may also be conditional. It may depend on the required concessions, or it may rely on how expansive they think the peace would be. For instance, a Masorti Mizrahi woman in her thirties in the Jerusalem area with a university education said, "We want peace without terrorism." This could imply that these citizens think that peace would only be accepted on certain terms or that peace negotiations are not complete without controlling for nonstate forces. Recent research has called into question how the public construes the terms *political violence* and *terrorism* (Huff and Kertzer 2018; Westwood et al. 2022; Kalmoe and Mason 2022). The threshold for calling any action terrorism in a context this tense could be quite low though. Some Israelis will apply the name to any Palestinian who challenges the state.

Others object to the two-state solution as a viable path. Two workable states would require allowing the Palestinians land and political authority. That was not acceptable to all participants. One respondent, a 50+-year-old secular Mizrahi woman in the central area with an advanced degree, particularly noted that her support for peace—support she gave in the direct question—did not extend that far: "We must emphasize in the questions that peace with the Arab states does not include Iran and the Palestinians." In contrast to the comment in Chapter 3 that the Israeli public does not care about Iran,[6] this response shows that some members of the public clearly do. Furthermore, although she claims to want peace, she does not want peace with Palestinians, despite preferring a state within the Green Line in the direct questions. Notably, peace is only made with enemies. Thus, the peace process must require engaging with states these publics do not like.

Some acknowledged that Israel plays a role in the conflict and peace process. However, they were not in accord about whether there is fault to be found in that. A secular Ashkenazi woman in her forties from the Sharon area with an advanced degree stated, "Peace with the Arab states depends on us, but not just [on us]." Another described his martial sentiments in conjunction with his desire for an expanded state. The Dati Ashkenazi man in his thirties from the Jerusalem area with vocational education expressed detailed preferences:

> I am in favor of a complete Israel within the Green Line and outside the Green Line, a Jewish majority in the Land of Israel and a stable one.
>
> A democratic country where everyone will be able to live here in peace and quiet according to the laws of the State of Israel, the dismantling of every existing weapon.
>
> No regional wars.
>
> By the way, it depends entirely on the Palestinians, as soon as they lower their arms, Israel will also lower them.
>
> Israel is only on the defensive. If Israel wanted to fight the Arabs they would have fought with the whole region long ago.

This representation skirts the history of regional conflict, in which Israel has hardly been a passive player (Oren 2019). The wholly defensive posture of Israel was also espoused by only some of the respondents. Unlike the previous woman, he sees only the Palestinians, not his own government, as responsible for securing peace.

The Pew Research Center asked respondents whether they thought the Israeli government and Palestinian leadership respectively are "making a sincere effort to bring about a peace settlement." A spare majority thought Netanyahu's government was making a sincere effort: 57.0 percent indicated that the Israeli government was sincerely trying, while 38.3 percent thought they were not. Conversely, 8.7 percent thought that the Palestinian government was sincerely trying, while 89.2 percent thought they were not.

Mizrahi/Sephardi Jewish Israelis were more likely to say that the Israeli government was making an effort (Model 1), even when the religiosity stick was pulled from the bundle (Model 2). Those who are foreign born, those for whom religion is important, and those who are satisfied with Israel's circumstances are more likely to credit the regime. Mizrahi/Sephardi Jewish Israelis are less likely to believe that the Palestinian leadership is making an effort, even after the religiosity stick has been removed from the bundle (Models 3 and 4). The more religious, those from the former USSR, and other foreign-born individuals were less likely to credit the Palestinians; those who were satisfied with Israel's circumstances and older respondents were more likely to do so. This result is consistent with the increased group protectiveness among marginal group members. In this case, they are more willing to blame the out-group for the failures to reach comity and more willing to defend the behavior of in-group members.

The iPanel respondents were divided on whether or not they favored the one- or two-state solution. 56.2 percent indicated they preferred "the future

TABLE 5.3 SINCERE EFFORTS IN THE PEACE PROCESS				
	Israeli Government		Palestinian Leaders	
(Intercept)	0.10*	−0.51***	−1.98***	−1.80***
	(0.05)	(0.14)	(0.07)	(0.22)
Mixed	−0.37**	−0.30*	−0.85***	−1.27***
	(0.13)	(0.14)	(0.26)	(0.28)
Mizrahi/Sephardi	0.53***	0.34***	−0.28**	−0.40***
	(0.06)	(0.08)	(0.10)	(0.12)
Other	−12.65	−12.65	−10.58	−10.91
	(231.67)	(213.37)	(231.67)	(231.34)
Covariates	No	Yes	No	Yes
AIC	5,670.37	4,997.74	2,958.76	2,633.05
N	3,609	3,387	3,709	3,476

Source: Pew Research Center (2014–2015), binary logistic regression models.
*$p<0.05$; **$p<0.01$; ***$p<0.001$

State of Israel [to] include the territories within and beyond the Green Line."
With these extensive holdings, only one state would be possible; in practice,
those borders could present obstacles for maintaining a Jewish majority, the
aforementioned demographic crisis. Those who favored expanding the state
did not necessarily perceive this issue. A Masorti Mizrahi man in his forties
from the Sharon area with a university education stated, "Israel should have
a clear Jewish majority that determines the conduct of the state. Anyone who
is not Jewish is welcome to live here under a clear Jewish government. Israel's
borders should not be reduced but only expanded." The government formed
after the 2022 elections supports such an expansion. On the other hand, 43.8
percent preferred "the future State of Israel [to] include the territories with-

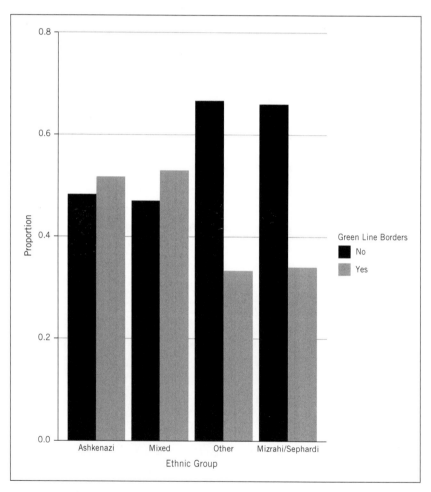

Figure 5.2 Ethnic Group Proportion Supporting or Opposing the Green Line Borders
(iPanel)

in the Green Line, with slight territorial changes." This is the structure proposed in the two-state solution. In practice, these territorial changes and swaps have proved difficult to choose. Devorah Manekin, Guy Grossman, and Tamar Mitts (2019) have documented this difficulty.[7]

The iPanel respondents were offered the choice between a state within the Green Line, with some territorial adjustments to account for subsequent population movements, or a state that included that territory and beyond. The distribution by ethnic group shows greater between-group disparities than were observed for some of the other features (Figure 5.2); the darker bar indicates support for the enlarged borders, while the lighter column indicates support for retrenching within the Green Line borders. Mizrahi/Sephardi Jewish Israelis were less likely to side with keeping the state within the Green Line borders (Model 3 in Table 5.1). More-religious individuals were less likely to support that choice; removing this stick from the bundle reduces the significance of the ethnic difference residuum (Model 4 in Table 5.1). Older and more educated respondents were also more likely to favor the two-state solution.

These opinions are consistent with the Pew Research Center survey responses about establishing a Palestinian state. When asked, "Do you think a way can be found for Israel and an independent Palestinian state to coexist peacefully with each other, or not?" 39.7 percent said yes, 47.8 percent said no, and 9.8 percent volunteered "it depends." Mizrahi/Sephardi Jewish Israelis are less likely to report that peace could form between Israel and an independent Palestinian state, either directly or conditionally (Table 5.4). This pattern holds even when the religiosity and education sticks are plucked from the ethnic bundle. This belief is consistent with less favorable attitudes to-

TABLE 5.4 PEACE WITH PALESTINE POSSIBLE				
	It Depends		Peace with Palestine	
(Intercept)	−1.255***	−1.325***	0.201***	0.226
	(0.075)	(0.226)	(0.048)	(0.147)
Mixed	0.281	0.250	0.167	0.036
	(0.197)	(0.213)	(0.133)	(0.148)
Mizrahi/Sephardi	−0.572***	−0.540***	−0.523***	−0.345***
	(0.110)	(0.136)	(0.066)	(0.085)
Other	−3.190	−9.317***	−0.257	−0.359
	(9.316)	(0.00004)	(1.440)	(1.450)
Covariates	No	Yes	No	Yes
AIC	8,336.118	7,363.277	8,336.118	7,363.277
N	3,687	3,459	3,687	3,459

Source: Pew Research Center (2014–2015), multinomial logistic regression models.
*p<0.05; **p<0.01; ***p<0.001

ward peace in general and especially toward the idea of an independent Palestine, which would undermine the vision of an expansive Israel.

At least one respondent did not shy away from the threat that expanded borders posed to peace. A secular man in his thirties in the central area who had a university education and whose family came from the USSR wrote the following:

> Yes, I wish for the state of Israel to reach a state where it is a democratic state with equal rights for all without differences of religion, sex and race, who strive for peace with their neighbors but will not lower their heads. Let there be a stable Jewish majority here, but certainly there will be room for other religions and populations with mutual respect and tolerance. And about the border? If the need arises to conquer, we will conquer. At the moment it is possible to get by just fine within the limits of the Green Line.

This man, who votes for the right-wing nationalist Yisrael Beitenu, theoretically supports peace. The other factors—especially the size of a Jewish state—just seem to matter more. For ethnicity, he chose "other" and wrote in Jewish. Per Lewin-Epstein and Cohen (2019) and Saperstein (2006), this deflection and the choice of Jewish instead of Israeli suggests that he is Mizrahi. The greater emphasis on majoritarianism and the willingness to "conquer" for the group's sake are then consistent with the within-group marginalization.

Belief in peace does not mean that all the other policy preferences are well aligned with achieving that goal. The Pew Research Center asked, "In your opinion, does the continued building of settlements help the security of Israel, hurt the security of Israel, or does it not make a difference?" 45.2 percent of Jewish Israelis thought that it helped security. Only 25.5 percent noted that it did not help security, and 25.8 percent thought that it depended on the case or that it did not make a difference. Manekin, Grossman, and Mitts (2019, 680) show that Jewish Israelis are "willing to pay substantial material costs to deepen territorial control of the West Bank." For some people, the territorial control is a question of security, and for some it is about ideology; those on the left "do not exhibit any attachment to the disputed territory," while those in the "center and the right blocs attach the highest priority to territorial control" (686). Figure 5.3 shows the great differences across the ethnic blocs. The black bar indicates support for the settlements, while the gray line indicates recognizing that the settlements hurt security.

One iPanel respondent questioned the utility of the settlements. A 50+-year-old secular Ashkenazi woman from the central area with vocational training wrote, "There are too many Jews who are pushed into Arab cities and regions and then there's an army at the expense of my taxes that keep them

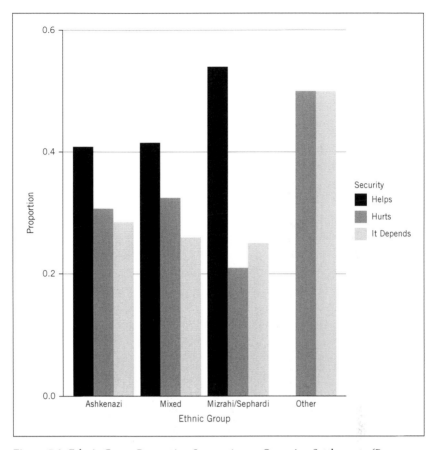

Figure 5.3 Ethnic Group Proportion Supporting or Opposing Settlements *(Pew Research Center)*

safe.—Why[?]" She was the only respondent to spontaneously criticize these establishments, though her objections seem logistical rather than philosophical. The expense and security threat these settlements posed was discussed during the 2023–2024 Gaza War. The deployment of resources to the West Bank settlements was seen as leaving the state economically and militarily vulnerable. These settlements also operated as bases for anti-Palestinian violence.

The Mizrahim also have an economic reason to support the settlements for which the respondent complains of paying. The arrival of new Israelis from the former Soviet Union—largely Ashkenazi and their families—"caused housing costs to skyrocket, pushing Mizraḥi families from the ghettos and barrios into the gentrified center," and Mizrahim in search of cheap housing could join the Zionists in the settlements for cheaper housing (Lavie 2018, 11). This may be what she means by "pushed." Between the violence to create new settlements over time and reprisals plus the extension of the state security apparatus, the settlements are not cheap for the state, and they do not constitute an avenue to peace. However, they provide some Israelis and some administrations a means to forestall addressing larger social issues in the short term. This respondent, for one, did not relish supporting these settlers.

Mizrahi/Sephardi Jewish Israelis are more likely to say that building these settlements in the Occupied Territories is useful for Israeli security (Model 2), even when the religiosity stick is pulled from the bundle (Model 4). They are even more willing to be equivocal (Models 1 and 3). More-religious individuals are more willing to assert that settlements improve Israel's security, as are men and individuals who are satisfied with the way things are going currently in Israel.

This finding is consistent with the 2018 Basic Law, which says, "The State views the development of Jewish settlement as a national value, and shall act to encourage and promote its establishment and consolidation." While this language can refer to Ingathering the diaspora into Israel, it can also cover distributing the Jewish population throughout all the potential territory. These settlements further the nationalist objective of promoting a Jewish state, and an extensive one at that. However, they make a two-state solution—or any peace requiring land swaps—a more challenging endeavor. Settlement supporters are trading the more durable security of a peace agreement for the unclear security of the settlements. Between undermining the ability to negotiate a state that could have a stable Jewish majority (via the two-state solu-

TABLE 5.5 SETTLEMENTS AND SECURITY				
	Dependent Variable:			
	It Depends	Settlements Help	It Depends	Settlements Help
	(1)	(2)	(3)	(4)
Constant	−0.392***	−0.046	−0.932***	−0.836***
	(0.057)	(0.052)	(0.179)	(0.166)
Mixed	−0.183	0.121	−0.072	0.233
	(0.165)	(0.139)	(0.179)	(0.159)
Mizrahi/Sephardi	0.505***	0.786***	0.358***	0.410***
	(0.084)	(0.075)	(0.104)	(0.096)
Other	0.390	−6.714	0.656	−9.746***
	(1.436)	(29.803)	(1.460)	(0.0001)
Covariates	No	Yes	No	Yes
AIC	9,347.51	9,347.51	8,255.40	8,255.40
N	3,655	3,655	3,424	3,424

Source: Pew Research Center, multinomial logistic regression model.
$*p<0.05; **p<0.01; ***p<0.001$

tion) and promoting discord through aggressive engagement with and dislocation of the Palestinian population, they would seem to undermine the viability of a Jewish state in the long term. There have also been assertions that they violate international law (Galchinsky 2004; Dugard and Reynolds 2013). The Hague Regulations and the Geneva Convention regulate military occupations, including with respect to the treatment of civilians and property rights. Ultimately, the settlements represent inconsistencies in the public reasoning and with Israel's international self-image.

Trading Off

Thus far this book has evaluated public opinion expressed in response to direct questions. These questions naturally separate the potentially intertwined policy areas. Public opinion research in Israel "highlights the necessity for trade-offs among values, which are inherent in the situation" (Shamir, Ziskind, and Blum-Kulka 1999, 366). To understand citizens' attitudes and preferences, it is necessary to consider their opinions on whole packages of options, rather than items in isolation. In trade-off scenarios, citizens are contending with an inability to achieve all their desires simultaneously. When choosing among packages, a displeasing reality in one category can be offset by a preferred outcome in another domain. To evaluate the *relative valuation* of these features, this chapter turns now to a conjoint analysis embedded in the iPanel survey.

A conjoint experiment is potentially fruitful for considering preferences over such a complex issue. Conjoint analysis has proliferated in MENA politics studies in recent years, including in studies of sectarianism and ethnic politics. Studies in Lebanon have probed the role of ethnicity in attitudes toward clientelism (Cammett, Kruszewska-Eduardo, et al. 2022) and sectarianism in security policy preferences (Cammett, Parreira, et al. 2022). Conjoint analyses have been used to study Arabs' propensities toward emigration (Ferwerda and Gest 2020) and attitudes toward women's labor force participation in Qatar (Blaydes, Gengler, and Lari 2021) and Jordan (Barnett, Jamal, and Monroe 2021). Ridge (2023a) uses a conjoint analysis to study attitudes toward democracy and Islamism in Egypt and Morocco. Conjoint designs have also been applied to conflict opinions in Colombia (Tellez 2019).

Conjoint designs have also been employed in Israel. Manekin, Grossman, and Mitts (2019) use a conjoint to study attitudes toward territorial control in Israel from a land value, security, economic, and budgetary perspective. Grossman, Manekin, and Yotam Margalit (2018) employed this technique to compare Israelis' policy preferences after a European Union decision to label products produced in the settlements, which Israelis linked to public boycotts of settlement products.

This study follows the conjoint model used by Shamir and Shamir (1995) to assess Israeli opinion during the First Intifada. Their study touches on several key issues. Namely, it engages with the principles of liberal democracy, the idea of a Jewish-majority state, the geographical scope of the state, and the desire for peace. They had expected that each of these positions would be popular. Lavie (2018, 18) calls this "the State of Israel's Zionist doctrine"—"maximum land, minimum non-Jews." In evaluating Israelis' preferences over these features, Shamir and Shamir (1995) find that having a Jewish majority in the state and having peace are the most important state features. "Greater Israel" and democracy are not significant factors by themselves. Democracy is only significant if there is a durable Jewish majority or, to a lesser extent, if there is peace: "It seems that in the present context of war and threat to the national identity, the commitment to democratic norms among Israeli Jews is weaker than in other Western countries, yet if one could 'control for' the context, Israelis would probably be as democratic as other people, possibly even more so" (Shamir and Shamir 1995, 120).

The conjoint design helps reduce intentional bias—such as social desirability bias and cheap talk—in responses to direct questions (Hainmueller, Hopkins, and Yamamoto 2014). It is easy to state a preference for two objectives when they are not presented as potentially in conflict. A rank-ordering question is possible, but observed rankings "are probably more affected by social desirability bias" than conjoint choices because the conjoint design does not require the respondents to spell out their order of preference or even to be conscious of it (Shamir and Shamir 1995, 121). At the same time, the technique is "agnostic about how respondents reach their observed decisions" (Hainmueller, Hopkins, and Yamamoto 2014, 3). The conjoint design can thus reduce bias by reducing the perceptibility of the potentially triggering item and by allowing for rationalization (Horiuchi, Markovich, and Yamamoto 2022).

In this case, the responders were presented with descriptions of potential scenarios for the future of the State of Israel. They had seen the sentences used in the description in the direct questions. Thus, they would be familiar with the options being presented. The instructions then stated, "Please rate to what extent you support or oppose the scenario described as a whole from 1 (strongly oppose) to 10 (strongly support). You can consider certain characteristics described in the scenario or all of their characteristics together when making the decision, but the rating you are asked to give should be general. We will present you with 10 different descriptions." The descriptive categories were drawn from Shamir and Shamir (1995), but the language was modified.[8]

The options for the scope of the state were "The future State of Israel will include the territories within and beyond the Green Line" and "The future

State of Israel will include the territories within the Green Line, with slight territorial changes." The Jewish character of the state is described in terms of the stability of the Jewish-majority population; they could choose "Israel's population could be made up of a clear, stable, long-term Jewish majority" or "Israel's population could be made up of a small Jewish majority that may become a minority in the future." They could indicate a preference for liberal democracy, "Israel could be a democratic state with equal political rights to all residents, regardless of religion, race, or sex," or an alternative, "Israel could be a non-democratic state, denying political rights, such as voting, to non-Jewish residents residing in the state." The choices for the conflict status were "Israel will conduct a lasting peace with Arab countries, and the chances of war with these countries will be low" and "Israel will not reach peace agreements with Arab countries and the chances of war with other countries will be high." Shamir and Shamir (1995) assumed that the respondents would prefer a large democratic state with a Jewish majority at peace with its neighbors. While the direct questions—already discussed in this book—show strong public support for peace, democracy, and a Jewish majority, the opinion was more divided with respect to the size of the state. The anti-peace minority, however, held strongly to that view.

Just because the conjoint technique does not require participants to be aware of their preferences or to avow them openly does not mean that people cannot. Some respondents used the open-ended space after the conjoint to express their opinions more discursively. Because they were only shown ten of the sixteen potential options, they did not all see their most preferred structure, and many respondents chose to share that structure in the free-response space. A secular Ashkenazi man in his forties from the Jerusalem area who had attended university described a state very much in line with Shamir and Shamir's expectations: "Of course, the ideal situation does not appear—a state that would include the Green Line areas and areas of Judea and Samaria where there is substantial Jewish settlement, a Jewish majority, a democratic state and a lasting peace." Judea and Samaria refer to the West Bank, whose annexation would undermine both peace and the Jewish majority.

It is evident that these goals conflict with each other. An enlarged state border would naturally include non-Jewish populations. In theory, the state can persist without having a Jewish majority or being a Jewish state. It would, though, be moving away from its supposed raison d'être. According to the Basic Law and the Declaration of Independence, this was to be a place of Jewish Ingathering and the homeland. Expanding the borders to include territories currently inhabited by non-Jews conflicts with the desire to perpetuate a Jewish-majority state. As noted in Chapter 2, many respondents felt that the state could not be a Jewish state without being a Jewish-majority state. For instance, a secular Mizrahi woman in her thirties with secondary education emphasized "a democratic state with a Jewish majority and peace with Arab states." The other features would then appear less crucial. In fact, she opted for the state within the Green Line boundaries, which would be consistent with her expressed central preferences.

Similarly, establishing a liberal democracy could challenge the Jewishness of the regime structure. Liberalism would shy away from giving one subpopulation special privileges. It cannot coexist with a separate and unequal regime that would suppress the non-Jewish population. Chapter 3 has noted that some Jewish Israelis would favor addressing this tension by expelling the non-Jewish population. Others have advocated a nondemocratic or illiberal regime in this circumstance. A 50+-year-old Dati Mizrahi woman from the north area with secondary education proposed an illiberal democracy: "A democratic country, a Jewish majority, equal rights for law-abiding residents, whoever betrays the country, take away all their rights." This description would be somewhat at odds with her selection of the liberal democratic option. Thus, she may prefer liberal democracy to a nondemocracy, but the liberalism is not necessary for her.

The enlarged state would also run against desires for peace. The other states and populations would likely contest the land claim or seek independence: "Although highly self-centered, Israeli discourse on the territories has acknowledged from the outset the need to trade territories for peace" (Shamir, Ziskind, and Blum-Kulka, 1999, 365). For instance, a secular Mizrahi 18–22-year-old man in the Sharon region with a secondary education said, "If we have to choose between a complete state of Israel and peace, we will choose peace, but the state's identity will remain Jewish and democratic." By using the word *we*, he functionally spoke for the group in his statement, although the opinion was not, in fact, universal; in his own choices, he preferred that the state remain within the Green Line borders. Although democracies supposedly are more likely to sue for peace, public opinion could constrain the trades that the democratic system makes.

Some respondents were aware of these potential conflicts. A secular Sephardi man in his forties from the Sharon area with vocational training described the challenge these realities pose: "I think we're in a huge paradox that makes it difficult to make decisions and form opinions. I'm all for peace, equality, free love and a country with no difference in race or gender." In the direct questions, he favored liberal democracy, peace, and a Jewish majority. A secular mixed-ethnicity man in his thirties from the Jerusalem area with a university education acknowledged that difficulty while enumerating his key features: "Some of the scenarios are impossible. And the most desirable scenario does not appear—that Israel withdraws from the territories, thus saving both the Jewish majority and the democratic government." His selections in the binary-choice questions aligned with his description. Recognizing the practical impossibility of some of these outcomes puts him ahead of the curve. A secular Ashkenazi woman in her thirties in the central area with an advanced degree put a more positive spin on the impossibility: "It feels like there are things here that are a dream." In light of this difficulty, respondents who were aware of the potential conflicts would have to make choices. A 50+-year-old Haredi Ashkenazi woman from the north area with a university education wrote, "Each of the components is significant, but the issue of peace and democracy are critical in my eyes." This difficulty is fundamental to Israel's politics.

Another respondent suggested resolving the tension by ceasing to be concerned with all of the factors. In particular, she ruled out caring about Israel's global standing. The Masorti Sephardi woman in her twenties from the central area with a university education stated, "All the options that have been given, there really isn't an option that is realistic for managing the State of Israel, everything here is very dynamic and in general it's time to stop being accountable to the world, they don't see us in any way." States are not really accountable internationally, but they can lose face. Ignoring Israel's international standing would facilitate illiberalism, expansion and settlements, and violence. Many activists argue that this has already happened. While the respondent endorsed democracy and peace in the direct questions, she also wanted a stable Jewish majority and enlarged state. While she is not specific about what she would do with openness to infamy, it cannot be something laudable.

Others chose not to see the contradictions at all. A 50+-year-old Haredi Ashkenazi man from the central area with only elementary education stated, "I think it is possible to control all the territories and remain democratic and establish peace with many countries and preserve the Jewish majority." He did not specify how. An 18–22-year-old Dati Mizrahi woman from the north area with vocational training wrote, "It is not for nothing that the name of the country is Israel, which means that the majority is supposed to be Jewish. The territories beyond the Green Line are also supposed to belong to the state, and, in addition, this does not contradict, and it is even desirable that there should be peace and that there should be equal rights for every citizen, regardless of race, religion, or gender." These individuals favored an enlarged Jewish-majority democratic state at peace with its neighbors. That does not mean there is a clear plan for achieving that goal.

One respondent explained away contradictions with divine prophecy. The 50+-year-old Dati Ashkenazi woman in the south area with a college education explained the situation as follows:

The assumption that the possession of the liberated territories will cause war and a Jewish minority in the Land of Israel does not correspond to my assessment, the vision of the prophets, the correctness, the successes of Zionism so far and it is just a defeatist statement resulting from the failure to recognize the historical right of the people of Israel to the Land of Israel and the failure to study Jewish history and faith.

Her statements recall those in Chapter 3 about God's giving the state to the Jewish people. The assumption in her statement is that those who knew the history of Zionist success would see that it would continue going forward. She even espoused a preference for a future with a higher chance of renewed conflict. Maybe she assumed that the wars would always go well for Israel.

Deep Divisions

It should be acknowledged that the conjoint technique has a limitation. The results are generated by compiling the ratings given by the many survey respondents and averaging them. The results are thus the average in terms of both the direction and the intensity of preferences. For instance, a minority that feels very strongly about electing female candidates can make the average result a small preference for female candidates although the majority would slightly prefer a male candidate (Abramson, Koçak, and Magazinnik 2022). A strongly held minority view can skew the figures.

The minorities in this survey who chose perpetuating the conflict or opted against illiberal democracy appear staunchly committed to that side. This manifests in the overall averages, which run counter to Shamir and Shamir's (1995) expectations. The iPanel conjoint results show lower averages for democracy, peace, an enlarged state, and the large Jewish majority. The conjoint technique averages over both the direction and the intensity of preferences, indicating two distinct camps with intense opinions. This pattern points to the relative strength of these bimodal preferences. The results in the direct questions are also more split than Shamir and Shamir had predicted, especially with regard to enlarging the borders. Even the lopsided preferences toward one side, like peace, can have negative averages, though, if the other side has a more vociferous opinion.

The focus here is not on the pooled sample but rather on the difference between the subgroups. Namely, the focus is on those who identify as Ashkenazi as opposed to those who do not. For comparability with the prior discussions, the discussion here will also explore the differences between those who are Mizrahi/Sephardi and the Ashkenazim. For this, the difference in marginal means is the appropriate focus measurement.

The marginal mean "describes the level of favorability toward profiles that have a particular feature level, ignoring all other features" (Leeper, Hobolt, and Tilley 2020, 6). A marginal mean above the midpoint indicates that the feature increases the support for a given profile, while a marginal mean below the midpoint means that the feature decreases favorability for that profile. The difference in the marginal means reveals the relative favorability or item weight, net of any influence from the other features, across the subgroups. Do the ethnic subgroups answer the conjoint differently from each other?[9]

In Chapter 4, the marginal Jewish Israelis were less likely to express support for a liberal democracy, but they were more likely to say that the state could be both a Jewish state and a democracy. They also define democracy differently, especially with respect to economic outcomes. As such, they may construe what being a democratic state means slightly differently from how the other blocs do. In Chapter 3, they were also more committed to a Jewish state, including Jewish privileges. This is consistent with the relatively reduced support for an explicitly liberal democracy.

In the conjoint results, the Ashkenazim were more open to a nondemocracy than the non-Ashkenazi respondents, while they were less open to a liberal democracy (Figure 1). This was true even if the model also included the covariates used in the regression analyses. The pattern also held if the sample was subset to just the Ashkenazi versus the Mizrahi/Sephardi Jews. The difference in these preference propensities could indicate that the role religion would play in the state is important. Without a clarification on this point, it could be that democracy is assumed to be a threat to the Jewish character of the state. Once the state is described more holistically (e.g., as a liberal democracy that can still maintain the Jewish majority), the focus and interpretation shifts. Majoritarian systems may be fine as long as their group is in the majority, and redistributive systems may be more favorable to those who would benefit from redistribution. It could also be a function of the relative staunchness of the anti-liberal or antidemocracy factions in each group. Less-vociferous support or strong opposition could make differences in the conjoint framework because the results are averages of both direction and intensity.

The impact from the other features on the ratings was not significantly different across the ethnic groups. Thus, although these groups express different preferences, they are not trading these preferences off differently against each other. This could stem from a shared *relative* value of most of these items, although the preferences are distinct. It could also indicate that the respondents are differently cognizant of these points. Although a vote choice can draw on subconscious preferences or include rationalization, it also draws on the conscious mind. The citizens' public statements are also what would inform elites' actions. As such, the differences in their direct choices indicate

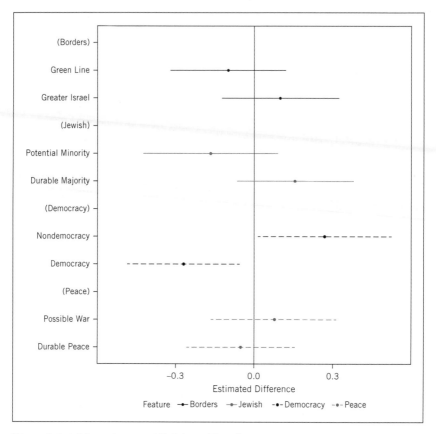

Figure 5.4 Ashkenazi versus All Others *(iPanel)*

that they would likely make different choices in the voting booth and demand different policies of their politicians. This is consistent with the diverging propensities to support left- and right-wing parties observed in Israeli politics.

Those who identify as secular (Hiloni) place more choice weight on having an expanded state and a Jewish majority. They are also more tolerant of a nondemocracy than other groups (Figure 5.5). The same pattern is evident when secularism is assessed by looking at those who do not pray as opposed to those who do (Figure 5.6). This pattern could reflect the discrepancy between cultural Jews and religious Jews. For the secular Jews, the state is a cultural proposition rather than a fulfillment of prophecy constrained by religious debates (Yadgar 2020). The pattern is at least consistent in some respects. As noted already, having a Jewish majority *and* the enlarged boundaries would be a demographic impossibility without substantial reapportionments of current

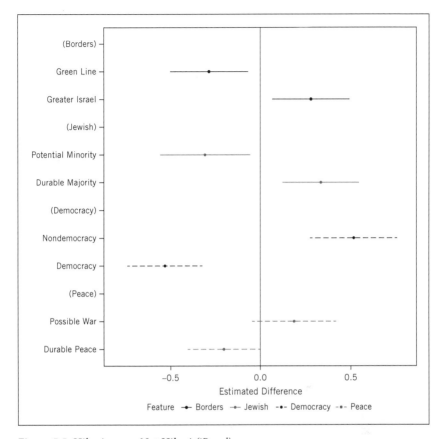

Figure 5.5 Hiloni versus Not Hiloni *(iPanel)*

populations. An illiberal or nondemocratic regime would be better philosophically equipped for such actions.

Discussion and Conclusions

This chapter has broached a domain of particular importance to Israeli politics: Israel's conflict with neighboring states and some of its own territorial inhabitants. Marginal group membership theory posits that marginal group members are more sensitive to threats to that group. In turn, they are more likely to engage in group-protective posturing and more likely to adopt conservative attitudes. In the case of marginal Jewish Israelis, compared to prototypicals, this can manifest in supporting conservative parties, in being aggressive in expanding the state's boundaries, and being less interested in making peace with the out-group.

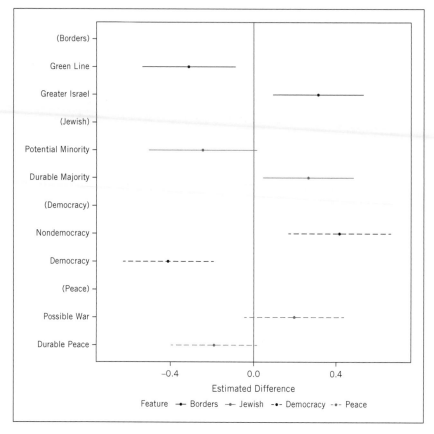

Figure 5.6 Never Pray versus Pray *(iPanel)*

The results shown here demonstrate that marginal group members are less likely to desire to keep the state to the Green Line borders. Consistent with that, they are more likely to think that the settlements are a security aid. These settlements, even if they were better for security—a doubtful proposition in itself—undermine the potential for a two-state solution, often framed as the best chance for peace. This group is less likely to believe that. These respondents are not all peaceniks, even though a large majority support peace. Hence the tension in contemporary politics and the respondents' descriptive preferences. There are many competing objectives. Even respondents who claim to speak for the masses contradict one another.

Remember, though, that these are differences in propensities for support. They do not indicate that one ethnic group is uniformly supporting peace and the other is manifestly promoting conflict. The modal respondent endorsed peace. Public opinion, however, was less uniform with respect to the execution of that peace, which would naturally touch on other goals citizens have for the state. The surveys reveal divisions over interest in a one- or two-state solution, which requires weighing both the scope of the territory the regime would control and the likely demographics of the resultant populations. The respondents were also split on whether or not the settlements—which promote an extended state but undermine peace negotiations—are improving the security situation. Security, a Jewish majority, and an enlarged state are all goals for sizable segments of the population. These divisions bespeak challenges for any kind of democratic solution. How can any state—even if it could resolve the situation alone—enact such divided will?

The challenges posed by these divisions are magnified on two fronts. First, these are not objectives that any state could necessarily fulfill all at once. How to be a democracy and an ethno-state and how to set the borders while securing peace are challenging questions. Future studies should do more to examine the potential trade-offs implied in some of these Jewish Israelis' expressed preferences.

Second, changing the state of play cannot be done alone. Even if the Jewish Israeli public opinion were united, all the voices singing in unison, any peace would require the assent and compliance of the other parties. Those include but are not necessarily limited to the non-Jewish inhabitants of Israel, the Palestinians in the Occupied Territories, and even the surrounding states and foreign powers. These parties would return to the questions described in Chapters 3 and 4 about support for Jewish privileges, right of return for Palestinians, and democratic regimes. These questions could justifiably be put as well to those populations. That, however, must be left to future research.

6

Conclusion

In 1947, a divided United Nations affirmed Resolution 181, recognizing the Partition Plan for ending the British Mandate in Palestine. In the words of the Israeli Ministry of Foreign Affairs, "Resolution 181 confirmed the 1922 recognition by the international community that the Jewish people deserve their own state, a Jewish state, in their historical homeland." The UN admitted Israel as a full member in 1949, and, according to the ministry, Israel "has been a fully democratic country with equal rights for all its citizens from its inception until today" (Israel Ministry of Foreign Affairs 2013).[1]

This book has focused on these questions of a Jewish state, democracy, and equality in Israel by looking within the Jewish population. Not all Jewish Israelis are treated as social equals. When Israel was created, the Jewish state did not simply relocate the diaspora. A state identity was forged. In particular, choices were made to build a modern, Western state on the model of European nation-states. In this process of Ingathering, in forming a secular, Western state identity, preference was thus given to Jews from European countries (Ashkenazi Jews) compared to those coming from the Asian and North African states (Mizrahi or Sephardi Jews). This normalization of Ashkenazi Jewishness has been called Ashkenormativity.

Despite the expectations of a melting pot that would inculcate these Eastern Jews into the Ashkenazi culture, a profile formed in which the Eastern Jews were Orientalized as backward, too religious, and too traditional (Smooha 2004; Khazzoom 2008). Over the years, that perception translated into circumstances in which Mizrahim and Sephardim are (or are perceived to be) less well educated, poorer, and more religious. They do not fit as well to the prototype image being created. The contemporary political relevance of these ethnic blocs and the social hierarchy has been challenged, but the results shown here indicate that these strata in the Jewish population are still politically relevant. In particular, the marginal group members—the Mizrahi and Sephardi Jews—report different preferences with respect to ethno-religious nationalism and democracy in Israel.

Ethnicity and Hierarchy in Israel

This study has drawn heavily on two elements of race and ethnic politics research. The first is the concept of race or ethnicity as a bundle of sticks (Sen and Wasow 2016). In this framework, the lived experience within a society as part of an ethnic group is part and parcel of group membership—not separate. Thus, the fact that Mizrahi/Sephardi Jews may be of a lower socioeconomic class or be more religiously engaged than the Ashkenazi Jewish Israelis are is not separated from their ethnic bundle. It is part of it. While these sticks are occasionally plucked from the bundle for analytic purposes, they are not ignored. The argument draws on the hierarchized experience writ large to anticipate differences in political attitudes—such as different propensities toward religious ethno-nationalism—among the ethnic blocs.

Second, the study draws on analyses of within-group distinctions. In any group, some members possess more group-defining features than others. These individuals are the prototypical group members (Ostfeld and Yadon 2022b; Ellemers and Jetten 2013). Other group members share enough features to be part of the group but do not share them all. For instance, although the majority of both major American political parties are white, middle-class Christians, the public would readily view a Black lesbian atheist as a prototypical Democrat and a southern Evangelical millionaire as a prototypical Republican (Ahler and Sood 2018). Gay Republicans and Evangelical Democrats fit the mold a little less. Their groupishness is then occasionally doubted (Campbell, Green, and Layman 2011). These nonprototypical members can be called the marginal group members.

Marginal group members are called upon to demonstrate their membership and loyalty. To access group privileges—or even achieve the identity concordance of being seen by others as they see themselves—they must perform membership sufficiently to be recognized by the in-group. This is particularly true in times of crisis, when marginal group members could be suspected of moving away from group identification to avoid costs or when the group would benefit from enlarged membership numbers. Marginal group members must be more aware of asserting group status than those prototypicals to whom membership is more readily afforded. They are more reactive to perceived threats against the group and its social position. Race-group threat reactivity has been linked to a heightened propensity to adopt conservative positions on both racial and nonracial issues.

By focusing on ethnicity in the Jewish community in Israel, this study parallels work on whiteness in American politics. Diversity within the white population can be overlooked, masking some manifestations of racial politics among white populations: "A lack of attention to skin color dynamics among White people makes Whiteness appear to be relatively uniform, stable, and essentialized compared to what happens within other ethnoracial categories, thus falsely positioning Whites as unaffected by or uninvolved with this dimension of American racial dynamics" (Ostfeld and Yadon 2022b, 80). Within that macro-group, however, "many people who were identified as White—including many Arab Americans, Latinos, and multiracial Americans—were clearly not able to fully experience Whiteness" (Ostfeld and Yadon 2022b, 86; see also d'Urso 2022). Similarly, within the Jewish community in Israel, there are subgroups with different levels of privilege and different policy preferences.

Because of the social construction of Israel as a Western secular state, which led to the privileging of Ashkenazi Jews, Ashkenazi Jewishness is prototypified (Khazzoom 2008). The non-Ashkenazi Jews are then the marginal group members. The largest bloc of these marginal group members is the "Arab Jews," the Mizrahim and Sephardim. The secularization of the Jewish state in this framework is a double whammy for these marginal group members. They are linked by their religion to the dominant group but are othered by being too religious for the developing secular prototype. Subsequent immigrant arrivals further diversified the population. Most immigrants from the former Soviet Union are Ashkenazi, but they are sometimes held apart socially and analytically because of their experiences behind the Iron Curtain and because some immigrants in that wave were the non-Jewish relatives of the Jewish diaspora. Jews from sub-Saharan African communities (e.g., Ethiopia's Beta Israel) arrived as well, but their total population is smaller than the Mizrahi population. These minorities also experience otherization.

The hypersalience of the proximity of non-Jewish residents and the surrounding Arab-majority states means that Israel is regularly operating in a crisis mindset. As such, there are many calls and opportunities for demonstrating loyalty and promoting status benefits for the in-group. Several surveys taken in Israel over the past decade demonstrate these effects.

Summary of the Results

Despite arguments questioning Ashkenormativity in Israel and asserting a declining role for ethnicity, these surveys indicate that biases exist. Sizable minorities report that "a lot of discrimination" against Mizrahim and Ethiopian Jews exists in Israel (Chapter 2). Although identifying themselves with discrimination is rare, the marginal group members (Mizrahim/Sephardim) are more likely to be aware of the biases against non-Ashkenazi Jews. Nonetheless, these citizens are *more* likely to express a sense of macro-group affinity. They are more likely to say that being Jewish is important in their lives, that they feel a sense of belonging in the group, and that they are proud to be Jewish. They are even more likely to say they feel a responsibility for Jews outside of Israel. Thus, the marginal Jewish Israelis are strongly asserting their groupishness, despite the constructed marginality.

The marginal group members show greater affinity to ethno-religious nationalism for Israel (Chapter 3). First, they demonstrate greater connection to their religious in-group by asserting a value for Judaism in the Jewish state. They need, in particular, to distinguish themselves from the Arab population, as (descendants of) largely Arab-state-origin immigrants. Supporting the Jewish character of the state is consistent with this objective. Second, as a lower-socioeconomic-status group, they benefit more from a system that privileges their macro-group identity. Without in-group privilege, they would slide down the hierarchy even further. At least this way they are on a higher rung.

This relative propensity toward ethno-religious nationalism appears in several ways. They are more likely to say that the government in Israel should grant privileges to Jewish citizens, enact religious law, and promote Jewish values. They are more likely to assert that a Jewish state is necessary to secure the survival of the Jewish people—a condition, several respondents were quick to say, that can only be fulfilled by its being a Jewish-majority state. They are also more likely to endorse policies that would protect the Jewish majority in the population. For instance, they are more likely to support restricting Christian migration, and they are less likely to support a generous policy toward refugees. They would be displeased if their children married outside the faith, and they are less accepting of people converted by non-Orthodox rabbis. These policies promote group perpetuation and endorse a conservative interpretation of who is part of the group. Furthermore, they are more likely to oppose Palestinians' presence in Israel. That includes opposing a right of return and supporting the forced removal of Palestinians from the state. Some survey respondents were quite literal in their expression here, even calling for driving them "into the sea." This is not to say that only marginal group members express these preferences. However, the marginal group members are more likely to endorse Jewish majoritarian policies and statements. Thus, not only are marginal group members evincing a stronger group connection, they are more likely to favor privileges for that group, even at the expense of out-group members.

As part of this confluence of propensities, marginal Jewish Israelis are less likely to focus on upholding liberal democracy in Israel (Chapter 4). This propensity manifests in two ways. One, they are less likely to say that liberal democracy—which would provide equal rights to the non-Jewish inhabitants—is preferable to a less liberal regime. For instance, citizens who view Arabs as enemies of the state are willing to take away (non-Jewish) Arabs' social and political rights. This is despite the recurrent assertions from the Israeli government that Israel is a democracy and the arguments that Israel, in the Middle East, represents a superior ally for countries like the United States because of its democratic credentials. The regime overtly wants the international cachet of being a democracy and presents itself as such, although others have challenged that identity. The respondents largely, if unevenly, see Israel as fulfilling the electoral institutional requirements for democracy. They are less convinced of—or committed to—liberal credentials for the current state.[2]

While "democracy" polls well in Israel, the respondents did differ somewhat in what it means to them. The marginal group members placed more weight on the voice of the people, direct democracy, and redistributive economic policies. Thus, they can support a democracy (particularly an illiberal democracy) that they think will equalize things for them, rather than equalizing things for the rest. As Israel actively considers the form the regime should take, how its citizens view democracy and how much they value they potential features are of tremendous import.

Many citizens endorsed liberal democracy, but that support was not unequivocal. Although the marginal group members are more likely to assert that the regime can be both democratic and Jewish nationalist, they are less likely to favor democracy in instances when those ideals are in conflict. Again, most Jewish Israelis favor democracy and even privilege democracy over Jewish law; the marginal group members, however, are less likely to espouse that commitment. Where sociopolitical impulses toward democracy and toward religious nationalism co-occur, this differential is informative and politically salient. As long as Israel perpetuates the exclusion or denigration of Palestinians, including the Palestinian Citizens of Israel, establishing Jewish privileges in the society, then the marginal Jewish Israelis will be more likely to lean, comparatively, toward that perpetuation of privilege by favoring religious bent over democracy. If citizens want to diffuse that religious-nationalist pull, they must reduce the need for these marginal group members to prove they belong—by reducing Ashkenormativity—or reduce the in-group privileges so there is nothing to win by such group-identity affirmation demonstrations. That could mitigate the Mizrahim-Ashkenazim gap. It would not, however, by itself, resolve all tensions between religious nationalism and democracy in a diverse, multinational state.

This Jewish majoritarianism also manifests in diverging views about what Israel's future should look like (Chapter 5). Prototypical and nonprototypical Jewish Israelis favored peace on balance. However, they have different views on attaining it. The marginal group members were more likely to believe that the Israeli government was making a sincere effort to bring about peace; they were less likely to say the same of the Palestinian leadership. This pattern is consistent with the heightened group-protective tendency. They blame the out-group for the failures to reach comity.

They also have different visions for the scope of this Jewish state. Mizrahi/Sephardi Jewish Israelis were less likely to support keeping the state within the Green Line borders—with territorial exchanges—in keeping with a two-state solution. They were also less likely to see peace with an independent Palestine as viable. Overall opinion was nearly evenly divided on this point. Marginal group members were also more willing to endorse Jewish settlements in the Occupied Territories as benefiting Israeli security, although they represent a challenge to achieving the aforementioned territorial exchanges and peaceful two-state solution. This group-affirming pattern is not a movement in the long-term interests of the group. If citizens want a Jewish-majority state (Chapter 3), then demographics suggest a two-state solution is required. Chapter 5 unpacks the contradictions that these reactive preferences represent in conjunction with one another. Respondents had detailed opinions, but they did not bring them together to a clear and shared path forward.

Ashkenormativity beyond Israel

While this text has focused on the sociopolitical implications of normalizing a particular form of Jewishness in Israel, this is not singularly an Israeli phenomenon. Every Jewish community has the potential for multiethnic Judaism. The immigration-based Jewish communities are the most likely cases, as they would have more diverse populations. The vast majority of the world's Jewish population lives in either the United States or Israel, and both of these populations derive from migration from multiple regions. Although Jewish immigrants to the United States in the late nineteenth and early twentieth century were socially coded as non-white, the community was socially whitened over time, becoming framed primarily as a religious group rather than an ethnic community, let alone a diverse ethnic community (Tapper, Kelman, and Saperstein 2023; Kalev and Maor 2015).

Unlike in Israel, however, a sizable majority of American Jews are Ashkenazi identifiers. According to the Pew Research Center (2021), 66 percent of American Jews "think of themselves as Ashkenazi." Only 3 percent identified as Sephardic and 1 percent as Mizrahi; 6 percent identified as mixed.

Unlike in Israel, a larger fraction (17 percent) identified as "just Jewish," and 8 percent were unsure or declined to answer. Intra-Jewish ethnicity seems to be declining in salience faster in the United States than in Israel. That said, the American cultural conception of Jewishness is still grounded in "Jewish customs from Europe" (2021, 38). American ideas of things like Jewish food, Jewish appearance, or Jewish clothing are often rooted in Ashkenazi cultural norms or countries of origin. The Pew report quotes a rabbi from New York describing an Ashkenazi congregation encountering Iranian Jews: "It has forced us to be more mindful of certain assumptions that we have about what it means to be Jewish" (186). Such questions can counteract Ashkenormativity.

The American Jewish population is so proportionally small—approximately 2 percent of the overall population—that it is usually treated as a single bloc in analyses. However, this masks internal heterogeneity that can merit consideration. These patterns of identity themselves are worthy of investigation by scholars of religion and of ethnicity. Researchers could consider American Jews' self-identification as "just Jewish" and the forces that are pushing or pulling them in this direction, compared to those who maintain a particular ethno-religious identity.

Other countries have Jewish populations of great duration that might also be considered. For instance, several Latin American countries have Jewish communities, many dating to the Sephardim's flight from persecution in Iberia; Jewish immigrants also arrived from the Ottoman Empire in the nineteenth century (Brodsky and Leibman 2023). Ashkenazim moved to Latin America to avoid nineteenth- and twentieth-century violence in Europe. Given the nuanced racial attitudes and hierarchies in Latin America, the positionality of these Jewish communities merits consideration.

France presents another potential case. It has the third-largest Jewish population, though it is an order of magnitude smaller than that in the United States or Israel. Recent high-profile incidents of violent antisemitism have spurred some French Jews to relocate to Israel. Although France has had an Ashkenazi community for centuries, it has a Mizrahi-majority Jewish population because of Jewish migration from the former French protectorates and colonies. It also has a large population of Muslim and Christian immigrants from those same territories. Scholars could consider the interplay of ethnicity, immigration generation, xenophobia, and political attitudes in France.

Examinations of intragroup prototypicality and heterogeneity should also be ported over into analyses of religion and politics. Especially in policy domains for which Jewish populations are particular foci of analysis, researchers must be mindful of these variations. Future studies of American Jewish opinions on topics like foreign policy (including but not limited to Israel/

Palestine), religious freedom and secularism politics, immigration, or family and identity issues should be mindful of these differences. Just as scholars should not ground all interpretations of Judaism in Hasidism or secularism, they should not ground them singularly in Ashkenazi Jewishness.

Ethnic and Religious Nationalism

Movements toward cosmopolitanism, internationalism, and regionalism could give the impression that the world is giving up on nationalism, particularly ethnic and religious nationalism. The recursive turn taken by European nation-states in recent years, however, suggests otherwise. Large-scale migration, for instance by Muslim Arabs, into Europe is exposing the extent to which religion and ethnic identity still shape citizens' views of what it means to be part of a nation (Shady 2022; Choi, Poertner, and Sambanis 2022). Some leaders, like Hungary's Victor Orban, make overt appeals to a Christian heritage or an ethnic unity. Even as Israel sought to frame itself as a Western state, the system fomented both religious and ethnic hierarchies and prototypes. Assertion of (non)prototypicality can readily shape political attitudes, such as anti-immigrant sentiment (Kalmar 2022).

Contemporary political discourse and public opinion surveys suggest that nationalism has ultimately not fallen by the wayside. Furthermore, these debates highlight the fact that, even within the dominant social group in a social hierarchy, there can be internal diversities that play their own role in shaping these sentiments. The most committed to maintaining a social hierarchy, for instance, may not be the most privileged individuals. The distribution of a group may also be more nuanced than a macro-group suggests. For instance, in Muslim-majority countries, sectarian differences are sometimes highly salient and inform citizens' positionality for benefits and inclusion (e.g., anti-Shiite bias in a Sunni-majority context); the macro-group Muslim would then be an inaccurate reflection of the social order. Similarly, citizens may equate religious and ethnic group membership, such as Russian Orthodoxy (Karpov, Lisovskaya, and Barry 2012) and Arab Muslims (Ridge 2023b). These groups tend to be more nationalistic. Ethnic and religious nationalism can feed off each other.

Boundaries of group inclusion may be more fluid than overt divisions imply. Citizens may contextually move themselves or be moved by others depending on the situation. For instance, white-passing or straight-passing individuals may or may not (choose to) be read as part of their identity group in a particular instance. Additionally, popular understandings of group membership could deviate from legalistic definitions. The definition of *white* in the United States has shifted over time, and popular conceptions of which ethnic groups are white do not align with U.S. Census classifications (d'Urso

2022; Tapper, Kelman, and Saperstein 2023). Scholars should be alert to the sectarian and ethnic diversity that might exist within social cleavages. They may not all play an equal role in their country's ethnic or religious-nationalist frames.

Race and Ethnic Politics

Discrete and uniform racial groups make incorporating race into political analysis simple. The simplicity of these variables obscures the complexity of the formation and implementation of these identities: "Adding race as a statistical control in quantitative models is now a common practice that signals disciplinary concern with the importance of race and ethnicity; but paradoxically, the ease of statistical controls offers the dangerous potential for reifying race as a category for social analysis without a concordant focus on what 'race' and 'ethnicity' mean" (Hitlin, Brown, and Elder 2007, 588).

This study has extended prior work that has looked at marginal group members. Excellent work is probing how forces like skin color shape individuals' sense of group inclusion and mutual recognition (Ostfeld and Yadon 2022b). Scholars of race and politics should expand on this kind of group nuance to better delineate the role that race and ethnicity play in politics. Macro-group distinctions have been found to matter in domains like health and criminalization as well as in vote choice and issue preference. Within these blocs, though, group hierarchies are still pertinent.

The hierarchies merit recognition on their own terms. They are the internal or near boundaries that individuals encounter. They are not merely aesthetic or epiphenomenal. They are implicated in access to power. Focusing only on the power differentials *between* groups, then misses the variations in power and privilege *within* groups. These distances from the loci of power inform citizens' lived experiences and their political preferences and practices. These disparities warrant further study. That includes considering behavior around the world. How do the ethnic hierarchies in countries like Türkiye, Singapore, and Russia map onto national prototypes? How do marginality and prototypicality affect the politics of other states?

As global diversity and the postmigration generations increase, the native-immigrant binary will cease to be the only or most important lens for many contexts' race politics. Increasing rates of intermarriage and ethnic mixing will expand the number of marginal group members and the forms of group liminality. Will memberships be decided by blood, by behavior, by location, by religion, by political affiliation, or by appearance? Will the ethnic bundle of sticks change with these transmutations, or will these populations form new groups with bundles of their own?

There are many domains yet to be explored in which the distinction between marginal and prototypical group members could be salient. For instance, marginal group members are more likely to be defensive of their group and, in contexts of higher social status, of its position in the social hierarchy. Are marginal group members more likely to show high social dominance orientation (SDO) generally or just with respect to their group? Do they show lower SDO when they are in lower-status groups? They are also more likely to be threat responsive. This has been demonstrated with racial threat; does it extend to other kinds of marginality/prototypicality? Does the reactiveness of racial marginal group members extend to less racialized threats? For instance, does a nonracial threat of violence trigger marginal white/Latino/Black Americans more than the respective prototypical Americans?

Do marginal group members behave differently across contexts? For instance, do marginal white people exhibit parallel preference patterns in England or Canada to those they exhibit in the United States? Marginality relates both to individuals' self-conception and to others' conceptions of these individuals. How do these factors come together to establish individuals' view of their own marginality, and which is the more potent force? Is this an internal sense of precarity or a case of perpetual reminding by the prototypicals? Are these forces different for different kinds of group membership (e.g., religion, race, sexuality)? Public opinion and experimental work could probe these domains and more.

Evolving standards of group inclusion and mutual (non)recognition are to be expected. The sense of inclusion, exclusion, and hierarchy will in turn influence citizens' self-conception, national conception, and policy preferences. Incorporating these patterns into analyses will be far more challenging than a white/not-white binary or nominal race-group variable. Importantly, such analyses will only be possible with sufficient group and cultural knowledge to recognize and measure the boundaries of group inclusion and the social hierarchies that are created.

Israeli Ethnic Politics

The Israeli Bureau of Statistics treats Israel-born children of Israel-born men as Israeli, nonethnic. They are Sabra. This is an optimistic classification system. It is also true that when given the option to use a grouping identity—Israeli or Jewish—instead of an ethnic one, most respondents do. This suggests that many Jewish Israelis at least want to identify that way. However, it does not truly erase the different lived experiences or their potential sociopolitical ramifications. Obtaining an outcome in which citizens not only see themselves as Sabra but are seen by others that way and see others that way in turn could be fruitful for reducing biases and social tensions. How that can be achieved—and it was not achieved by heavy-handed assimilationist programs—is a matter for future consideration.

In the meantime, the decline of ethnicity's role in Israeli politics has been exaggerated. At least in these domains of nationalism, democracy, and intergroup attitudes, intra-Jewish ethnicity continues to be a significant predictor of public opinion. This book has focused on policy issues overtly linked to marginality and group affirmation. However, other areas of Israeli politics should be examined for ethnic group and marginality effects. Some of the ideas already noted readily apply to the Israeli case. Additional domains are more specific to Israel.

For instance, ethnicity remains a salient factor in Israelis' vote choice, and it does so in defiance of voters' economic interest. As Mizrahim are more likely to be economically precarious and of lower socioeconomic status, one might assume that they would support leftist parties, like Labor. However, in practice they are more likely to vote for right-wing parties, like Likud, or ethnic parties, like Shas. This is demonstrable in the iPanel and European Social Survey datasets.

This pattern has historical antecedents. In the early period, Labor was largely Ashkenazi, giving the impression that it was an Ashkenazi party. As Lavie (2018, 28) puts it, to this day, "the main reason the Mizraḥim support the Right is the foundational role of the Zionist Left political parties that established and maintained the intra-Jewish racial formations of Zionism." These constituents also, though, support the hawkish and anti-Palestinian policies that Likud adopted and maintains (Yuchtman-Yaar, Alkalay, and Aival 2018). One of Lavie's interlocutors (62) stated, "Yes they hate us because we vote Likud. Of course we vote for the Right. They didn't do these crimes to us. It was the Labor Party and the rest of 'em Left." Another shot back, "Likud screwed with us too. . . . But we must support them. They're not wishy-washy with peace mumbo-jumbo." In fact, many of the wars have taken place under Left administrations, while the Right administrations have bubbling tensions, despite the parties' stated preferences. The 2023–2024 Gaza War was under Likud. None of that means that Likud has empowered a Mizrahi leadership; all of the Israeli prime ministers have been Ashkenazi, including the Likud ones. Between feeling alienated from the left by ethnicity and needing to affirm Jewish nationalism against the idea that they are "lesser" or "other," the Mizrahim/Sephardim are nonetheless pushed to the right. This pattern can create a partisan stick for these ethnic bundles.

Their (forebears') connection to the Arab states leaves unequal association with Arab identity. The Mizrahim are sometimes characterized as "Arab Jews." Propensity to hold this dual identity itself merits investigation.[3] This book is not meant to argue that these Mizrahim should adopt an Arab identity as a response to Ashkenormativity or merely on the basis of familial history. A crosscutting identity is unlikely to solve these circumstances by itself, although identity complexity has been associated with increased out-group tolerance (Roccas and Brewer 2002; Brewer and Pierce 2005). In some cases, those family histories were not positive experiences—Jewish minorities were subject to discrimination in many countries—which could discourage alignment with those states. Additionally, the fusion of Muslim and Arab identity has pushed some religious minorities out of the pan-Arab political terrain, even in domains where religious minorities thought it could be a way to reduce discrimination. Performative adoption of an Arab identity could ultimately undercut discussions of the non-Jewish Arabs' circumstances in Israel. As Ostfeld and Yadon (2022b, 259) note about Americans who misreport or misperceive their own ethnicity or color, "it is valuable to recognize that identifying with darker skin color or the associated ethoracial [sic] categories—particularly when it is done by people with lighter skin—can detract from productive conversations around color-based privilege and discrimination." The so-called Arab Jews who do possess this identity risk being cross-pressured. The proximity to Palestinian Arabs is, for some, leading to more emphasis on the Jewish identity rather than openness to Arab proximity. Could the crosscutting identity encourage rapprochement if there were less sociopolitical benefit to being on the "right" side of the divide? Whether a crosscutting identity could be converted to openness and under what conditions it would operate are worth consideration.

American race research has shown that redistributive attitudes are informed by citizens' affiliations and their expectations about which groups will benefit from policies. Does this pattern translate to the Israeli context? Is this effect conditional on that intergroup hierarchy as well? For instance, are marginal group members more likely to favor redistributive programs? Would they only favor them if the benefit is restricted (in their minds or in practice) to coreligionists, thus preserving the inter-religious-group hierarchy?

Future research can also address methods for reducing these disparities. Scholars have argued that the ethnic element is declining in Israeli politics in favor of religious bloc politics (Yuchtman-Yaar, Alkalay, and Aival 2018). This reflects both the philosophical desire to see the assimilation process as successful and the empirical effect of removing important sticks (e.g., religiosity and class) from the ethnic bundles. Evidently, differences between the groups persist; in some domains, the differences persist even when religiosity and political-party sticks are removed from the ethnic bundles. Ameliorating the differences in lived experiences could reduce some of the between-group political differences, although it may not totally remove them. Where the differences in political beliefs are not a manifestation of the within-group differences but are rather aimed at maintaining between-group differences

(Ostfeld and Yadon 2022b), the ethnic voting patterns may be harder to shift. Reducing social biases on that scale, however, is not an easy task.

These kinds of questions can be examined using observational data from the several surveys conducted regularly in Israel or from targeted surveys and experiments. In the meantime, scholars of Israeli politics should not omit the role that intragroup diversity plays in shaping citizens' lived experiences or the political manifestations of this diversity. Demarginalization may mitigate these disparities. The formation of the prototypical, however, was a substantial and wide-ranging endeavor, and prior attempts to "melt" the Mizrahim/ Sephardim into the "neutral" position were unsuccessful and have even exacerbated some citizens' sense of alienation. De-ethnicizing Israeli politics then is not just a matter of time, and equity is unlikely to arise from ignoring these intra-ethnic disparities.

APPENDIX A

Sample Characteristics

TABLE A.1 IPANEL SAMPLE CHARACTERISTICS	
Characteristic	Percentage (%)
Ethnicity	
Ashkenazi	40.4
Mizrahi	29.0
Sephardi	13.1
Mixed	13.5
Other	4.0
Religious Group	
Haredi	4.3
Dati	14.8
Masorti	29.7
Hiloni	51.2
Age	
18–22	10.2
23–29	16.8
30–39	21.7
40–49	18.8
50+	32.5
College Education	
Yes	51.2
No	48.8
Income (In)sufficiency	
Sufficient Income	70.8
Insufficient Income	29.1
Area of Residence	
Jerusalem Area	11.9
Central Area	32.5
North Area	26.3
South Area	20.3
Sharon Area	9.0

TABLE A.2 EUROPEAN SOCIAL SURVEY 8 SAMPLE CHARACTERISTICS	
Characteristic	Percentage (%)
Ethnicity	
Ashkenazi	34.8
Mizrahi/Sephardi	39.4
Mixed	11.0
Other	3.7
Do not identify ethnically	9.1
NA/DK	2.1
Identify as a Minority	
Yes	3.4
No	95.6
NA/DK	1.0
Foreign Born	
Yes	35.0
No	65.0
NA/DK	0.05
Decade of Birth	
Before 1930	1.3
1930–1939	6.8
1940–1949	15.5
1950–1959	15.5
1960–1969	13.1
1970–1979	13.9
1980–1989	15.2
1990–1999	15.8
2000 or later	1.5
NA	1.2
College Education	
Yes	32.9
No	66.6
NA	0.5
(Un)employment	
Paid Employment	55.1
No Paid Employment	44.9
Hebrew Spoken at Home	
Hebrew	86.6
Other	13.4

TABLE A.3 EUROPEAN SOCIAL SURVEY 10 SAMPLE CHARACTERISTICS	
Characteristic	Percentage (%)
Ethnicity	
Ashkenazi	29.6
Mizrahi/Sephardi	34.0
Mixed	4.9
Other	4.2
Israeli	24.6
NA/DK	2.7
Foreign Born	
Yes	20.4
No	77.6
NA/DK	1.9
Decade of Birth	
1930–1939	1.5
1940–1949	6.4
1950–1959	10.9
1960–1969	12.1
1970–1979	14.3
1980–1989	19.1
1990–1999	16.9
2000 or later	11.3
NA	7.5
College Education	
Yes	41.6
No	47.9
NA	10.4
(Un)employment	
Paid Employment	59.6
No Paid Employment	40.4
Hebrew Spoken at Home	
Hebrew	84.0
Other	13.4
NA	2.5

TABLE A.4 PEW RESEARCH CENTER SAMPLE CHARACTERISTICS

Characteristic	Percentage (%)
Ethnicity	
Ashkenazi	47.1
Sephardi	17.4
Mizrahi	27.9
Mixed	7.3
Other	0.05
NA/DK	0.3
Religious Group	
Haredi	18.6
Dati	15.4
Masorti	24.3
Hiloni	41.7
NA/DK	0.05
Foreign Born	
Yes	26.7
No	72.9
NA/DK	0.3
Age	
18–21	7.6
22–29	17.9
30–39	21.8
40–49	17.8
50–59	14.0
60–69	13.4
70–79	6.2
80+	1.1
College Education	
Yes	28.2
No	71.8
(Un)employment	
Unemployed	3.6
Not Unemployed	96.4
Language Spoken at Home	
Hebrew	83.9
Arabic	0.2
Russian	9.4
Other	6.5

APPENDIX B

Question Wording and Variable Coding

TABLE B.1 IPANEL QUESTION WORDING AND VARIABLE CODING		
Variable	Question	Coding
Age	How old are you? 1) 18–22 2) 23–29 3) 30–39 4) 40–49 5) 50+	1 Forty or older 0 Less than 40
College	What is the highest level of education you have completed? 1) Elementary school 2) Secondary school 3) Vocational school 4) University degree (BA, BS) 5) Higher university degree (MA, Ph.D., MD, MBA) 6) None of these	1 BA/BA/MA/Ph.D./MD/MBA 0 All else
Male	Do you identify as male, female, or something else?	1 Male 0 Female
Income Insufficiency	Which statement best describes your usual household income? 1) Our household income covers our expenses. 2) Our household income does not cover our expenses.	1 Insufficient Income 0 Sufficient Income
Group	How would you describe yourself?	Haredi Dati Masorti Hiloni

(continued)

TABLE B.1 IPANEL QUESTION WORDING AND VARIABLE CODING
(*continued*)

Variable	Question	Coding
Secular	Apart from when you are at religious services, how often, if at all, do you pray? 1) Every day 2) More than once a week 3) Once a week 4) At least once a month 5) Only on special holy days 6) Less often 7) Never	1 Only on special holy days/less often/never 0 All else
Minority	Do you belong to a minority ethnic group in Israel?	1 Yes 0 No
Ethnicity	How would you describe your ancestry? 1) Ashkenazi 2) Eastern/Mizrahi 3) Sephardi 4) Mixed ethnicity 5) Other (Specify: _____)	1 Ashkenazi 2 Sephardi 3 Mizrahi 4 Mixed ethnicity 5 Other OR 1 Ashkenazi 23 Sephardi/Mizrahi 4 Mixed ethnicity 5 Other
NOT Former USSR	Did you or your family come from the USSR after 1989?	0 Yes 1 No
Political Interest	How interested would you say you are in politics?	1 Very interested/quite interested 0 Hardly interested/not at all interested
European Immigration	To what extent do you think Israel should allow Christians from Europe to come and live here?	1 Allow few/allow none 0 Allow many to come and live here/allow some
African Immigration	To what extent do you think Israel should allow Ethiopian Jews to come and live here?	1 Allow few/allow none 0 Allow many to come and live here/allow some
Party	Is there a political party you feel closer to than to other parties?	Left - HaAvoda - Meretz - Yesh Atid - Kahol-Lavan (Blue & White) Right - Likud - Yisraeli Beitenu - Shas - Yehadut HaTora - Yamina - Tikva Hadasa - Hatzionut Hadatit - HaMiflaga HaCalcalit Other None/DK/Refused

TABLE B.2 EUROPEAN SOCIAL SURVEY 8 QUESTION WORDING AND VARIABLE CODING		
Variable	Question Label and Wording	Coding
Religion	rlgdnm Do you consider yourself as belonging to any particular religion or denomination? If yes, which one?	Subset to Jewish
Ethnicity	IL11_J If you had to define yourself in terms of ethnic origin, which options would you choose?	1 Mizrahi, Sephardi, or Eastern 2 Ashkenazi 3 Mixed 5 Other (6 Do not define myself according to ethnic origin)
Identify as a Minority	blgetmg Do you belong to a minority ethnic group in Israel	1 Yes 0 No
Hebrew	lnghom1 What language or languages do you speak most often at home?	1 Speaks Hebrew at home 0 All else
Life Satisfaction	stflife All things considered, how satisfied are you with your life as a whole nowadays? Please answer using this card, where 0 means extremely dissatisfied and 10 means extremely satisfied.	10 Extremely Satisfied 9 8 7 6 5 4 3 2 1 0 Extremely Dissatisfied
Economic Satisfaction	stfeco On the whole, how satisfied are you with the present state of the economy in Israel?	10 Extremely Satisfied 9 8 7 6 5 4 3 2 1 0 Extremely Dissatisfied
Religiosity	rlgdgr Regardless of whether you belong to a particular religion, how religious would you say you are?	10 Very religious 9 8 7 6 5 4 3 2 1 0 Not at all religious

(continued)

TABLE B.2 EUROPEAN SOCIAL SURVEY 8 QUESTION WORDING AND VARIABLE CODING (*continued*)

Variable	Question Label and Wording	Coding
Foreign Born/ Immigrant	brncntr Were you born in Israel?	1 Born in Israel 0 Born abroad
College Educated	eisced Highest level of education	1 BA/MA/Ph.D. 0 All else
Employed	pdwrk Using this card, which of these descriptions applies to what you have been doing for the last 7 days? In paid work (or away temporarily) (employee, self-employed, working for your family business)	1 Employed 0 All else
Female	gndr CODE SEX, respondent	0 Male 1 Female
Age	yrbrn In what year were you born	Year
Left/Right/ Other	clsprty, prtcldil Is there a particular political party you feel closer to than all the other parties? Which one?	Left - Kadima - Avoda - Meretz - Yesh Atid - Chadash - HaTnua - Balad - Zionist Union Right - Likud - Israeli Beitenu - Shas - Yehadut HaTora - HaBait HaYehudi - Kulanu - Yachad Other None/DK/Refused
Judge Refugee Petitions Generously	gvrfgap Some people come to this country and apply for refugee status on the grounds that they fear persecution in their own country. Using this card, please say how much you agree or disagree with the following statements. Firstly . . . the government should be generous in judging people's applications for refugee status.	1 Agree strongly 2 Agree 3 Neither agree nor disagree 4 Disagree 5 Disagree strongly

(*continued*)

Variable	Question Label and Wording	Coding
TABLE B.2 EUROPEAN SOCIAL SURVEY 8 QUESTION WORDING AND VARIABLE CODING (*continued*)		
Refugees Lie	rfgfrpc Some people come to this country and apply for refugee status on the grounds that they fear persecution in their own country. Using this card, please say how much you agree or disagree with the following statements. Firstly . . . most applicants for refugee status aren't in real fear of persecution in their own countries.	1 Agree strongly 2 Agree 3 Neither agree nor disagree 4 Disagree 5 Disagree strongly
Experience Discrimination	dscrgrp Would you describe yourself as being a member of a group that is discriminated against in this country?	1 Yes 0 No
Racial Discrimination	dscrrce On what grounds is your group discriminated against? Colour or race.	1 Marked 0 Not marked
Ethnic Discrimination	dscretn On what grounds is your group discriminated against? Ethnic group.	1 Marked 0 Not marked

TABLE B.3 EUROPEAN SOCIAL SURVEY 10 QUESTION WORDING AND VARIABLE CODING

Variable	Question Label and Wording	Coding
Religion	rlgdnm/rlgdnme Do you consider yourself as belonging to any particular religion or denomination? Which religion do/did you belong to? anctry1 How would you describe your ancestry?	Subset to Jewish by declared religious denomination or reported ancestry (Jewish, Ashkenazi, Sephardi, or Mizrahi)
Ethnicity	mocntr Was your mother born in [country]? In which country was your mother born? fbrncntc Was your father born in [country]? In which country was your father born? anctry1 How would you describe your ancestry? anctry2 How would you describe your ancestry?	Assign by parents' country of birth. Where both parents were born in Israel, use the reported ancestry. Mizrahi/Sephardi Ashkenazi Mixed Other Israeli
Hebrew	lnghom1 What language or languages do you speak most often at home?	1 Speaks Hebrew at home 0 All else
Life Satisfaction	stflife All things considered, how satisfied are you with your life as a whole nowadays? Please answer using this card, where 0 means extremely dissatisfied and 10 means extremely satisfied	10 Extremely Satisfied 9 8 7 6 5 4 3 2 1 0 Extremely Dissatisfied
Economic Satisfaction	stfeco On the whole, how satisfied are you with the present state of the economy in Israel?	10 Extremely Satisfied 9 8 7 6 5 4 3 2 1 0 Extremely Dissatisfied

(continued)

TABLE B.3 EUROPEAN SOCIAL SURVEY 10 QUESTION WORDING AND VARIABLE CODING (*continued*)

Variable	Question Label and Wording	Coding
Religiosity	rlgdgr Regardless of whether you belong to a particular religion, how religious would you say you are?	10 Very religious 9 8 7 6 5 4 3 2 1 0 Not at all religious
Foreign Born/ Immigrant	brncntr Were you born in Israel?	1 Born in Israel 0 Born abroad
College Educated	eisced What is the highest level of education you have successfully completed?	1 BA/MA/Ph.D. 0 All else
Employed	pdwrk Using this card, which of these descriptions applies to what you have been doing for the last 7 days? In paid work (or away temporarily) (employee, self-employed, working for your family business)	1 Employed 0 All else
Female	gndr CODE SEX, respondent	0 Male 1 Female
Age	yrbrn In what year were you born?	Year

Left/Right/Other	clsprty, prtcldil
	Is there a particular political party you feel closer to than all the other parties? Which one?
		Left
		  - Chachol-Lavan
		  - Avoda
		  - Meretz
		  - Yesh Atid
		  - Tikva Hadasha
		  - HaReshima HaMeshutefet
		Right
		  - Likud
		  - Israeli Beitenu
		  - Shas
		  - Yehadut HaTora
		  - HaBait HaYehudi
		  - HaZionut HaDatit
		  - Yamina
		Other
		None/DK/Refused

(*continued*)

TABLE B.3 EUROPEAN SOCIAL SURVEY 10 QUESTION WORDING AND VARIABLE CODING (*continued*)

Variable	Question Label and Wording	Coding
Say in Government	psppsgva How much would you say the political system in Israel allows people like you to have a say in what the government does?	1 Not at all 2 Very little 3 Some 4 A lot 5 A great deal
Influence in Government	psppipla And how much would you say that the political system in Israel allows people like you to have an influence on politics?	1 Not at all 2 Very little 3 Some 4 A lot 5 A great deal
Experience Discrimination	dscrgrp Would you describe yourself as being a member of a group that is discriminated against in this country?	1 Yes 0 No
Racial Discrimination	dscrrce On what grounds is your group discriminated against? Colour or race.	1 Marked 0 Not marked
Ethnic Discrimination	dscretn On what grounds is your group discriminated against? Ethnic group.	1 Marked 0 Not marked
National Attachment	atchctr How emotionally attached do you feel to Israel?	10 Very emotionally attached 9 8 7 6 5 4 3 2 1 0 Not at all emotionally attached
Importance of Democracy	Implvdm How important is it for you to live in a country that is governed democratically? Choose your answer from this card, where 0 is not at all important and 10 is extremely important.	10 Very important 9 8 7 6 5 4 3 2 1 0 Not at all important

(*continued*)

TABLE B.3 EUROPEAN SOCIAL SURVEY 10 QUESTION WORDING AND VARIABLE CODING (*continued*)		
Variable	Question Label and Wording	Coding
Strong Leader Acceptance	accalaw How acceptable would it be for Israel to have a strong leader who is above the law?	10 Completely acceptable 9 8 7 6 5 4 3 2 1 0 Not at all acceptable
Meaning of Democracy	Using this card, please tell me how important you think it is for democracy in general . . . fairelc that national elections are free and fair. medcrgv that the media are free to criticize the government. rghmgpr that the rights of minority groups are protected. votedir that citizens have the final say on the most important political issues by voting on them directly in referendums. cttresa that the courts treat everyone the same. gvctzpv that the government protects all citizens against poverty. grdfinc that the government takes measures to reduce differences in income levels. viepol that the views of ordinary people prevail over the views of the political elite. wpestop that the will of the people cannot be stopped.	10 Extremely important for democracy in general 9 8 7 6 5 4 3 2 1 0 Not at all important for democracy in general

TABLE B.4 PEW RESEARCH CENTER QUESTION WORDING AND VARIABLE CODING

Variable	Question Label and Wording	Coding
Religion	Q526 What is your nationhood (Le'om)? Jewish, Arab, or other?	Subset to Jewish
Ethnicity	QA89 What is your ethnicity?	1 Ashkenazi 2 Sephardi 3 Mizrahi 4 Mixed ethnicity OR 1 Ashkenazi 23 Sephardi/Mizrahi 4 Mixed ethnicity
USSR	QFSU For respondents who took the survey in Hebrew or Russian, this variable identifies respondents born in countries that were part of the former Soviet Union.	1 Former Soviet Union 0 All else
Hebrew	QLANG What language do you most commonly speak at home?	1 Speaks Hebrew at home 0 All else
Personal Satisfaction	Q501 All in all, are you satisfied or dissatisfied with the way things are going in Israel today?	1 Satisfied 0 Dissatisfied
Personal Economic Circumstances	Q503 Thinking about your personal economic situation, how would you describe it—is it very good, somewhat good, somewhat bad, or very bad?	1 Very good/Somewhat good 0 Very bad/Somewhat bad
Religious Group	QA30 How would you define yourself religiously? Haredi, Dati, Masorti, Hiloni, or something else?	1 Haredi 2 Dati 3 Masorti 4 Hiloni
Religion Is Important	QIMPORTcmb How important is religion in your life—very important, somewhat important, not too important, or not at all important?	1 Very important/Somewhat important 0 Not too important/Not at all important
Foreign Born	Q113CMB In what country were you born?	1 Born abroad 0 Born in Israel
College Educated	QEDU1 What is the highest level of education that you have completed?	1 BA/MA/Ph.D. 0 All else
Unemployed	QEMPLOY Which of the following employment situations best describes your current status?	1 Unemployed and looking for a job 0 All else
Male	QGEN Gender	1 Male 0 Female

(continued)

TABLE B.4 PEW RESEARCH CENTER QUESTION WORDING AND VARIABLE CODING (*continued*)		
Variable	Question Label and Wording	Coding
Age	QAGE How old were you at your last birthday?	Age in years
Left/Right/Other	QPARTY Which political party, if any, do you feel closest to?	Left - Kadima - Avoda - Meretz - Yesh Atid - Chadash - HaTnua - Balad Right - Likud - Israeli Beitenu - Shas - Yehadut HaTora - HaBait HaYehudi Other None/DK/Refused
Discrimination against Mizrahim	Q506 Just your impression, in Israel today, is there a lot of discrimination against [INSERT] or not? Mizrahim.	1 Yes, there is a lot of discrimination 2 No, don't think so
Discrimination against Ethiopians	Q506 Just your impression, in Israel today, is there a lot of discrimination against [INSERT] or not? Ethiopian Jews.	1 Yes, there is a lot of discrimination 2 No, don't think so
Being Jewish Is Important to Identity	Q63cmb How important is being Jewish in your life—very important, somewhat important, not too important, or not at all important?	1 Very important/Somewhat important 0 Not too important/Not at all important
Proud to Be Jewish	Q13CMB As I read a few statements, please tell me if you agree or disagree with each one. I am proud to be Jewish.	1 Agree 0 Disagree
Sense of Belonging	Q13CMB As I read a few statements, please tell me if you agree or disagree with each one. I have a strong sense of belonging to the Jewish people.	1 Agree 0 Disagree
Global Responsibility	Q13CMB As I read a few statements, please tell me if you agree or disagree with each one. I have a special responsibility to take care of Jews in need around the world.	1 Agree 0 Disagree
Jewish First	QA17 Would you describe yourself as Jewish first or as Israeli first?	−1 Israeli 1 Jewish 0 Unsure

(*continued*)

TABLE B.4 PEW RESEARCH CENTER QUESTION WORDING AND VARIABLE CODING (*continued*)

Variable	Question Label and Wording	Coding
Enact Halakha	Q44cmb Do you favor or oppose making halakha the state law for Jews in Israel?	1 Favor 0 Oppose
Non-Orthodox Conversion	QA10e In your opinion, can a person be Jewish if they [INSERT] or not? Were converted to Judaism by a non-Orthodox Rabbi.	1 Yes, can be Jewish 0 No, cannot be Jewish
Palestinian Return	Q10Fcmb In your opinion, can a person be Jewish if they [INSERT] or not? Support the Palestinian's [*sic*] right of return.	1 Yes, can be Jewish 0 No, cannot be Jewish
Israel Is Necessary	QA18 Do you think a Jewish state is necessary for the long-term survival of the Jewish people, or not?	1 Yes 0 No
Stay in Israel	QA22 Which comes closer to your view, even if neither is exactly right?	0 Jews in Israel should feel free to pursue the good life anywhere in the world, even if it means leaving Israel 1 Jews in Israel should remain in Israel, even if it means giving up the good life elsewhere
Jewish Privileges	QA26 Please tell me if you strongly agree, agree, disagree or strongly disagree with the following statements. Jews deserve preferential treatment in Israel.	1 Strongly agree/Agree 0 Strongly disagree/Disagree
Expel Palestinians	QA26 Please tell me if you strongly agree, agree, disagree or strongly disagree with the following statements. Arabs should be expelled or transferred from Israel	1 Strongly agree/Agree 0 Strongly disagree/Disagree
Oppose Christian Marriage	Q36cmb How comfortable would you be if a child of yours someday married a Christian?	1 Not too comfortable/Not at all comfortable 0 Very comfortable/somewhat comfortable
Oppose Muslim Marriage	Q38cmb How comfortable would you be if a child of yours someday married a Muslim?	1 Not too comfortable/Not at all comfortable 0 Very comfortable/somewhat comfortable

(*continued*)

TABLE B.4 PEW RESEARCH CENTER QUESTION WORDING AND VARIABLE CODING (*continued*)

Variable	Question Label and Wording	Coding
Jewish Values	QA41 People have different views on the role of religion in government. Which comes closer to your view?	1 Government policies should promote religious values and beliefs in our country 0 Religion should be kept separate from government policies
Jewish State and Democracy	Q509 In your opinion, can Israel be both a Jewish state and a democratic state, or not?	1 Yes 0 No
Privilege Halakha	Q510 And if there is a contradiction between halakhah and democratic principles, should the state of Israel give preference to democratic principles or halakhah?	1 Democracy should be given preference –1 halakhah [*sic*] should be given preference 0 Depends on the situation/Both/Neither
Two-State Solution Possible	Q523 Do you think a way can be found for Israel and an independent Palestinian state to coexist peacefully with each other, or not?	1 Yes 0 No
Settlements and Security	Q522 In your opinion, does the continued building of settlements help the security of Israel, hurt the security of Israel, or does it not make a difference?	1 Help the security of Israel –1 Hurt the security of Israel 0 It does not make a difference
Israeli Government Is Trying	Q508 Do you think the current Israeli government is making a sincere effort to bring about a peace settlement with the Palestinians, or don't you think so?	1 Yes, making a sincere effort 0 No, don't think so
Palestinian Leaders Are Trying	Q511 Do you think the current Palestinian leadership is making a sincere effort to bring about a peace settlement with Israel, or don't you think so?	1 Yes, making a sincere effort 0 No, don't think so

Appendix C

Tables with Covariates

Appendix C reports the models with the covariates. The table numeration matches the abbreviated tables in the chapters.

TABLE C.2.2 EXPERIENCES OF DISCRIMINATION (EUROPEAN SOCIAL SURVEY 8)

	Any Discrimination		Racial Discrimination		Ethnic Discrimination	
(Intercept)	−1.79***	−51.87*	−4.92***	−76.82	−4.28***	−42.92
	(0.24)	(21.19)	(1.00)	(39.38)	(0.73)	(45.32)
Mizrahi/Sephardi	−0.46	−0.72	1.51	1.24	−0.27	0.11
	(0.34)	(0.38)	(1.07)	(0.91)	(0.99)	(0.91)
Mixed	−0.16	−0.44	0.60	0.37	0.16	0.40
	(0.46)	(0.49)	(1.51)	(1.28)	(1.26)	(1.10)
Other	0.08	−0.07	3.03*	2.47*	1.04	1.11
	(0.65)	(0.69)	(1.19)	(1.05)	(1.36)	(1.26)
Year of Birth		0.03*		0.04		0.02
		(0.01)		(0.02)		(0.02)
Female		0.17		−0.51		−0.08
		(0.33)		(0.60)		(0.73)
College Education		0.49		0.08		1.13
		(0.39)		(0.85)		(0.82)
Life Satisfaction		−0.06		0.01		−0.16
		(0.09)		(0.17)		(0.19)
Economic Satisfaction		−0.07		0.04		0.00
		(0.07)		(0.13)		(0.17)
Paid Employment		0.43		0.61		0.71
		(0.35)		(0.63)		(0.81)
Religiosity		0.10*		0.03		0.04
		(0.05)		(0.09)		(0.11)
Foreign Born		−0.32		0.72		1.23
		(0.44)		(0.71)		(0.76)
Identify as a Minority		1.38*		1.48		1.94*
		(0.60)		(0.92)		(0.92)
AIC	102.98	117.01	40.34	59.83	11.46	30.25
N	1,722	1,623	1,726	1,627	1,726	1,627

Source: European Social Survey 8 (2016–2017), models 1–2: binary logistic regression, models 3–6: rare events logistic regression model.
*$p<0.05$; **$p<0.01$; ***$p<0.001$

TABLE C.2.3 EXPERIENCES OF DISCRIMINATION (EUROPEAN SOCIAL SURVEY 10)

	Any Discrimination		Racial Discrimination		Ethnic Discrimination	
(Intercept)	−0.82***	−22.74	−4.47***	−38.02	−4.03***	−70.37
	(0.22)	(15.70)	(0.98)	(33.74)	(0.79)	(39.76)
Israeli	−0.21	−0.60	0.02	−0.55	0.92	0.73
	(0.33)	(0.38)	(1.40)	(1.27)	(0.95)	(0.91)
Mixed	−2.29*	−3.35	0.72	0.62	0.27	0.11
	(1.10)	(1.77)	(1.76)	(1.59)	(1.66)	(1.54)
Mizrahi/Sephardi	0.20	0.16	1.92	1.62	1.18	1.45
	(0.29)	(0.32)	(1.03)	(0.91)	(0.87)	(0.82)
Other	−1.67	−2.13	1.26	1.03	0.56	0.57
	(0.98)	(1.24)	(1.64)	(1.52)	(1.68)	(1.62)
Year of Birth		0.01		0.02		0.03
		(0.01)		(0.02)		(0.02)
Female		−0.46		−0.39		−0.90
		(0.28)		(0.56)		(0.58)
College Education		0.68*		0.92		1.19
		(0.34)		(0.67)		(0.61)
Life Satisfaction		−0.04		−0.22*		0.25
		(0.06)		(0.11)		(0.15)
Economic Satisfaction		−0.07		−0.04		−0.08
		(0.05)		(0.11)		(0.10)
Paid Employment		−0.31		−0.00		1.01
		(0.29)		(0.60)		(0.71)
Religiosity		0.16***		0.14		0.01
		(0.04)		(0.08)		(0.08)
Foreign Born		−0.76		−1.10		0.74
		(0.40)		(1.00)		(0.71)
AIC	314.64	298.07	72.11	76.17	90.71	88.73
N	628	550	633	551	633	551

Source: European Social Survey 10 (2022), models 1–2: binary logistic regression, models 3–6: rare events logistic regression model.
*p<0.05; **p<0.01; ***p<0.001

TABLE C.2.4 DISCRIMINATION AGAINST ETHNIC GROUPS

	Discrimination against Ethiopian Jews		Discrimination against Mizrahi Jews	
(Intercept)	−0.60***	0.20	−2.20***	−1.18***
	(0.05)	(0.14)	(0.07)	(0.17)
Mixed	0.35**	0.07	0.65***	0.30
	(0.13)	(0.14)	(0.17)	(0.18)
Mizrahi/Sephardi	0.16*	−0.01	1.52***	1.20***
	(0.07)	(0.08)	(0.09)	(0.10)
Other	12.15	12.09	−9.35	−9.80
	(198.96)	(198.96)	(198.96)	(198.96)
From the Former USSR		−0.92***		−1.15***
		(0.14)		(0.22)
Dati		−0.22		−0.10
		(0.13)		(0.15)
Haredi		−0.80***		−0.07
		(0.15)		(0.17)
Masorti		−0.12		−0.14
		(0.10)		(0.12)
Male		−0.05		0.00
		(0.07)		(0.08)
Age in Years		−0.01***		−0.01***
		(0.00)		(0.00)
College Education		0.24**		−0.05
		(0.08)		(0.10)
Religion Is Important		0.14		0.29*
		(0.10)		(0.12)
Foreign Born		0.17		0.28*
		(0.11)		(0.13)
Satisfied with Israel		−0.58***		−0.62***
		(0.07)		(0.09)
Personal Economic Circumstances		0.19*		−0.23**
		(0.08)		(0.09)
Unemployed		0.46*		0.09
		(0.18)		(0.21)
AIC	5,572.59	5,053.69	4,110.17	3,747.50
N	3,638	3,412	3,685	3,454

Source: Pew Research Center (2014–2015), binary logistic regression models.
*p<0.05; **p<0.01; ***p<0.001

TABLE C.2.5 INFLUENCE ON POLITICS

	Have a Say in Government		Influence on Politics	
(Intercept)	2.05***	5.09	2.06***	−0.43
	(0.07)	(4.41)	(0.07)	(4.18)
Israeli	−0.14	−0.01	−0.18	−0.12
	(0.10)	(0.11)	(0.09)	(0.11)
Mixed	0.28	0.43*	0.10	0.18
	(0.16)	(0.17)	(0.15)	(0.16)
Mizrahi/Sephardi	−0.07	0.03	−0.24**	−0.16
	(0.09)	(0.10)	(0.08)	(0.09)
Other	0.04	0.24	0.23	0.35
	(0.18)	(0.20)	(0.17)	(0.19)
Year of Birth		−0.00		0.00
		(0.00)		(0.00)
Female		−0.07		−0.08
		(0.08)		(0.07)
College Education		0.02		0.08
		(0.10)		(0.09)
Life Satisfaction		−0.01		−0.01
		(0.02)		(0.02)
Economic Satisfaction		0.08***		0.05***
		(0.02)		(0.01)
Paid Employment		−0.20*		0.07
		(0.08)		(0.08)
Religiosity		−0.01		−0.02
		(0.01)		(0.01)
Foreign Born		0.17		0.15
		(0.10)		(0.10)
R^2	0.01	0.10	0.03	0.08
Adj. R^2	0.01	0.08	0.02	0.06
N	632	551	632	551

Source: European Social Survey 10 (2022), OLS regression models.
*$p<0.05$; **$p<0.01$; ***$p<0.001$

TABLE C.2.6 JEWISH GROUP IDENTIFICATION

	Important in Life		Proud to Be		Belonging		Responsibility	
(Intercept)	1.64***	-0.03	2.51***	1.57***	1.89***	0.67**	0.16***	-0.51***
	(0.06)	(0.21)	(0.09)	(0.31)	(0.07)	(0.21)	(0.05)	(0.14)
Mixed	0.08	0.12	-0.31	-0.53*	0.19	0.08	0.09	0.01
	(0.17)	(0.19)	(0.21)	(0.24)	(0.19)	(0.21)	(0.13)	(0.14)
Mizrahi/Sephardi	1.49***	0.80***	2.41***	1.51***	0.62***	-0.00	0.48***	-0.01
	(0.12)	(0.15)	(0.27)	(0.29)	(0.11)	(0.13)	(0.07)	(0.08)
Other	-14.20	-19.18	11.05	17.54	-1.90	-1.10	-12.71	-12.36
	(231.67)	(4,633.37)	(381.96)	(7,669.52)	(1.44)	(1.45)	(231.67)	(230.11)
From the Former USSR		-0.27		0.13		-0.44*		-0.95***
		(0.24)		(0.29)		(0.22)		(0.14)
Dati		1.77		1.15		0.86**		0.88***
		(0.94)		(1.02)		(0.29)		(0.14)
Haredi		14.43		14.80		0.58*		1.17***
		(319.36)		(516.02)		(0.29)		(0.16)
Masorti		0.52*		0.35		0.70***		0.47***
		(0.20)		(0.29)		(0.18)		(0.10)
Male		-0.18		-0.19		-0.19		0.04
		(0.11)		(0.16)		(0.11)		(0.07)
Age in Years		0.02***		0.02**		0.01***		0.00
		(0.00)		(0.01)		(0.00)		(0.00)
College Educated		-0.03		-0.46**		0.00		0.05
		(0.12)		(0.17)		(0.12)		(0.08)

(continued)

TABLE C.2.6 JEWISH GROUP IDENTIFICATION (*continued*)

	Important in Life	Proud to Be	Belonging	Responsibility
Religion is Important	3.04***	2.39***	0.97***	0.47***
	(0.31)	(0.40)	(0.17)	(0.10)
Foreign Born	0.30	−0.59*	0.01	0.23
	(0.23)	(0.29)	(0.20)	(0.12)
Satisfied with Israel	0.42***	0.87***	0.31**	0.17*
	(0.12)	(0.18)	(0.12)	(0.07)
Personal Economic Circumstances	0.30*	−0.22	0.35**	0.14
	(0.13)	(0.19)	(0.12)	(0.08)
Unemployed	−0.37	−0.66	−0.23	−0.12
	(0.27)	(0.35)	(0.26)	(0.20)
AIC	2,812.85 2,088.95	1,455.72 1,230.14	2,867.88 2,447.37	5,446.81 4,761.16
N	3,789 3,550	3,707 3,479	3,710 3,482	3,504 3,290

Source: Pew Research Center (2014–2015), binary logistic regression models.
*$p<0.05$; **$p<0.01$; ***$p<0.001$

TABLE C.3.2 EMOTIONAL ATTACHMENT		
	Model 1	Model 2
(Intercept)	8.53***	64.37***
	(0.16)	(9.74)
Israeli	−0.09	0.21
	(0.23)	(0.25)
Mixed	0.26	0.51
	(0.37)	(0.38)
Mizrahi/Sephardi	0.48*	0.32
	(0.21)	(0.21)
Other	−1.27**	−0.43
	(0.42)	(0.45)
Year of Birth		−0.03***
		(0.00)
Female		0.26
		(0.17)
College Education		−0.01
		(0.21)
Life Satisfaction		0.06
		(0.04)
Economic Satisfaction		0.02
		(0.03)
Paid Employment		0.08
		(0.18)
Religiosity		0.07**
		(0.02)
Foreign Born		−0.15
		(0.23)
R^2	0.04	0.12
Adj. R^2	0.03	0.10
N	632	550

Source: European Social Survey 10 (2022), OLS regression model.
*$p<0.05$; **$p<0.01$; ***$p<0.001$

TABLE C.3.3 JEWISH FIRST		
	Model 1	Model 2
(Intercept)	−0.06	−1.82***
	(0.05)	(0.20)
Mixed	−0.04	0.14
	(0.14)	(0.19)
Mizrahi/Sephardi	0.73***	0.02
	(0.07)	(0.12)
Other	−12.49	−10.98
	(231.67)	(231.53)
From the Former USSR		0.59**
		(0.18)
Dati		2.92***
		(0.22)
Haredi		3.87***
		(0.36)
Masorti		1.67***
		(0.12)
Male		−0.05
		(0.09)
Age in Years		0.01***
		(0.00)
College Education		−0.37***
		(0.10)
Religion Is Important		1.35***
		(0.12)
Foreign Born		0.43**
		(0.16)
Satisfied with Israel		−0.41***
		(0.10)
Personal Economic Circumstances		0.05
		(0.11)
Unemployed		0.21
		(0.25)
AIC	4,748.13	2,912.12
N	3,055	2,851

Source: Pew Research Center (2014–2015), binary logistic regression models.
*p<0.05; **p<0.01; ***p<0.001

TABLE C.3.4 JEWISH PRIVILEGES, VALUES, AND LAW

	Preferential Treatment		Promote Values		Enact Halakha	
(Intercept)	1.10***	0.76***	−1.01***	−2.29***	−1.28***	−2.65***
	(0.05)	(0.18)	(0.05)	(0.19)	(0.06)	(0.22)
Mixed	−0.03	0.00	0.39**	0.41*	0.17	0.39
	(0.14)	(0.16)	(0.13)	(0.18)	(0.15)	(0.21)
Mizrahi/Sephardi	0.71***	0.35***	0.96***	0.05	0.90***	0.25*
	(0.08)	(0.10)	(0.07)	(0.11)	(0.07)	(0.12)
Other	11.45	11.48	1.02	2.21	−11.28	−9.91
	(231.67)	(229.24)	(1.44)	(1.45)	(231.67)	(230.34)
From the Former USSR		1.10***		−0.59**		−0.48*
		(0.17)		(0.20)		(0.23)
Dati		1.88***		3.03***		3.17***
		(0.25)		(0.16)		(0.18)
Haredi		2.29***		3.21***		3.83***
		(0.32)		(0.19)		(0.21)
Masorti		0.57***		1.63***		1.22***
		(0.12)		(0.12)		(0.14)
Male		0.01		0.14		0.46***
		(0.08)		(0.09)		(0.10)
Age in Years		0.00		−0.00		−0.01**
		(0.00)		(0.00)		(0.00)
College Education		−0.41***		−0.70***		−0.69***
		(0.09)		(0.11)		(0.12)
Religion Is Important		0.63***		1.19***		1.36***
		(0.12)		(0.12)		(0.15)
Foreign Born		−0.28*		0.29*		0.31*
		(0.14)		(0.14)		(0.15)
Satisfied with Israel		0.91***		−0.25**		−0.30**
		(0.09)		(0.09)		(0.10)
Personal Economic Circumstances		−0.68***		−0.20*		−0.11
		(0.11)		(0.10)		(0.11)
Unemployed		−0.57**		−0.18		−0.72**
		(0.22)		(0.24)		(0.27)
AIC	4,310.95	3,538.17	5,331.26	3,298.95	4,778.80	2,758.13
N	3,751	3,514	3,611	3,382	3,524	3,307

Source: Pew Research Center (2014–2015), binary logistic regression models.
*$p<0.05$; **$p<0.01$; ***$p<0.001$

TABLE C.3.5 JEWISH MAJORITY AND MIGRATION

	Stable Jewish Majority		Restrict Christian Immigration		Restrict Ethiopian Immigration	
(Intercept)	3.03***	17.17	−0.28**	−0.21	−2.13***	−0.36
	(0.24)	(1,592.95)	(0.10)	(0.69)	(0.16)	(0.87)
Identify as an Ethnic Minority	−1.04	−1.03	0.65	0.29	−0.09	−0.52
	(0.64)	(0.68)	(0.34)	(0.37)	(0.54)	(0.56)
Mixed	0.81	0.65	0.31	0.40	−0.93*	−0.80
	(0.63)	(0.66)	(0.20)	(0.22)	(0.45)	(0.47)
Other	14.80	15.88	0.39	0.55	−0.38	−0.67
	(750.99)	(1,207.06)	(0.40)	(0.43)	(0.76)	(0.78)
Mizrahi/Sephardi	1.47**	1.23*	1.10***	0.88***	−0.05	0.18
	(0.51)	(0.57)	(0.15)	(0.18)	(0.23)	(0.28)
40+ Years Old		−0.40		−0.31*		−0.00
		(0.42)		(0.15)		(0.23)
Female		0.05		−0.01		−0.14
		(0.41)		(0.15)		(0.23)
College Education		0.38		−0.25		−0.59
		(0.41)		(0.63)		(0.80)
Haredi		0.55		−0.28		−0.07
		(1.11)		(0.15)		(0.23)
Dati		1.36		2.84***		1.10*
		(1.05)		(0.62)		(0.45)
Masorti		0.07		2.56***		−0.54
		(0.53)		(0.30)		(0.43)
Income Is Insufficient		−0.05		0.67***		0.24
		(0.44)		(0.17)		(0.29)
Political Interest		0.09		0.17		0.42
		(0.45)		(0.16)		(0.24)
Family NOT from the USSR		0.87		−0.18		−0.63*
		(0.47)		(0.17)		(0.25)
President Question Correct		−14.96		0.10		−1.09***
		(1,592.95)		(0.24)		(0.31)
AIC	250.39	260.09	1,303.20	1,157.38	625.89	611.00
N	991	988	991	988	991	988

Source: iPanel, binary logistic regression models.
*$p<0.05$; **$p<0.01$; ***$p<0.001$

TABLE C.3.6 REFUGEE ATTITUDES

	Judge Conservatively		True Fear	
(Intercept)	3.30***	15.97***	2.99***	−1.55
	(0.05)	(2.94)	(0.05)	(3.31)
Mizrahi/Sephardi	0.41***	0.31***	−0.25***	−0.25***
	(0.06)	(0.07)	(0.07)	(0.08)
Mixed	0.10	0.12	0.01	−0.02
	(0.09)	(0.09)	(0.10)	(0.10)
Other	0.31*	0.27	−0.33*	−0.38*
	(0.13)	(0.14)	(0.15)	(0.15)
Year of Birth		−0.01***		0.00
		(0.00)		(0.00)
Female		−0.04		0.12
		(0.06)		(0.06)
College Educated		−0.14		−0.04
		(0.07)		(0.08)
Life Satisfaction		0.00		0.02
		(0.02)		(0.02)
Economic Satisfaction		0.01		−0.01
		(0.01)		(0.01)
Employed		0.09		0.01
		(0.06)		(0.06)
Religiosity		0.05***		−0.03**
		(0.01)		(0.01)
Identify as a Minority		−0.17		0.32*
		(0.15)		(0.16)
R^2	0.03	0.07	0.01	0.03
Adj. R^2	0.03	0.06	0.01	0.02
N	1,652	1,565	1,494	1,427

Source: European Social Survey 8 (2016–2017), OLS regression models.
*p<0.05; **p<0.01; ***p<0.001

TABLE C.3.7 TREATMENT OF PALESTINIAN POPULATION

	Expel Arabs		Palestinian Right of Return	
(Intercept)	−0.28***	−0.72***	0.42***	0.75***
	(0.05)	(0.14)	(0.05)	(0.14)
Mixed	−0.08	0.12	−0.09	−0.22
	(0.13)	(0.14)	(0.13)	(0.14)
Mizrahi/Sephardi	0.65***	0.49***	−0.34***	−0.27**
	(0.06)	(0.08)	(0.07)	(0.08)
Other	12.83	13.31	12.13	11.90
	(231.67)	(231.48)	(231.67)	(231.60)
From the Former USSR		1.36***		−0.86***
		(0.14)		(0.14)
Dati		1.02***		−0.71***
		(0.14)		(0.13)
Haredi		0.62***		0.68***
		(0.15)		(0.15)
Masorti		0.40***		−0.31**
		(0.10)		(0.10)
Male		0.16*		0.01
		(0.07)		(0.07)
Age in Years		−0.00		−0.00
		(0.00)		(0.00)
College Education		−0.34***		0.21**
		(0.08)		(0.08)
Religion Is Important		0.67***		−0.47***
		(0.10)		(0.10)
Foreign Born		−0.10		−0.17
		(0.11)		(0.11)
Satisfied with Israel		0.07		0.05
		(0.07)		(0.07)
Personal Economic Circumstances		−0.22**		0.23**
		(0.08)		(0.08)
Unemployed		0.15		−0.22
		(0.19)		(0.19)
AIC	5,642.98	4,863.51	5,458.61	4,845.99
N	3,579	3,354	3,473	3,253

Source: Pew Research Center (2014–2015), binary logistic regression models.
*$p<0.05$; **$p<0.01$; ***$p<0.001$

TABLE C.3.8 NON-ORTHODOX CONVERSIONS ARE VALID		
	Model 1	Model 2
(Intercept)	0.16***	1.14***
	(0.05)	(0.16)
Mixed	0.54***	0.74***
	(0.13)	(0.16)
Mizrahi/Sephardi	−1.19***	−0.68***
	(0.07)	(0.09)
Other	−0.17	−0.59
	(1.44)	(1.49)
From the Former USSR		0.64***
		(0.15)
Dati		−2.07***
		(0.18)
Haredi		−2.94***
		(0.25)
Masorti		−0.69***
		(0.11)
Male		−0.08
		(0.08)
Age in Years		−0.00
		(0.00)
College Education		0.05
		(0.09)
Religion Is Important		−0.74***
		(0.10)
Foreign Born		−0.34**
		(0.13)
Satisfied with Israel		−0.63***
		(0.08)
Personal Economic Circumstances		0.23*
		(0.09)
Unemployed		0.01
		(0.22)
AIC	5,192.77	4,013.78
N	3,534	3,312

Source: Pew Research Center (2014–2015), binary logistic regression models.
*$p<0.05$; **$p<0.01$; ***$p<0.001$

TABLE C.3.9 OPPOSITION TO OUT-MARRIAGE

	Christian Marriage		Muslim Marriage	
(Intercept)	1.89***	0.69**	4.13***	2.62***
	(0.07)	(0.25)	(0.18)	(0.69)
Mixed	0.45*	0.09	−0.17	0.23
	(0.22)	(0.25)	(0.46)	(0.55)
Mizrahi/Sephardi	2.21***	1.15***	2.02***	1.53**
	(0.18)	(0.22)	(0.50)	(0.53)
Other	−1.88	−1.41	10.43	17.05
	(1.44)	(1.46)	(629.75)	(12,604.23)
From the Former USSR		−1.16***		2.15**
		(0.29)		(0.76)
Dati		3.86***		15.64
		(1.10)		(744.41)
Haredi		16.30		0.44
		(316.31)		(0.82)
Masorti		2.02***		0.88
		(0.31)		(0.61)
Male		−0.02		−0.63
		(0.13)		(0.34)
Age in Years		0.02***		0.05***
		(0.00)		(0.01)
College Education		−0.26		−0.69
		(0.14)		(0.36)
Religion Is Important		0.24		0.65
		(0.19)		(0.54)
Foreign Born		0.01		−1.09
		(0.29)		(0.57)
Satisfied with Israel		0.57***		1.37***
		(0.15)		(0.41)
Personal Economic Circumstances		0.33*		−0.72
		(0.15)		(0.47)
Unemployed		0.58		1.02
		(0.41)		(1.59)
AIC	2,033.18	1,592.81	446.76	386.59
N	3,643	3,415	3,720	3,485

Source: Pew Research Center (2014–2015), binary logistic regression models.
*p<0.05; **p<0.01; ***p<0.001

TABLE C.3.10 MAINTAINING ISRAEL				
	Remain in Israel		Israel Is Necessary	
(Intercept)	−0.31***	−1.77***	2.19***	1.53***
	(0.05)	(0.15)	(0.07)	(0.26)
Mixed	−0.27*	−0.35*	0.15	0.22
	(0.13)	(0.15)	(0.21)	(0.24)
Mizrahi/Sephardi	0.64***	0.21*	1.05***	1.14***
	(0.06)	(0.08)	(0.14)	(0.16)
Other	12.87	13.84	−2.19	−1.92
	(231.67)	(231.66)	(1.44)	(1.45)
From the Former USSR		−0.15		0.66*
		(0.14)		(0.29)
Dati		1.75***		−0.54
		(0.14)		(0.34)
Haredi		1.59***		−2.76***
		(0.16)		(0.28)
Masorti		0.74***		0.03
		(0.10)		(0.25)
Male		0.26***		−0.34*
		(0.07)		(0.13)
Age in Years		0.02***		0.01**
		(0.00)		(0.00)
College Education		0.13		0.28
		(0.08)		(0.16)
Religion Is Important		0.43***		0.93***
		(0.10)		(0.26)
Foreign Born		−0.17		−0.05
		(0.12)		(0.23)
Satisfied with Israel		0.01		0.54***
		(0.07)		(0.15)
Personal Economic Circumstances		−0.04		0.06
		(0.08)		(0.15)
Unemployed		−0.50*		−0.09
		(0.21)		(0.33)
AIC	5,573.35	4,696.81	2,087.55	1,703.25
N	3,467	3,254	3,720	3,486

Source: Pew Research Center (2014–2015), binary logistic regression models.
*p<0.05; **p<0.01; ***p<0.001

TABLE C.4.2 PREFERENCE FOR LIBERAL DEMOCRACY

	Model 1	Model 2
(Intercept)	1.86***	0.22
	(0.15)	(0.70)
Identify as an Ethnic Minority	0.25	0.75
	(0.45)	(0.47)
Mixed	−0.13	−0.28
	(0.28)	(0.31)
Other	0.17	0.24
	(0.63)	(0.65)
Mizrahi/Sephardi	−0.51**	−0.30
	(0.19)	(0.23)
40+ Years Old		0.38*
		(0.19)
Female		0.42*
		(0.19)
College Education		0.20
		(0.19)
Haredi		−1.85***
		(0.39)
Dati		−1.46***
		(0.26)
Masorti		−1.02***
		(0.24)
Income Is Insufficient		−0.23
		(0.20)
Political Interest		0.30
		(0.22)
Family NOT from the USSR		0.71*
		(0.31)
President Question Correct		1.03
		(0.62)
AIC	887.45	829.17
N	991	988

Source: iPanel, binary logistic regression model.
*$p<0.05$; **$p<0.01$; ***$p<0.001$

TABLE C.4.3 REGIME-TYPE PREFERENCES				
	Important to Live in Democracy		Strong Leader Acceptable	
(Intercept)	9.22***	23.74*	2.34***	−16.37
	(0.15)	(9.67)	(0.26)	(16.09)
Israeli	−0.39	−0.27	−0.08	−0.52
	(0.22)	(0.24)	(0.38)	(0.41)
Mixed	0.22	0.17	−0.41	−0.50
	(0.36)	(0.38)	(0.60)	(0.63)
Mizrahi/Sephardi	0.02	0.12	0.03	−0.49
	(0.20)	(0.21)	(0.34)	(0.35)
Other	−0.52	−0.38	−0.78	−1.22
	(0.41)	(0.45)	(0.68)	(0.74)
Year of Birth		−0.01		0.01
		(0.00)		(0.01)
Female		−0.09		0.45
		(0.17)		(0.29)
College Education		0.15		−0.81*
		(0.21)		(0.35)
Life Satisfaction		0.09*		−0.15*
		(0.04)		(0.06)
Economic Satisfaction		−0.02		−0.01
		(0.03)		(0.06)
Paid Employment		−0.15		−0.02
		(0.18)		(0.29)
Religiosity		−0.07**		0.24***
		(0.02)		(0.04)
Foreign Born		−0.38		0.24
		(0.23)		(0.38)
R^2	0.01	0.05	0.00	0.11
Adj. R^2	0.00	0.03	−0.00	0.09
N	627	548	622	547

Source: European Social Survey 10 (2022), OLS regression models.
*p<0.05; **p<0.01; ***p<0.001

TABLE C.4.4 DEMOCRACY AND JEWISH STATE		
	Model 1	Model 2
(Intercept)	1.07***	1.58***
	(0.05)	(0.17)
Mixed	0.16	−0.20
	(0.15)	(0.16)
Mizrahi/Sephardi	0.51***	0.14
	(0.08)	(0.10)
Other	−1.06	−1.51
	(1.44)	(1.44)
From the Former USSR		−0.58***
		(0.15)
Dati		0.05
		(0.16)
Haredi		−1.00***
		(0.16)
Masorti		0.28*
		(0.13)
Male		−0.25**
		(0.08)
Age in Years		0.00
		(0.00)
College Education		−0.19*
		(0.09)
Religion Is Important		−0.01
		(0.12)
Foreign Born		−0.13
		(0.13)
Satisfied with Israel		0.14
		(0.08)
Personal Economic Circumstances		−0.17
		(0.09)
Unemployed		−0.27
		(0.21)
AIC	4,317.80	3,957.50
N	3,640	3,412

Source: Pew Research Center (2014–2015), binary logistic regression models.
*p<0.05; **p<0.01; ***p<0.001

TABLE C.4.5 JEWISH LAW VERSUS DEMOCRACY				
	Dependent Variable:			
	It Depends	Privilege Democracy	It Depends	Privilege Democracy
	(1)	(2)	(3)	(4)
Constant	−0.341***	1.349***	3.177***	5.238***
	(0.081)	(0.059)	(0.386)	(0.371)
Mixed	0.382	0.338	0.210	0.128
	(0.232)	(0.179)	(0.287)	(0.280)
Mizrahi/Sephardi	−0.567**	−0.777***	−0.337**	−0.151
	(0.109)	(0.076)	(0.151)	(0.145)
Other	−3.966	−1.418	−13.361***	−5.023***
	(8.680)	(1.442)	(0.00004)	(1.486)
From the Former USSR			0.582	−0.347
			(0.301)	(0.296)
Dati			−2.954***	−5.581***
			(0.316)	(0.314)
Haredi			−4.518***	−6.952***
			(0.360)	(0.397)
Masorti			−2.050***	−2.818***
			(0.302)	(0.281)
Male			−0.658***	−0.773***
			(0.124)	(0.116)
Age in Years			−0.007	0.001
			(0.004)	(0.004)
College Educated			0.583***	0.593***
			(0.153)	(0.147)
Religion Is Important			−0.720*	−1.808***
			(0.282)	(0.258)
Foreign Born			−0.056	−0.158
			(0.197)	(0.179)
Satisfied with Israel			−0.254	0.444***
			(0.132)	(0.122)
Personal Economic Circumstances			0.154	0.488***
			(0.139)	(0.131)
Unemployed			0.104	0.140
			(0.322)	(0.304)
AIC	7,878.59	7,878.59	4,644.68	4,644.68
N	3,719	3,719	3,486	3,486

Source: Pew Research Center (2014–2015), multinomial logistic regression models.
*p<0.1; **p<0.05; ***p<0.01

TABLE C.5.2 PREFERENCES FOR PEACE AND BORDERS

	Lasting Peace		Green Line Borders	
(Intercept)	2.83***	16.67	0.09	−0.54
	(0.22)	(628.96)	(0.10)	(0.69)
Identify as an Ethnic Minority	−0.41	−0.20	−0.48	0.01
	(0.50)	(0.51)	(0.33)	(0.37)
Mixed	−0.40	−0.64	0.05	0.19
	(0.38)	(0.40)	(0.20)	(0.23)
Other	−0.67	−0.69	−0.70	−0.83
	(0.66)	(0.67)	(0.42)	(0.46)
Mizrahi/Sephardi	−0.47	−0.59	−0.75***	−0.25
	(0.28)	(0.31)	(0.14)	(0.18)
40+ Years Old		−0.16		0.77***
		(0.25)		(0.15)
Female		−0.03		0.30
		(0.26)		(0.15)
College Education		0.38		0.47**
		(0.26)		(0.15)
Haredi		−0.96		−2.49***
		(0.52)		(0.55)
Dati		−0.68		−2.67***
		(0.35)		(0.29)
Masorti		−0.08		−1.18***
		(0.32)		(0.18)
Income Is Insufficient		−0.21		0.09
		(0.26)		(0.16)
Political Interest		0.02		0.14
		(0.30)		(0.18)
Family NOT from the USSR		0.88*		0.04
		(0.38)		(0.24)
President Question Correct		−14.35		0.13
		(628.96)		(0.64)
AIC	532.17	536.07	1,331.85	1,132.40
N	991	988	991	988

Source: iPanel, binary logistic regression model.
*$p<0.05$; **$p<0.01$; ***$p<0.001$

TABLE C.5.3 SINCERE EFFORTS IN THE PEACE PROCESS				
	Israeli Government		Palestinian Leaders	
(Intercept)	0.10*	−0.51***	−1.98***	−1.80***
	(0.05)	(0.14)	(0.07)	(0.22)
Mixed	−0.37**	−0.30*	−0.85***	−1.27***
	(0.13)	(0.14)	(0.26)	(0.28)
Mizrahi/Sephardi	0.53***	0.34***	−0.28**	−0.40***
	(0.06)	(0.08)	(0.10)	(0.12)
Other	−12.65	−12.65	−10.58	−10.91
	(231.67)	(213.37)	(231.67)	(231.34)
From the Former USSR		0.16		−1.31***
		(0.14)		(0.26)
Dati		−0.18		−0.90***
		(0.13)		(0.23)
Haredi		−0.16		−0.98***
		(0.15)		(0.26)
Masorti		0.01		−0.43**
		(0.10)		(0.16)
Male		−0.10		0.03
		(0.07)		(0.10)
Age in Years		−0.00		0.01**
		(0.00)		(0.00)
College Education		−0.11		−0.09
		(0.08)		(0.12)
Religion Is Important		0.85***		−0.07
		(0.10)		(0.15)
Foreign Born		0.31**		−0.50**
		(0.11)		(0.17)
Satisfied with Israel		1.09***		0.29**
		(0.07)		(0.11)
Personal Economic Circumstances		−0.16*		−0.11
		(0.08)		(0.13)
Unemployed		0.06		−0.64
		(0.19)		(0.39)
AIC	5,670.37	4,997.74	2,958.76	2,633.05
N	3,609	3,387	3,709	3,476

Source: Pew Research Center (2014–2015), binary logistic regression models.
*p<0.05; **p<0.01; ***p<0.001

TABLE C.5.4 PEACE WITH PALESTINE POSSIBLE

	It Depends		Peace with Palestine	
(Intercept)	−1.255***	−1.325***	0.201***	0.226
	(0.075)	(0.226)	(0.048)	(0.147)
Mixed	0.281	0.250	0.167	0.036
	(0.197)	(0.213)	(0.133)	(0.148)
Mizrahi/Sephardi	−0.572***	−0.540***	−0.523***	−0.345***
	(0.110)	(0.136)	(0.066)	(0.085)
Other	−3.190	−9.317***	−0.257	−0.359
	(9.316)	(0.00004)	(1.440)	(1.450)
From the Former USSR		0.490**		−0.551***
		(0.215)		(0.142)
Dati		0.174		−1.093***
		(0.207)		(0.140)
Haredi		−0.054		−1.318***
		(0.225)		(0.160)
Masorti		0.233		−0.555***
		(0.168)		(0.104)
Male		−0.111		−0.056
		(0.109)		(0.070)
Age in Years		0.011***		0.014***
		(0.004)		(0.003)
College Education		0.279**		0.269***
		(0.126)		(0.080)
Religion Is Important		−0.031		−0.455***
		(0.166)		(0.101)
Foreign Born		−0.471**		−0.431***
		(0.188)		(0.117)
Satisfied with Israel		0.058		0.071
		(0.116)		(0.074)
Personal Economic Circumstances		−0.727***		0.066
		(0.120)		(0.084)
Unemployed		−0.050		−0.382*
		(0.264)		(0.202)
AIC	8,336.118	7,363.277	8,336.118	7,363.277
N	3,687	3,459	3,687	3,459

Source: Pew Research Center (2014–2015), multinomial logistic regression models.
*p<0.05; **p<0.01; ***p<0.001

TABLE C.5.5 SETTLEMENTS AND SECURITY

	Dependent Variable:			
	It Depends (1)	Settlements Help (2)	It Depends (3)	Settlements Help (4)
Mixed	−0.183	0.121	−0.072	0.233
	(0.165)	(0.139)	(0.179)	(0.159)
Mizrahi/Sephardi	0.505***	0.786***	0.358***	0.410***
	(0.084)	(0.075)	(0.104)	(0.096)
Other	0.390	−6.714	0.656	−9.746***
	(1.436)	(29.803)	(1.460)	(0.0001)
From the Former USSR			0.584***	0.577***
			(0.172)	(0.158)
Dati			0.694***	1.351***
			(0.200)	(0.171)
Haredi			1.299***	1.066***
			(0.206)	(0.191)
Masorti			0.621***	0.470***
			(0.129)	(0.118)
Male			0.274**	0.281***
			(0.086)	(0.080)
Age in Years			−0.002	−0.004
			(0.003)	(0.003)
College Education			−0.100	−0.090
			(0.097)	(0.090)
Religion Is Important			0.308**	0.903***
			(0.125)	(0.114)
Foreign Born			−0.178	−0.013
			(0.143)	(0.130)
Satisfied with Israel			0.513***	0.592***
			(0.091)	(0.085)
Personal Economic Circumstances			−0.179	−0.208*
			(0.103)	(0.095)
Unemployed			0.011	0.167
			(0.245)	(0.224)
Constant	−0.392***	−0.046	−0.932***	−0.836***
	(0.057)	(0.052)	(0.179)	(0.166)
AIC	9,347.51	9,347.51	8,255.40	8,255.40
N	3,655	3,655	3,424	3,424

Source: Pew Research Center, multinomial logistic regression model.
*$p<0.05$; **$p<0.01$; ***$p<0.001$

Notes

CHAPTER 1

1. *Halakha* means "the way to behave," and it guides religious practice and daily life. It includes biblical commandments, Talmud, and tradition.

2. In this way, this study parallels the race and ethnic politics work in the United States that is complicating the evaluation of white Americans' racialized politics (Jardina 2019; Yadon and Ostfeld 2020).

3. A short note on the terminology Arab Jews is in order. In piloting survey questions for this project, some Jewish Israelis used the "other" space to identify their ethnic group as Arab. While Arab is used in most writings and questions to refer to non-Jewish—usually Muslim—populations, there are some Mizrahi Jews who use the terminology to describe themselves. Thus, the word Arab was avoided in subsequent versions of the original survey. The word Arab is often used in surveys like the European Social Survey and Pew Research Survey, though, to mean non-Jewish people.

4. Members of a minority group who cannot pass or do not wish to pass as white may ridicule members who can for doing so (Hitlin, Brown, and Elder 2007). Those who pass as members of another group may also experience cognitive identity discordance at being classed by observers with an identity group they do not share. Thus, in theory, the strategic choice is not costless to make. As the focus in the Israeli case is on marginal group members and not on individuals moving between groups (or pretending to), the concern is less pertinent here. Future research could unpack passing as a phenomenon in this arena.

5. Nonreligious people are not a separate category for this purpose. Secular Jews are still Jews in this classification. It is a distinction between those identifying as Jewish and those identifying with other religions—most importantly with Islam but also, to a lesser extent, with Christianity.

6. The language of race is taboo in Israel because of the association with the Holocaust and the racialization of Jewish identity. It is still invoked with respect to Ethiopian Jews

or other sub-Saharan African Jewish communities, who may be racially othered even within the Jewish community. However, the invocation of race is sometimes held against these groups because of the sensitivity around racializing Judaism and Jews and because it emphasizes within-community divisions that some people would prefer to ignore (Kalev and Maor 2015; Mizrachi and Herzog 2012).

7. Asian-country Jews are also considered Mizrahi. This includes, for instance, Indian Jews. Some Indian Jews were Sephardim fleeing the Inquisition, while other Jewish communities predated that arrival.

8. In theory, "other" could include individuals like the Black Hebrew Israelites, who are not necessarily recognized as Jewish and are largely not citizens of Israel although they may be permanent residents (Jackson 2013). This analysis, however, focuses on self-identified Jewish Israelis.

9. Converts and African Jews have sometimes faced difficulty getting recognized by Israeli law. This difficulty manifests during claims to the right of return if the religious validity of the conversion or community is questioned. Israeli law privileges Orthodox conversions when evaluating the acceptability for return; American converts, however, have been sometimes exempted from that standard (Yadgar 2020). Those individuals could be termed "rejected marginals" (Ellemers and Jetten 2013, 10). The focus here, though, is on Jews within Israel. Thus, all of the Jewish Israelis surveyed here have been at least *somewhat* accepted.

10. Referring to these individuals as "blacks" (*shchorim* or *shwartzes* in Hebrew or Yiddish respectively) is derogatory and not phenotypically based (Mizrachi and Herzog 2012). The later immigration of Ethiopian Jews exposing the existence of Black African Jews makes the use of "black" to describe Mizrahim particularly problematic. It foreshadows the skepticism with which Ethiopian Jews were treated when claiming right of return, and calling Mizrahim "black" indicates latent colorism. While the Mizrahim are treated as ethnically distinct, they are not racially othered in the way the Ethiopian Jews have been. More is said on this later in this chapter and Chapter 2.

11. The Israel Central Bureau of Statistics does not assign ethnic categories for later generations in Israel (Kalev and Maor 2015). Those who are born abroad are identified, as are the children of immigrants, who receive a designation based on their father's category. Subsequent generations are coded as Israeli. Lavie (2018) argues that this coding conceals the fact that the state should be considered majority Mizrahi, since the Mizrahim have more children than the Ashkenazim.

12. Smooha (2004, 52) also argues that the assimilationist pressures have declined such that "Mizrahim and later immigrants, like Russian and Ethiopian newcomers, are no longer expected to fully dispose of their cultural heritage and are allowed instead to keep their particularity while integrating into the wider society." This view would be somewhat consistent with the small population that takes surveys in Russian; however, the pressure to use Hebrew instead of Arabic would remain strong, given the condition of the Palestinians. It also does not mean the cultures are treated equally.

13. The American Jewish community skews much more heavily toward Ashkenazi ethnicity. Only "20 per cent of U.S. Jews are of colour" (Gonzalez-Lesser 2020, 492).

14. Noting this pattern is not meant to endorse differential treatment based on religion. However, the securitization of part of the "in-group" demonstrates their marginal group membership.

15. For more information on the European Social Survey and sampling, see the survey website (https://www.europeansocialsurvey.org) and Lynn et al. (2007).

16. In the ESS10, the surveys were self-completed. Of the respondents, 21.3 percent did not answer the religion question, which accounts for the lowered Jewish proportion. The Jewish sample includes those who religiously identified as Jewish currently, those who said they were raised Jewish, and those who identified Jewish ancestry.

17. In this dataset, none of the respondents who identified as Arab also identified as Jewish.

18. 1,141 panelists completed the quota questions; 134 responses were removed for speeding (less than 180 seconds).

19. A pilot study was fielded in June 2021. The pilot survey was scheduled to be fielded in May 2021; however, it was delayed because of the clashes over Sheikh Jarrah in Jerusalem. The main survey was delayed because of some high-profile public stabbings. Effort was made to put some temporal distance between a flash point and the survey. It would be unethical to conduct a survey that might cue ethnic conflict during a tense point in an ethnic conflict. The unpredictable nature of Israeli politics meant that eventually the project was fielded with the hope that additional violence would not occur. Given that crises have been shown to heighten in-group sentiment and group-protective behavior, fielding the surveys in times of relatively lower conflict shows lower bounds for group effects.

20. This might be akin to the language stick being larger for some bundles in American racial groups than other bundles of sticks (e.g., Hispanic Americans as compared to white Americans). Neither the bundles nor the stick sizes have to be the same across groups.

21. Lewin-Epstein and Cohen note that some Mizrahim attempted to skirt classification by claiming they were "mixed" or "other" rather than Mizrahi, especially among generations born in Israel. "An individual's self report of race can draw not only from her ancestry, but also from social cues about which identity would be appropriate to claim (perhaps based on her physical appearance) and which identity would be valued in a given context" (Saperstein 2006, 59–60). The analysis thus focuses on the ethnicity identified, separate from those clumping, ethnicity-concealing options.

22. ESS10 did not include the supplemental form that identified respondents as Ashkenazi, Mizrahi/Sephardi, or other. The respondent's group was identified by the parents' country of birth; if both parents were born in Israel, the respondent was labeled Israeli. The result was compared with the stated ancestry—the question for which the most common answers were Jewish and Israeli. If a respondent had marked Ashkenazi, Sephardi, or Mizrahi or had identified specific countries, the classification was updated to reflect the answers. Based on the balance of probability and statements in ethnographic sources, the United States and Canada are treated as Ashkenazi source countries, and India, Georgia, and France are treated as Mizrahi source countries.

23. For those born in Israel, the father's country of birth is used for the ICBS coding. With successive generations, Israel-born fathers are more common; in that case, those citizens are marked as Israeli without an ethnic designation (Lewin-Epstein and Cohen 2019).

24. Mizrachi and Weiss (2020, 195) note that the term Sephardi "originally referred to the Jewish Diaspora in Spain but today" is used for "Mizrahi Jews who have adopted a Sephardic liturgical style." Thus, it is considered appropriate to put all of the "Eastern" Jews into one group. For readers who are interested in models that keep Mizrahi and Sephardi respondents separately coded, those results are shown in the Online Appendix (available at https://scholarshare.temple.edu/handle/20.500.12613/9253). Models that use

Mizrahi as a reference category to identify differences between the Mizrahi and Sephardi respondents are also shown in the Online Appendix. The Mizrahim and Sephardim
are generally not significantly different. The discussion focuses on the ESS8-style coding
for comparability.

25. Theoretically, a superordinate religious or citizenship-based identity would be better because it could be more inclusive. For instance, Choi, Poertner, and Sambanis (2022)
argue that the development of cultural-citizenship identities in a country, instead of ethnic identities, can reduce anti-immigrant biases. However, the ESS surveys do not indicate what identity is favored by these respondents (e.g., Jewish writ large, Israeli broadly,
or something else). The nature of such an overarching identity could be probed in future
research. For readers who are interested in models that include those opting to live without an ethnic identity, see the Online Appendix (available at https://scholarshare.temple
.edu/handle/20.500.12613/9253). These respondents are not significantly different from
the Ashkenazim.

26. The iPanel survey used age quotas; 10.2 percent were 18–21, 16.8 percent were
22–29, 21.6 percent were 30–39, 18.8 percent were 40–49, and 32.5 percent were over 50.

27. This classification has been called into question. Mchenry and Mady (2006) argue
that this designation is only possible with a selective interpretation of Israel's borders. They
argue that the Palestinian Territories undermine this classification, but by only counting
part of the territory that Israel claims, focusing on the Jewish-majority terrains, the systems label Israel democracy. Oren (2019, 90) refers to Israel as a "hegemonic state"—"a
state that promotes the interest of a single ethnopolitical group in a multinational setting"—and concludes that that "makes Israel at best a 'flawed' democracy." For the purposes of this project, it suffices to note that Israel's governmental documents espouse democratic intention.

28. For a larger discussion of minimalist and maximalist conceptions of democracy
and the separation between liberalism and democracy, see Schmitter and Karl (1991),
Collier and Levitsky (1997), Plattner (2020), and Ridge (2023a).

29. The Green Line refers to the borders after the 1948 Arab-Israeli War and before
the 1967 Six-Day War. It would exclude the Occupied Territories. Contemporary negotiations often would slightly modify these borders with "territory swaps" to account for
the subsequent population movements and the settlements.

CHAPTER 2

1. Experiencing bias is not the key defining trait of being Jewish. However, Jewish traditions and Israeli culture invoke histories of repression regularly. Many Jewish and Israeli holidays commemorate surviving danger or repression. In the Pew Research Center
Israel studies, 63.6 percent of adult Jewish Israelis said antisemitism is very common
around the world, and 35.2 percent said it is somewhat common. Of Jewish Israelis, 61.3
percent said that remembering the Holocaust was an "essential part of what being Jewish
means to" them. For comparison, 32.1 percent said living in Israel was essential, 41.7
percent said observing Jewish law was essential, and 49.9 percent said "leading an ethical
and moral life" was essential.

2. Territorial distribution was crucial in the early state because the government believed that disbursing the incoming Jewish population widely would prevent Palestinians
from returning to the land (Pearlman and Atzili 2018). Thus, they were more concerned
with the state interest in territorial acquisition than with the interests or preferences of
the immigrants.

3. Linked fate is the concept that what happens to some members of a group informs or predicts what happens to all members of that group (Dawson 1994). In theory, class-based linked fate is also possible, especially among those experiencing economic precarity (Donnelly 2021). However, the salience of ethnicity, as well as the Palestinian-Israeli distinction, could undermine the countervailing effects of social class. The Mizrahim are more likely to evince or seek linked fate with the Jewish population than the non-Jewish Arab population.

4. A workshop discussant noted that I could conduct such a systematic analysis using the photo-reflectance tools Ostfeld and Yadon (2020; 2022b) used in their work. However, such measurements risk recalling the racial appearance testing conducted during the Holocaust. A study, then, could be very upsetting to the participants and would have to be undertaken with great care. Future research could evaluate Israelis' ability to conduct such classifications, citizens' understanding of how others perceive them, and their feelings about these issues in a qualitative fashion.

5. Bagno-Moldavski (2015, 519) compares the intra-Jewish ethnic hierarchy in Israel to "the politically acute racial divides in the South Africa [sic] and the United States." These groups' middle position might be compared to darker-skinned white people in the United States or the Coloured ethnic group in South Africa.

6. Conversely, non-Jewish respondents readily reported discrimination against Muslims. Muslim respondents divided 84.6–14.2 on that point, and Christian respondents divided 58.6–35.5.

7. For reference, 65.1 percent of non-Jews in the overall ESS8 sample and 64.4 percent of individuals who did not identify their current or prior religious affiliation as Jewish in the overall ESS10 sample reported identification with a discriminated-against group.

8. In the reverse, Sasson-Levy (2013) notes that some Ashkenazim were reluctant to own their own biases, even while exhibiting them. For instance, they would rather describe other people's biases, like their parents' biases, or blame the Mizrahim for the social order.

9. Few respondents reported identifying as part of a group experiencing ethnic or racial discrimination. To account for this distribution, rare events logits are used in those models (Kosmidis 2022).

10. Phoenix and Chan (2022) argue that these questions should be formulated to explicitly mention racial groups for more accurate predictions of racial efficacy belief. This study is constrained by the existing ESS survey questions.

CHAPTER 3

1. Benefiting from perpetuating Jewish majoritarianism does not mean that they benefit from Ashkenormativity. There is no supposition that they endorse within-group biases; however, they do benefit from perpetuating a hierarchy against out-groups.

2. For marginal members who can choose different groups, such as multiracial individuals, relative group status can inform their strategic identification (Telles and Paschel 2014). One could imagine scenarios in which "Arab Jews" would benefit from being viewed as Arab. However, ethnodoxy—the fusion of Arab and Muslim identities by Muslim Arabs—would undermine that potential because they would be othered on the religion dimension in the Arab states (Ridge 2023b). The formation of Israel and the anti-Israel stance of parts of the Arab nationalist movement complicate this process. For Jews in Arab countries, "their religion (Jewishness) was rapidly turning into a national marker in the international arena, which gradually conflicted with their affiliation with the Arab nation-

state" (Shohat 2003, 53). Although strong Arab nationalists would likely have avoided moving to Israel, participation in a pan-Arab identity would work against finding an ethnicity effect here.

3. The socioeconomic circumstances supposedly synonymous with ethnic marginalization are also linked to exclusionary policies. Regulation and control of the Palestinian population serves the economic interests of the lower-socioeconomic-status groups. Cheap Palestinian labor could threaten the economic conditions of Mizrahi Jews because they are more likely to "occupy the bottom sections of the occupational scale" and thus compete with Palestinians (Peled 1998). Israel's permitting regime—domestic migration permissions for residents of the Occupied Territories to enter and work in Israel—has been used as a labor market control device (Berda 2018).

4. Peled is citing Erik Cohen.

5. The same pattern presents if those who are unsure (19.5 percent) are counted as a separate group rather than omitted.

6. For the refugee petitions, the economic precarity factor could have heterogenous effects. The interactions between ethnicity and economic satisfaction are not significant, but the interaction models for ethnicity and employment status are. The difference between the Mizrahim and Ashkenazim is reduced, but not brought to zero, for those who are employed. Among the unemployed, the Mizrahim express greater disagreement than the Ashkenazim.

7. The phrasing of these questions does not specify the borders within which the respondent should construe Israel or *return* for the purposes of this question.

8. He reported supporting Yesh Atid, which was part of the coalition government at the time of the survey. He may have soured on the leadership.

9. Sheikh Jarrah is a Palestinian neighborhood in East Jerusalem that experienced violent clashes that year when Palestinian homes were seized.

10. Another respondent also noted the smallness of the country. A Masorti Mizrahi man in his twenties in the south area with a secondary education wrote, "We are one small nation among many big nations, and we should be united and not fight each other." He did not specify whether this *we* extends to non-Jewish residents of Israel. Nonetheless, his comment echoes the old American notion of "politics stopping at the water's edge."

11. Social identity theory has been linked to rioting and intergroup violence. Deindividuation shifts the locus of attention to the macro identity of the victim and the perpetrator, and "during and after a riot, participants often feel a strong sense of social identity" (Hornsey 2008, 210). Thus, participating in or suborning violence could be identity affirming for these respondents. Future work should continue to unpack this dimension.

12. Assertions that Israel systematically victimizes Palestinians has been called "genocide inversion" and "soft-core" Holocaust denial (Lipstadt 2019). Some people treat this view as antisemitism.

13. Civil-ceremony interfaith marriages are recognized if contracted outside of Israel and subsequently registered. Recent court rulings suggest that virtual weddings under the auspices of another country (e.g., the United States) could permit interfaith couples to marry "abroad" while remaining physically in Israel. The Orthodox rabbinate opposes this movement, which would challenge their control and facilitate out-marriage.

14. One conference attendee, during a presentation on material for this book, reported assuming Ashkenormativity derived from the Holocaust. She thought that it was because Mizrahim felt guilty that their states had been spared and were thus sympathetic toward the Ashkenazim on that basis.

15. While 61.3 percent of the respondents in the Pew Research Center survey said that remembering the Holocaust was to them an essential part of being Jewish, Mizrahi/Sephardi respondents were slightly but significantly more likely than Ashkenazi Jewish respondents to say that it was not part of what being Jewish means to them, but they were also more willing to call it essential as compared to important. Future work could unpack the role of the Holocaust and remembrance in these groups' identities and attitudes.

16. It would be a bit circular because Israel's existence and politics themselves play a role in that sentiment (Fox and Topor 2021).

CHAPTER 4

1. Freedom House (2022) acknowledges, "The numerical scores and status listed above do not reflect conditions in the Gaza Strip or the West Bank." Answering the question of whether or not Israel is a democracy is beyond the scope of this book, but the National Election Survey data shows that the point is disputed among Jewish Israelis.

2. Fox and Rynhold state that "Israel has a higher level of GIR than do other democracies, whether they are western or non-western. However, when examining the individual types of GIR that exist in Israel, all of them exist in other democratic states. Furthermore, the overall levels of official support for religion, religious regulation, and religious discrimination are no higher than they are in several other democratic states, but this is not true of religious legislation. That being said, the overall level of GIR in Israel is among the highest of any democratic state" (2008, 524). As such, they do not consider the government's engagement with religion (especially Judaism) an antidemocratic force in the state.

3. In the original, this entire quote is in italics.

4. As with Chapter 3, the models are replicated including a political ideology variable in the appendixes. Although the more religious and the Mizrahim are associated with voting for right-wing parties and the secular and the Ashkenazim are linked to the left-wing parties, "after the 1996 elections, the effect of ethnicity on voting patterns had weakened, while that of religious identity had strengthened" (Yuchtman-Yaar, Alkalay, and Aival 2018, 2). This pattern would move against finding any effects here—although religiosity and political affiliation are also potentially part of the ethnic bundle of sticks (Sen and Wasow 2016). It should also be noted that the second-axis issue of the conflict has increasingly complicated the Left-Right divide in Israel into a three-bloc system by cross-pressuring some citizens (Yakter and Tessler 2023).

5. She was from the former USSR and was notable as the only respondent to write the open-ended statement in Russian.

6. If one assigns a normative value to democracy, then one could suspect citizens of overstating their democratic preferences in these raw figures. However, there is no reason to suspect differential interest in overstating among the different ethnic groups. As such, the regression model results would not be biased by it.

7. Studies of Africa, the Middle East, and Muslim-majority states have suggested that women are less committed to democracy because they may fear that women's rights would be curtailed by the likely electoral winners. Specification of women's rights can clarify that potentiality and make up that difference (Rizzo, Abdel-Latif, and Meyer 2007; Ridge 2022a, 2022b).

8. Asking how important a feature is to democracy is a common construction. For instance, the World Values Survey uses this technique. A weakness is the opportunity

for cheap talk, like saying that every feature is important (Ridge 2023a). This book's discussion, though, is constrained to the questions as posed in the ESS.

9. While it may seem strange for Muslims or Christians to favor halakha, there are reasons for it. Respectively 5.2 percent and 3.8 percent indicated "depends on the situation/both/neither." Israel allows for certain areas of law, such as family law, to be governed by religious sect. This carves out a domain for these groups to follow their own laws, which they could fear a democracy would otherwise contradict. The religious minorities might also figure that a halakha-grounded regime could be friendlier to religious minorities than some of the elected governments have been. For instance, recent studies have shown that states around the world with more religious population are less likely to enact anti-Muslim policies (Hoffman and Rosenberg 2023) or evince anti-Jewish policies or attitudes (Fox and Topor 2021).

CHAPTER 5

1. As noted in Chapter 1, the terminology used in this domain can be controversial in itself. The word *conflict* is used here for simplicity, not to comment on the scale or legitimacy of the violence. In keeping with international recognition, Gaza and the West Bank are described as (Occupied) Palestinian Territories. Where sources used other language, their terminology is maintained.

2. Israelis from the former Soviet Union are somewhat of an exception here because they lean to the right although 80 percent are Ashkenazi (Yuchtman-Yaar, Alkalay, and Aival 2018).

3. Models incorporating political affiliation are included in the appendixes. The conflict is connected heavily with politics in Israel. Typically the right is seen as more hawkish and the left more dovish; additionally, Mizrahim are often associated with the right, while Ashkenazim are associated with the left historically. Recent work suggests that the conflict now operates as a second-axis issue driving the development of three blocs by cross-pressuring citizens who support peace in theory but doubt its practicality (Yakter and Tessler 2023).

4. Taking matters still further, only 9.2 percent were willing to stop the fighting to swap prisoners for hostages; 26.6 percent opposed the swap under any circumstance.

5. Her assertions are not consistent with the Arab Barometer data. In Wave 7, 51.1 percent of respondents (including 53.7 percent of Palestinians) endorsed a two-state solution along the 1967 borders as their preferred outcome to the conflict. The vast majority (74.4 percent overall and 85.6 percent of Palestinians) felt that occupation was a critical threat to regional security.

6. Iran is not an Arab state. Most Iranians are Persian. However, she is apparently not concerned with that nuance.

7. In fact, one respondent wished the swaps were specified in the survey questions. The college-educated Masorti Mizrahi woman in her thirties in the Sharon area also wanted to know about the parameters of the nondemocracy: "It is necessary to specify what is meant by small territorial changes. In addition, it is necessary to specify who is considered not able to vote. One who has an ID card? Foreign workers?"

8. The most important change from Shamir and Shamir (1995) was removing the word Arab from the sentences. In the pilot study, some of the Mizrahim had described themselves as Arab. This change would avoid potential confusion. On the advice of an Israeli researcher, the liberalness of the democracy was described in more detail.

9. Since the response was a rating rather than a forced choice, the ratings are demeaned per ethnic bloc so that the comparisons are against a shared zero point. The mean rating for members of an ethnic group is calculated and then subtracted from the members' ratings. Then the difference in marginal means for the groups is calculated. This is done using the *cregg* package designed by Leeper, Hobolt, and Tilley.

CHAPTER 6

1. As has been noted, the process rapidly induced contested claims, conflict and violence, and mass population transfers of disputed voluntariness. Equal rights were not afforded to noncitizens or even to all citizens in practice. The state, though, identifies itself—and is often identified by others—as a democracy.

2. On a 0 to 10 scale, the average score for Israel's having free and fair elections was 7.39. The average score for protecting minority rights was 5.53, for media freedom was 7.23, and for the rule of law was 4.54.

3. This terminology is not an assertion of dual loyalties or untrustworthiness. Any such assertion of dual loyalties would not be without irony. Anti-Jewish sentiment outside of Israel was previously justified by the claim that Jews were all at least partially loyal to the global Jewish community or a Jewish state as well as or instead of the country in which they reside (Fox and Topor 2021). Thus, questioning Arab Jewish Israelis' loyalty to Israel would harken back to a long history of justifying antisemitic bias.

Bibliography

Abramson, Scott F., Korhan Koçak, and Asya Magazinnik. "What Do We Learn about Voter Preferences from Conjoint Experiments?" *American Journal of Political Science* 66, no. 4 (2022): 1008–1020.

Abramson, Yehonatan. "Securitizing the Nation beyond the State: Diasporas as Threats, Victims, and Assets." *European Journal of International Relations* 30, no. 1 (2024): 78–103.

Ahler, Douglas J., and Gaurav Sood. "The Parties in Our Heads: Misperceptions about Party Composition and Their Consequences." *Journal of Politics* 80, no. 3 (2018): 964–981.

Alpert, Rebecca. "What Is a Jew? The Meaning of Genetic Disease for Jewish Identity." *Reconstructionist* 71, no. 2 (2007): 69–84.

Amnesty International. *Israel's Apartheid against Palestinians*. Amnesty International, 2022.

Anderson, Benedict. *Imagined Communities: Reflections on the Origin and Spread of Nationalism*. Verso Books, 2006.

Azoulay, Ariella, and Adi Ophir. *The One-State Condition: Occupation and Democracy in Israel/Palestine*. Stanford University Press, 2012.

Bagno-Moldavski, Olena. "The Effect of Religiosity on Political Attitudes in Israel." *Politics and Religion* 8, no. 3 (2015): 514–543.

Barnett, Carolyn, Amaney A. Jamal, and Steve L. Monroe. "Earned Income and Women's Segmented Empowerment: Experimental Evidence from Jordan." *American Journal of Political Science* 65, no. 4 (2021): 954–970.

Berda, Yael. *Living Emergency: Israel's Permit Regime in the Occupied West Bank*. Stanford University Press, 2018.

Blaydes, Lisa, Justin Gengler, and Noora Ahmed Lari. "Understanding Cultural Constraints to Female Labor Force Participation: How Family Dynamics Influence Women's Employment in Qatar and the Arab Gulf States." Working paper, March 2021.

Branigan, Amelia R., Christopher Wildeman, Jeremy Freese, and Catarina I. Kiefe. "Complicating Colorism: Race, Skin Color, and the Likelihood of Arrest." *Socius* 3 (2017): 2378023117725611.

Brewer, Marilynn B., and Kathleen P. Pierce. "Social Identity Complexity and Outgroup Tolerance." *Personality and Social Psychology Bulletin* 31, no. 3 (2005): 428–437.

Brodsky, Adriana M., and Laura Arnold Leibman, eds. *Jews across the Americas: A Sourcebook, 1492–Present.* Vol. 1. NYU Press, 2023.

Cammett, Melani, Dominika Kruszewska-Eduardo, Christiana Parreira, and Sami Atallah. "Coethnicity beyond Clientelism: Insights from an Experimental Study of Political Behavior in Lebanon." *Politics and Religion* 15, no. 2 (2022): 417–438.

Cammett, Melani, Christiana Parreira, Dominika Kruszewska-Eduardo, and Sami Atallah. "Commitment to the 'National' in Post-conflict Countries: Public and Private Security Provision in Lebanon." *Journal of Conflict Resolution* 66, no. 7–8 (2022): 1235–1262.

Campbell, David E., John C. Green, and Geoffrey C. Layman. "The Party Faithful: Partisan Images, Candidate Religion, and the Electoral Impact of Party Identification." *American Journal of Political Science* 55, no. 1 (2011): 42–58.

Canetti, Daphna, Ibrahim Khatib, Aviad Rubin, and Carly Wayne. "Framing and Fighting: The Impact of Conflict Frames on Political Attitudes." *Journal of Peace Research* 56, no. 6 (2019): 737–752.

Choi, Donghyun Danny, Mathias Poertner, and Nicholas Sambanis. *Native Bias: Overcoming Discrimination against Immigrants.* Vol. 33. Princeton University Press, 2022.

Collier, David, and Steven Levitsky. "Democracy with Adjectives: Conceptual Innovation in Comparative Research." *World Politics* 49, no. 3 (1997): 430–451.

Coppedge, Michael, John Gerring, Carl Henrik Knutsen, Staffan I. Lindberg, Jan Teorell, Nazifa Alizada, David Altman, et al. "V Dem [Country–Year/Country–Date] Dataset v12." Varieties of Democracy (V-Dem) Project. March 2022. Available at https://doi.org/10.23696/vdemds22.

Cortellessa, Eric. "Why Is There No Civil Marriage in Israel?" *Times of Israel.* 12 July 2015.

Craig, Maureen A., and Jennifer A. Richeson. "On the Precipice of a 'Majority-Minority' America: Perceived Status Threat from the Racial Demographic Shift Affects White Americans' Political Ideology." *Psychological Science* 25, no. 6 (2014): 1189–1197.

Daniller, Andrew. "Majorities of Americans See at Least Some Discrimination against Black, Hispanic, and Asian People in the U.S." Pew Research Center. 18 March 2021.

Dawson, Michael C. *Behind the Mule: Race and Class in African-American Politics.* Princeton University Press, 1994.

Donnelly, Michael J. "Material Interests, Identity and Linked Fate in Three Countries." *British Journal of Political Science* 51, no. 3 (2021): 1119–1137.

Dugard, John, and John Reynolds. "Apartheid, International Law, and the Occupied Palestinian Territory." *European Journal of International Law* 24, no. 3 (2013): 867–913.

d'Urso, Amanda Sahar. "A Boundary of White Inclusion: The Role of Religion in Ethnoracial Assignment." *Perspectives on Politics* (2022): 1–18.

Ellemers, Naomi, and Jolanda Jetten. "The Many Ways to Be Marginal in a Group." *Personality and Social Psychology Review* 17, no. 1 (2013): 3–21.

Enos, Ryan D., and Noam Gidron. "Exclusion and Cooperation in Diverse Societies: Experimental Evidence from Israel." *American Political Science Review* 112, no. 4 (2018): 742–757.

ESS Round 8: European Social Survey Round 8 Data (2016). Data file edition 2.2. Sikt—Norwegian Agency for Shared Services in Education and Research, Norway—Data archive and distributor of ESS data for ESS ERIC. Available at https://doi.org/10.21338 /NSD-ESS8-2016.

ESS Round 10: European Social Survey Round 10 Data (2020). Data file edition 1.2. Sikt— Norwegian Agency for Shared Services in Education and Research, Norway—Data archive and distributor of ESS data for ESS ERIC. Available at https://doi.org/10.21338 /NSD-ESS10-2020.

Ferwerda, Jeremy, and Justin Gest. "Pull Factors and Migration Preferences: Evidence from the Middle East and North Africa." *International Migration Review* 55, no. 2 (2021): 431–459.

Foster, Mindi D. "Positive and Negative Responses to Personal Discrimination: Does Coping Make a Difference?" *Journal of Social Psychology* 140, no. 1 (2000): 93–106.

Fox, Jonathan, and Jonathan Rynhold. "A Jewish and Democratic State? Comparing Government Involvement in Religion in Israel with Other Democracies." *Totalitarian Movements and Political Religions* 9, no. 4 (2008): 507–531.

Fox, Jonathan, and Lev Topor. *Why Do People Discriminate against Jews?* Oxford University Press, 2021.

Freedom House. "Israel." *Freedom in the World* (2022).

Galchinsky, Michael. "The Jewish Settlements in the West Bank: International Law and Israeli Jurisprudence." *Israel Studies* 9, no. 3 (2004): 115–136.

Gonzalez-Lesser, Emma. "Jewishness as Sui Generis: Extending Theorizations beyond the Debate of Race, Ethnicity, or Religion." *Ethnic and Racial Studies* 43, no. 3 (2020): 479–500.

Gross, Judah Ari. "Bid to Scrap Law of Return Grandchild Clause Likely to Fail, but Part of Wider Fight." *Times of Israel.* 11 November 2022.

Grossman, Guy, Devorah Manekin, and Yotam Margalit. "How Sanctions Affect Public Opinion in Target Countries: Experimental Evidence from Israel." *Comparative Political Studies* 51, no. 14 (2018): 1823–1857.

Hainmueller, Jens, Daniel J. Hopkins, and Teppei Yamamoto. "Causal Inference in Conjoint Analysis: Understanding Multidimensional Choices Via Stated Preference Experiments." *Political Analysis* 22, no. 1 (2014): 1–30.

Hartstone, Margaret, and Martha Augoustinos. "The Minimal Group Paradigm: Categorization into Two versus Three Groups." *European Journal of Social Psychology* 25, no. 2 (1995): 179–193.

Herzog, Hanna. "Social Construction of Reality in Ethnic Terms: The Case of Political Ethnicity in Israel." *International Review of Modern Sociology* 15, no. 1/2 (1985): 45–61.

Hitlin, Steven, J. Scott Brown, and Glen H. Elder Jr. "Measuring Latinos: Racial vs. ethnic Classification and Self-Understandings." *Social Forces* 86, no. 2 (2007): 587–611.

Hoffman, Michael, and Emma Rosenberg. "Religious Behavior and European Veil Bans." *Politics, Groups, and Identities* 11, no. 4 (2023): 854–875.

Hogg, Michael A., and Scott A. Reid. "Social Identity, Self-Categorization, and the Communication of Group Norms." *Communication Theory* 16, no. 1 (2006): 7–30.

Horiuchi, Yusaku, Zachary Markovich, and Teppei Yamamoto. "Does Conjoint Analysis Mitigate Social Desirability Bias?" *Political Analysis* 30, no. 4 (2022): 535–549.

Hornsey, Matthew J. "Social Identity Theory and Self-Categorization Theory: A Historical Review." *Social and Personality Psychology Compass* 2, no. 1 (2008): 204–222.

Huff, Connor, and Joshua D. Kertzer. "How the Public Defines Terrorism." *American Journal of Political Science* 62, no. 1 (2018): 55–71.

Israel Democracy Institute. "War in Gaza Public Opinion Survey (2)." 18–19 October 2023.

Israel Ministry of Foreign Affairs. "1947: The International Community Says YES to the Establishment of the State of Israel." 2013. Available at https://mfa.gov.il/Jubilee-years /Pages/1947-UN-General-Assembly-Resolution-181-The-international-community-says -Yes-to-the-establishment-of-the-State-of-Israel.aspx.

Jackson, John L. *Thin Description: Ethnography and the African Hebrew Israelites of Jerusalem*. Harvard University Press, 2013.

Jardina, Ashley. *White Identity Politics*. Cambridge University Press, 2019.

Jardina, Ashley, and Robert Mickey. "White Racial Solidarity and Opposition to American Democracy." *ANNALS of the American Academy of Political and Social Science* 699, no. 1 (2022): 79–89.

Kalev, Henriette Dahan, and Maya Maor. "Skin Color Stratification in Israel Revisited." *Journal of Levantine Studies* 5, no. 1 (2015): 9.

Kalmar, Ivan. *White but Not Quite: Central Europe's Illiberal Revolt*. Policy Press, 2022.

Kalmoe, Nathan P., and Lilliana Mason. *Radical American Partisanship: Mapping Violent Hostility, Its Causes, and the Consequences for Democracy*. University of Chicago Press, 2022.

Karpov, Vyacheslav, Elena Lisovskaya, and David Barry. "Ethnodoxy: How Popular Ideologies Fuse Religious and Ethnic Identities." *Journal for the Scientific Study of Religion* 51, no. 4 (2012): 638–655.

Khazzoom, Aziza. *Shifting Ethnic Boundaries and Inequality in Israel: Or, How the Polish Peddler Became a German Intellectual*. Stanford University Press, 2008.

Kimmerling, Baruch. *The Invention and Decline of Israeliness: State, Society, and the Military*. University of California Press, 2001.

Klein, Zivka. "New Movement Calls for Israelis to Leave, Establish Diaspora Communities." *Jerusalem Post*. 14 December 2022.

Kosmidis, Ioannis. "Package 'brglm.'" 12 October 2022. Available at https://mirrors.aliyun .com/CRAN/web/packages/brglm/brglm.pdf.

Lajevardi, Nazita, Kassra A. R. Oskooii, Hannah L. Walker, and Aubrey L. Westfall. "The Paradox between Integration and Perceived Discrimination among American Muslims." *Political Psychology* 41, no. 3 (2020): 587–606.

Lavie, Smadar. *Wrapped in the Flag of Israel: Mizrahi Single Mothers and Bureaucratic Torture*. University of Nebraska Press, 2018.

Lebovic, Matt. "When American Jews Described Their Own Intermarriage as a 'Second Holocaust.'" *Times of Israel*. 12 July 2019.

Leeper, Thomas J., Sara B. Hobolt, and James Tilley. "Measuring Subgroup Preferences in Conjoint Experiments." *Political Analysis* 28, no. 2 (2020): 207–221.

Lemi, Danielle Casarez, and Nadia E. Brown. "The Political Implications of Colorism Are Gendered." *PS: Political Science & Politics* 53, no. 4 (2020): 669–673.

Lewin-Epstein, Noah, and Yinon Cohen. "Ethnic Origin and Identity in the Jewish Population of Israel." *Journal of Ethnic and Migration Studies* 45, no. 11 (2019): 2118–2137.

Lipstadt, Deborah E. *Antisemitism: Here and Now*. Schocken, 2019.

Lis, Jonathan. "Israel Passes Law Permitting Nonreligious to Refuse to Work on Shabbat." *Haaretz*. 19 June 2018.

López, Nancy, Edward Vargas, Melina Juarez, Lisa Cacari-Stone, and Sonia Bettez. "What's Your 'Street Race'? Leveraging Multidimensional Measures of Race and Intersectionality for Examining Physical and Mental Health Status among Latinxs." *Sociology of Race and Ethnicity* 4, no. 1 (2018): 49–66.

Lynn, Peter, Sabine Hader, Siegfried Gabler, and Seppo Laaksonen. "Methods for Achieving Equivalence of Samples in Cross-National Surveys: The European Social Survey Experience." *Journal of Official Statistics* 23, no. 1 (2007): 107–124.

Manekin, Devorah, Guy Grossman, and Tamar Mitts. "Contested Ground: Disentangling Material and Symbolic Attachment to Disputed Territory." *Political Science Research and Methods* 7, no. 4 (2019): 679–697.

Marques, Jose, Dominic Abrams, Dario Paez, and Cristina Martinez-Taboada. "The Role of Categorization and In-Group Norms in Judgments of Groups and Their Members." *Journal of Personality and Social Psychology* 75, no. 4 (1998): 976.

Marshall, Monty G., and Ted Robert Gurr. *Polity5*. Center for Systemic Peace, 2020.

Mchenry, Dean, Jr., and Abdel-Fattah Mady. "A Critique of Quantitative Measures of the Degree of Democracy in Israel." *Democratization* 13, no. 2 (2006): 257–282.

McIntosh, Peggy. "White Privilege: Unpacking the Invisible Knapsack." *Peace and Freedom Magazine.* July/August 1989, 10–12.

Metzger, Jackie. "The Jews of North Africa." Yad Vashem. 2023. Available at https://www.yadvashem.org/articles/general/the-jews-of-north-africa.html.

Mizrachi, Nissim, and Hanna Herzog. "Participatory Destigmatization Strategies among Palestinian Citizens, Ethiopian Jews and Mizrahi Jews in Israel." *Ethnic and Racial Studies* 35, no. 3 (2012): 418–435.

Mizrachi, Nissim, and Erica Weiss. "'We Do Not Want to Assimilate!': Rethinking the Role of Group Boundaries in Peace Initiatives between Muslims and Jews in Israel and in the West Bank." *European Journal of Cultural and Political Sociology* 7, no. 2 (2020): 172–197.

Montgomery, Jacob M., Brendan Nyhan, and Michelle Torres. "How Conditioning on Posttreatment Variables Can Ruin Your Experiment and What to Do about It." *American Journal of Political Science* 62, no. 3 (2018): 760–775.

Napier, Jaime L., Alexandra Suppes, and Maria Laura Bettinsoli. "Denial of Gender Discrimination Is Associated with Better Subjective Well-Being among Women: A System Justification Account." *European Journal of Social Psychology* 50, no. 6 (2020): 1191–1209.

Oren, Neta. *Israel's National Identity: The Changing Ethos of Conflict.* Lynne Rienner Publishers, 2019.

Orey, Byron D'Andra, and Yu Zhang. "Melanated Millennials and the Politics of Black Hair." *Social Science Quarterly* 100, no. 6 (2019): 2458–2476.

Ostfeld, Mara Cecilia, and Nicole D. Yadon. "¿Mejorando La Raza? The Political Undertones of Latinos' Skin Color in the United States." *Social Forces* 100, no. 4 (2022a): 1806–1832.

———. *Skin Color, Power, and Politics in America.* Russell Sage Foundation, 2022b.

Pearlman, Wendy, and Boaz Atzili. *Triadic Coercion: Israel's Targeting of States That Host Nonstate Actors.* Columbia University Press, 2018.

Peled, Yoav. "Mizrahi Jews and Palestinian Arabs: Exclusionist Attitudes in Development Towns." In *Ethnic Frontiers and Peripheries,* edited by Oren Yiftachel and Avinoam Meir, pp. 87–111. Westview Press, 1998.

Pérez, Efrén O. "Xenophobic Rhetoric and Its Political Effects on Immigrants and Their Co-ethnics." *American Journal of Political Science* 59, no. 3 (2015): 549–564.

Pérez, Efren, Crystal Robertson, and Bianca Vicuña. "Prejudiced When Climbing Up or When Falling Down? Why Some People of Color Express Anti-Black Racism." *American Political Science Review* 117, no. 1 (2023): 168–183.

Phoenix, Davin L., and Nathan K. Chan. "Clarifying the 'People like Me': Racial Efficacy and Political Behavior." *Perspectives on Politics* (2022): 1–18.

Plattner, Marc F. "Illiberal Democracy and the Struggle on the Right." In *The Emergence of Illiberalism*, pp. 43–57. Routledge, 2020.

Renan, Ernest. *Qu'est-ce qu'une nation?* Calmann Levy, 1882.

Ridge, Hannah M. *Defining Democracy: Democratic Commitment in the Arab World.* Lynne Rienner Publishing, 2023a.

———. "Dismantling New Democracies: The Case of Tunisia." *Democratization* 29, no. 8 (2022a): 1539–1556.

———. "Effect of Religious Legislation on Religious Behavior: The Ramadan Fast." *Interdisciplinary Journal of Research on Religion* 15 (2019): 1–39.

———. "Ethnodoxy in Egypt." *Interdisciplinary Journal of Research on Religion* 19 (2023b): 1–32.

———. "Illiberal Democrats in Egypt." *Journal of the Middle East and Africa* 13, no. 4 (2022b): 363–384.

———. "State Regulation of Religion: The Effect of Religious Freedom on Muslims' Religiosity." *Religion, State & Society* 48, no. 4 (2020): 256–275.

Rizzo, Helen, Abdel-Hamid Abdel-Latif, and Katherine Meyer. "The Relationship between Gender Equality and Democracy: A Comparison of Arab versus Non-Arab Muslim Societies." *Sociology* 41, no. 6 (2007): 1151–1170.

Roccas, Sonia, and Marilynn B. Brewer. "Social Identity Complexity." *Personality and Social Psychology Review* 6, no. 2 (2002): 88–106.

Rudoren, Jodi. "In Exodus from Israel to Germany, a Young Nation's Fissures Show." *New York Times.* 16 October 2014.

Ruiter, Stijn, and Frank van Tubergen. "Religious Attendance in Cross-National Perspective: A Multilevel Analysis of 60 Countries." *American Journal of Sociology* 115, no. 3 (2009): 863–895.

Saperstein, Aliya. "Double-Checking the Race Box: Examining Inconsistency between Survey Measures of Observed and Self-Reported Race." *Social Forces* 85, no. 1 (2006): 57–74.

Saperstein, Aliya, and Andrew M. Penner. "Beyond the Looking Glass: Exploring Fluidity in Racial Self-Identification and Interviewer Classification." *Sociological Perspectives* 57, no. 2 (2014): 186–207.

Sasson-Levy, Orna. "A Different Kind of Whiteness: Marking and Unmarking of Social Boundaries in the Construction of Hegemonic Ethnicity." *Sociological Forum* 28, no. 1 (2013): 27–50.

Sasson-Levy, Orna, and Avi Shoshana. "'Passing' as (Non)Ethnic: The Israeli Version of Acting White." *Sociological Inquiry* 83, no. 3 (2013): 448–472.

Schaeffer, Katherine, and Khadija Edwards. "Black Americans Differ from Other U.S. Adults over Whether Individual or Structural Racism Is a Bigger Problem." Pew Research Center. 15 November 2022.

Schaeffer, Merlin, and Judith Kas. "The Integration Paradox: A Review and Meta-analysis of the Complex Relationship between Integration and Reports of Discrimination." *International Migration Review* (2023): 01979183231170809.

Schmitter, Philippe C., and Terry Lynn Karl. "What Democracy Is . . . and Is Not." *Journal of Democracy* 2, no. 3 (1991): 75–88.

Selinger, Guy Abutbul. "Hybridization and Purification: The Experiences of Mizrachi Middle-Class Adolescents in Israel." *Israel Studies Review* 28, no. 2 (2013): 122–139.

Sen, Maya, and Omar Wasow. "Race as a Bundle of Sticks: Designs That Estimate Effects of Seemingly Immutable Characteristics." *Annual Review of Political Science* 19, no. 1 (2016): 499–522.

Shady, Stephanie N. "Territory and the Divine: The Intersection of Religion and National Identity." *West European Politics* 45, no. 4 (2022): 744–766.

Shamir, Jacob, Neta Ziskind, and Shoshana Blum-Kulka. "What's in a Question? A Content Analysis of Survey Questions." *Communication Review* 3, no. 4 (1999): 353–377.

Shamir, Michal, and Jacob Shamir. "Competing Values in Public Opinion: A Conjoint Analysis." *Political Behavior* 17, no. 1 (1995): 107–133.

Shohat, Ella. "Rupture and Return: Zionist Discourse and the Study of Arab Jews." *Social Text* 21, no. 2 (2003): 49–74.

Shoshana, Avihu. "Ethnicity without Ethnicity: 'I'm Beyond That Story' State Arrangements, Re-education and (New) Ethnicity in Israel." *Social Identities* 22, no. 5 (2016): 487–501.

Smooha, Sammy. "Jewish Ethnicity in Israel: Symbolic or Real." *Jews in Israel: Contemporary Social and Cultural Patterns* 1 (2004): 47–80.

Strmic-Pawl, Hephzibah V., Vanessa Gonlin, and Steve Garner. "Color in Context: Three Angles on Contemporary Colorism." *Sociology of Race and Ethnicity* 7, no. 3 (2021): 289–303.

Tajfel, H., and J. C. Turner. "An Integrative Theory of Intergroup Conflict." In *The social psychology of intergroup relations*, edited by W. G. Austin and S. Worchel, pp. 33–47. Brooks/Cole, 1979.

Tapper, Aaron J. Hahn, Ari Y. Kelman, and Aliya Saperstein. "Counting on Whiteness: Religion, Race, Ethnicity, and the Politics of Jewish Demography." *Journal for the Scientific Study of Religion* 62, no. 1 (2023): 28–48.

Telles, Edward, and Tianna Paschel. "Who Is Black, White, or Mixed Race? How Skin Color, Status, and Nation Shape Racial Classification in Latin America." *American Journal of Sociology* 120, no. 3 (2014): 864–907.

Tellez, Juan Fernando. "Peace Agreement Design and Public Support for Peace: Evidence from Colombia." *Journal of Peace Research* 56, no. 6 (2019): 827–844.

TOI Staff. "Israel's Official Rules Limiting Shabbat Activity Increasingly Ignored—Research." *Times of Israel*. 20 September 2022.

Tsourapas, Gerasimos. "Theorizing State-Diaspora Relations in the Middle East: Authoritarian Emigration States in Comparative Perspective." *Mediterranean Politics* 25, no. 2 (2020): 135–159.

Turner, David. "Aliya to Germany! An Invite to Israelis from, 'the Young Generation of Israel.'" *Jerusalem Post*. 11 October 2014.

Turner, John C., Rupert J. Brown, and Henri Tajfel. "Social Comparison and Group Interest in Ingroup Favouritism." *European Journal of Social Psychology* 9, no. 2 (1979): 187–204.

Vandermaas-Peeler, Alex, Jelena Subotic, and Michael Barnett. "Constructing Victims: Suffering and Status in Modern World Order." *Review of International Studies* 50, no. 1 (2024): 171–189.

Weaver, Vesla M. "The Electoral Consequences of Skin Color: The 'Hidden' Side of Race in Politics." *Political Behavior* 34, no. 1 (2012): 159–192.

Weil, Julie Zauzmer. "Three Couples Marry in Washington. In Israel, It Would Be Illegal." *Washington Post*. 27 March 2019.

Weiss, Steward. "Will Jews Do 'Reverse Aliyah' and Leave Israel for Other Lands?" *Jerusalem Post*. 30 December 2022.

Westwood, Sean J., Justin Grimmer, Matthew Tyler, and Clayton Nall. "Current Research Overstates American Support for Political Violence." *Proceedings of the National Academy of Sciences* 119, no. 12 (2022): e2116870119.

Yadgar, Yaacov. *Israel's Jewish Identity Crisis: State and Politics in the Middle East.* Vol. 11. Cambridge University Press, 2020.

Yadon, Nicole, and Mara C. Ostfeld. "Shades of Privilege: The Relationship between Skin Color and Political Attitudes among White Americans." *Political Behavior* 42, no. 4 (2020): 1369–1392.

Yakter, Alon, and Mark Tessler. "The Long-Term Electoral Implications of Conflict Escalation: Doubtful Doves and the Breakdown of Israel's Left–Right Dichotomy." *Journal of Peace Research* 60, no. 3 (2023): 504–520.

Yuchtman-Yaar, Ephraim, Yasmin Alkalay, and Tom Aival. "Effects of Religious Identity and Ethnicity on the Israeli-Jewish Electorate." *Israel Studies Review* 33, no. 3 (2018): 1–20.

INDEX

Note: Page numbers followed by *f* and *t* indicate figures and tables, respectively.

Group-protective behavior: and authoritarianism, 84; crises and, 179n19; of group status, 10, 11, 18; of marginal group members, 25, 27–28, 54, 97
Group status, protection of, 10–11
Group stereotypes, 16–17, 16n
Group threats: and authoritarian institutional support, 83–84; group identification and reaction to, 55, 123–124; as part of Israeli ethos, 96; and political conservatism, 98, 124

Hady, Abdel-Fattah, 82
Halakha: defined, 177n1; democracy *vs.*, 85*t*, 92, 93*f*, 94, 94*t*, 126, 171*t*; importance of, 161*t*; and Jewish family lines, 2; and Jewish State, 56, 57, 58*t*, 63–64, 63*f*, 64*t*
Haredi, 13
Hebrew, pressure to use, 178n12
Hegemonic state, Israel as, 82, 92
Heritage: and Jewish identity, 12; and social benefits, 16–17, 17n; and subgroup identification, 23, 179n22
Herzog, Hanna, 40
Hierarchy(ies): cultural, 15; ethnicity and, 17, 123–124; in Israel, 2, 3
Hiloni: Ashkenazim as, 20; and Ashkenormativity, 16; in conjoint analysis, 118–119, 119*f*, 120*f*; defined, 13; and democracy, 28; and discrimination, 43–44; as Jews, 177n5
Holocaust: Jewishness and, 180n1, 183n15; and Jewish State, 77–78
Homeland, Israel as, 2, 51, 62

ICBS (Israel Central Bureau of Statistics) practices, 24
IDF (Israeli Defense Forces), 102
Illiberal democracy: in Central Europe, 84; group threat and, 83–84; Jewish State and, 63, 73; marginal group members and, 26–27, 126; preference for, 86–87, 114
Immigrants: assimilation of, 32–34; children of, 178n11; Jewish *vs.* non-Jewish, 26, 51, 65, 66*f*; natives *vs.*, 130; processing and territorial distribution of, 32–34, 180n2; resource distribution to, 32

Immigration: of Christians, 58*t*, 65, 66*f*, 67, 68*t*, 125, 162*t*; of Ethiopian Jews, 58*t*, 65, 68*t*, 162*t*; of European non-Jews, 58*t*, 65; to Mandate Palestine, 13–14; Mizrahi, 31, 51; to State of Israel, 14, 31–32
Inclusion, as Jews, 74–75, 74*t*
Income inequality, 30, 35, 88, 89
Indian Jews, 178n7
Ingathering: of African Jews, 178n9; of Arab Jews, 32; Basic Laws and Declaration of Independence on, 26, 51, 113; and conversion, 75; of converts, 178n9; of diasporic Jews, 14–15, 28–29; ethnic differences in, 31–32; non-Jewish Israelis and, 2; and right of return, 68; and settlements, 110; Zionist project of, 15
In-groups, 3, 4; securitization of part of, 16, 178n15
Institutional racism, 30–31
Integration paradox phenomenon, 33
Interfaith marriages. *See* Out-marriage
Intergroup tolerance, diversity and, 4
Intermarriage. *See* Out-marriage
International law, violation of, 101, 111
iPanel survey, 21–22; on conflicting values, 116–118, 118*f*–120*f*; consent process for, 22; delay of pilot, 179n19; on democracy, 85*t*, 116; demographics of, 24, 24*t*; on ethnic politics, 132; feedback on, 22; free-response space in, 22; on Green Line borders, 99*t*, 103*t*, 105–107, 106*f*, 116, 172*t*; on immigration, 162*t*; on Israel as necessary for Jewish people's survival, 77–78; on Jewish majority population, 65–66, 66*f*, 67*f*, 68*t*, 116, 162*t*; on Jewish nationalism, 55–57, 58*t*; on liberal democracy, 168*t*; marginality *vs.* group identity on, 22–23; on peace, 98–99, 99*t*, 101–103, 102*f*, 103*t*, 116, 172*t*; question wording and variable coding for, 139*t*–140*t*; quota sampling in, 21, 179n18, 180n26; sample characteristics for, 135*t*; self-identification in, 23; on settlements, 108–109; on state structural preferences, 86–88, 87*f*, 88*f*; subgroup identification in, 23, 24, 24*t*; on trade-offs, 111
Iraqi Jews, immigration of, 14, 32, 128
Isolation, of nonprototypical group members, 36–37
Isolationism, 43

Hannah M. Ridge is Assistant Professor of Political Science at Chapman University and the author of *Defining Democracy: Democratic Commitment in the Arab World.*